Sciences Content Knowledge: Study Guide

▶ ▶ ▶ ▶ ▶ ▶ ▶ ▶ ▶ ▶ ▶ ▶ ▶

A PUBLICATION OF EDUCATIONAL TESTING SERVICE

Table of Contents
Study Guide for the Praxis *Sciences: Content Knowledge* Tests

► ► ► ► ► ► ► ► ► ► ► ►

TABLE OF CONTENTS

TABLE OF CONTENTS

Chapter 1
Introduction to the Praxis *Sciences: Content Knowledge* Tests and Suggestions for Using this Study Guide

▶   ▶   ▶   ▶   ▶   ▶   ▶   ▶   ▶   ▶   ▶   ▶   ▶

Introduction to the Praxis *Sciences: Content Knowledge* Tests

The Praxis *Sciences: Content Knowledge* Tests are designed for prospective secondary science teachers. The tests are designed to reflect current standards for knowledge, skills, and abilities in science education. Educational Testing Service (ETS) works in collaboration with teacher educators, higher education content specialists, and accomplished practicing teachers in several fields of science to keep the tests updated and representative of current standards. All of the tests are not intended to assess teaching skills but rather to demonstrate the candidate's fundamental knowledge in the major areas of science.

This guide covers science tests related to five fields—Biology, Chemistry, Earth and Space Sciences, General Science, and Physics. The tests for each field are listed below.

Science Subject	Test Name and Code	Questions, Length of Test	Major Content Areas Covered and Approximate Percentage of Questions in Each Area
Biology (note: calculators prohibited)	*Biology: Content Knowledge, Part 1* (0231)	75 questions, one hour	• Basic Principles of Science (17%) • Molecular and Cellular Biology (16%) • Classical Genetics and Evolution (15%) • Diversity of Life, Plants, and Animals (26%) • Ecology (13%) • Science, Technology, and Society (13%)
	Biology: Content Knowledge, Part 2 (0232)	75 questions, one hour	• Molecular and Cellular Biology (21%) • Classical Genetics and Evolution (24%) • Diversity of Life, Plants, and Animals (37%) • Ecology (18%)
	Biology: Content Knowledge (0235)	150 questions, two hours	• Basic Principles of Science (8%) • Molecular and Cellular Biology (25%) • Classical Genetics and Evolution (15%) • Diversity of Life, Plants, and Animals (30%) • Ecology (15%) • Science, Technology, and Society (7%)

Science Subject	Test Name and Code	Questions, Length of Test	Major Content Areas Covered and Approximate Percentage of Questions in Each Area
Chemistry (note: calculators prohibited)	*Chemistry: Content Knowledge* (0241)	50 questions, one hour	• Atomic Structure/Chemical Periodicity/Thermodynamics of Chemical Reactions (24%) • Nomenclature/The Mole, Bonding, and Geometry (22%) • Solutions and Solubility (26%) • Chemical Reactions/Biochemistry (28%)
	Chemistry: Content Knowledge (0245)	100 questions, two hours	• Matter and Energy; Heat, Thermodynamics, and Thermochemistry (16%) • Atomic and Nuclear Structure (10%) • Nomenclature; The Mole, Chemical Bonding, and Geometry (14%) • Periodicity and Reactivity; Chemical Reactions; Biochemistry and Organic Chemistry (23%) • Solutions and Solubility; Acid/base Chemistry (12%) • Scientific Procedures and Techniques; History and Nature of Sciences; Science, Technology and Society (25%)
Earth and Space Sciences (note: calculators prohibited)	*Earth and Space Sciences: Content Knowledge* (0571)	100 questions, two hours	• Basic Scientific Principles of Earth and Space Sciences (8-12%) • Tectonics and Internal Earth Processes (18-22%) • Earth Materials and Surface Processes (23-27%) • History of the Earth and its Life Forms (13-17%) • Earth's Atmosphere and Hydrosphere (18-22%) • Astronomy (8-12%)

Science Subject	Test Name and Code	Questions, Length of Test	Major Content Areas Covered and Approximate Percentage of Questions in Each Area
General Science (note: calculators prohibited)	*General Science: Content Knowledge, Part 1* (0431)	60 questions, one hour	• Methodology/Philosophy; Math/ Measurement/Data; Laboratory/Safety (23%) • Basic Principles of Science (23%) • Life Science (22%) • Earth/Space Science; Science, Technology, and Society (32%)
	General Science: Content Knowledge, Part 2 (0432)	60 questions, one hour	• Physics (27%) • Chemistry (27%) • Life Science (18%) • Earth/Space Science; Science, Technology, and Society (28%)
	General Science: Content Knowledge (0435)	120 questions, two hours	• Scientific Methodology, Techniques, and History (10%) • The Physical Sciences (40%) • The Life Sciences (20%) • The Earth Sciences (20%) • Science, Technology, and Society (10%)
Physics (note: calculators prohibited)	*Physics: Content Knowledge* (0261)	50 questions, one hour	• Mechanics (40%) • Electricity and Magnetism (34%) • Optics and Waves; Special Topics in Modern Physics (26%)
	Physics: Content Knowledge (0265)	100 questions, two hours	• Mechanics (32%) • Electricity and Magnetism (23%) • Optics and Waves (17%) • Heat and Thermodynamics (8%) • Modern Physics; Atomic and Nuclear Structure (8%) • History and Nature of Science; Science Technology and Social Perspectives (STS) (12%)

Science Subject	Test Name and Code	Questions, Length of Test	Major Content Areas Covered and Approximate Percentage of Questions in Each Area
Combination Tests (note: calculators prohibited)	*Biology and General Science* (0030)	160 questions, two hours	• History, Philosophy, and Methodology of Science; Science, Technology, and Society (10%) • Molecular and Cellular Biology of Prokaryotes and Eukaryotes (15%) • Biology of Plants, Animals, Fungi, and Protists (20%) • Evolution (12%) • Ecology (13%) • Chemistry (10%) • Physics (10%) • Earth and Space Science (10%)
	Chemistry, Physics, and General Science (0070)	140 questions, two hours	• Major Ideas of Chemistry and Physics (20%) • Chemistry (30%) • Physics (30%) • Earth and Space Science (10%) • Life Science (10%)
	Physical Science: Content Knowledge (0481)	60 questions, one hour	• Methodology; Math, Measurement, Data; Science, Technology, and Society (33%) • Laboratory Procedures and Safety; Matter and Energy (37%) • Heat and Thermodynamics; Atomic and Nuclear Structure (30%)

Suggestions for Using the "Study Topics" Chapters of this Study Guide

The Praxis test you will take is different from a final exam or other tests you may have taken in that it is comprehensive—that is, it covers material you may have learned in several courses during more than one year. It requires you to synthesize information you have learned from many sources and to understand the subject as a whole.

This test is also very different from the SAT® or other assessments of your reading, writing, and mathematical skills. You may have heard it said that you can't study for the SAT—that is, you should have learned these skills throughout your school years, and you can't learn reading or reasoning skills shortly before you take the exam. You can *practice* taking the SAT and skills tests like it to become more adept at applying the skills to the particular format of the test. The Praxis *Sciences: Content Knowledge* Tests, on the other hand, assess domains you *can* review for and *can* prepare to be tested on. Therefore, you should review for and prepare for your test, not merely practice with the question formats. A thorough review of the material covered on the test will significantly increase your likelihood of success. Moreover, studying for your licensing exam is a great opportunity to reflect on your field and develop a deeper understanding of it before you begin to teach the subject matter to others. As you prepare to take the test, you may find it particularly helpful to think about how you would apply the study topics and sample exercises to your own clinical experience that you obtained in schools during your teacher preparation program. Your student teaching experience will be especially relevant to your thinking about the materials in the study guide.

We recommend the following approach for using the "Study Topics" chapters to prepare for the test.

Become familiar with the test content. Learn what will be assessed in the test, covered in the chapter with the study topics for your field of science. (See the Table of Contents.)

Assess how well you know the content in each subject area. It is quite likely that you will need to study in most or all of the areas. After you learn what the test contains, you should assess your knowledge in each area. How well do you know the material? In which areas do you need to learn more before you take the test?

Develop a study plan. Assess what you need to study and create a realistic plan for studying. You can develop your study plan in any way that works best for you. A "Study Plan" form is included in Appendix A at the end of the book as a possible way to structure your planning. Remember that this is a licensure test and covers a great deal of material. Plan to review carefully. You will need to allow time to find the books and other materials, time to read the material and take notes, and time to go over your notes.

Identify study materials. Most of the material covered by the test is contained in standard introductory textbooks. If you do not own introductory texts that cover all the areas, you may want to borrow one or more from friends or from a library. You may also want to obtain a copy of your state's standards for your field of science. (One way to find these standards quickly is to go to the Web site for your state's Department of Education.) The textbooks used in secondary classrooms may also prove useful to you, since they also present the material you need to know. Use standard school and college introductory textbooks and other reliable, professionally prepared materials. Don't rely heavily on information provided by friends or from searching the World Wide Web. Neither of these sources is as uniformly reliable as textbooks.

Work through your study plan. You may want to work alone, or you may find it more helpful to work with a group or with a mentor. Work through the topics and questions provided in the chapter with the study topics. Be able to define and discuss the topics in your own words rather than memorizing definitions from books. If you are working with a group or mentor, you can also try informal quizzes and questioning techniques.

Proceed to the practice questions. Once you have completed your review, you are ready to benefit from the "Practice Questions" portion of this guide.

Suggestions for Using the "Practice Questions" and "Right Answers and Explanations for the Practice Questions" Chapters

Read chapter 8 ("Don't Be Defeated by Multiple-Choice Questions"). This chapter will sharpen your skills in reading and answering questions. Succeeding on multiple-choice questions requires careful focus on the question, an eye for detail, and patient sifting of the answer choices.

Answer the practice questions. See the Table of Contents to identify the chapter with practice questions for your field of science. Make your own test-taking conditions as similar to actual testing conditions as you can. Work on the practice questions in a quiet place without distractions. Remember that the practice questions are only examples of the way the topics are covered in the test. The test you take will have different questions.

Score the practice questions. See the Table of Contents to identify the chapter with "Right Answers and Explanations" for your field of science. Go through the detailed answers in that chapter and mark the questions you answered correctly and the ones you missed. Look over the explanations of the questions you missed and see whether you understand them.

Decide whether you need more review. After you have looked at your results, decide whether you need to brush up on certain subject areas before taking the actual test. (The practice questions are grouped by topic, which may help you to spot areas of particular strength or weakness.) Go back to your textbooks and reference materials to see if the topics are covered there. You might also want to go over your questions with a friend or teacher who is familiar with the subjects.

Assess your readiness. Do you feel confident about your level of understanding in each of the areas? If not, where do you need more work? If you feel ready, complete the checklist in chapter 19 ("Are You Ready?") to double-check that you've thought through the details. If you need more information about registration or the testing situation itself, use the resources in Appendix B: "For More Information."

Chapter 2
Background Information on
The Praxis Series™ Assessments

▶   ▶   ▶   ▶   ▶   ▶   ▶   ▶   ▶   ▶   ▶   ▶   ▶

What are The Praxis Series Subject Assessments?

The Praxis Series Subject Assessments are designed by Educational Testing Service (ETS) to assess your knowledge of the subject area you plan to teach, and they are a part of the licensing procedure in many states. This study guide covers an assessment that tests your knowledge of the actual content you hope to be licensed to teach. Your state has adopted The Praxis Series tests because it wants to be certain that you have achieved a specified level of mastery of your subject area before it grants you a license to teach in a classroom.

The Praxis Series tests are part of a national testing program, meaning that the test covered in this study guide is used in more than one state. The advantage of taking Praxis tests is that if you want to move to another state that uses The Praxis Series tests, you can transfer your scores to that state. Passing scores are set by states, however, so if you are planning to apply for licensure in another state, you may find that passing scores are different. You can find passing scores for all states that use The Praxis Series tests in the *Understanding Your Praxis Scores* pamphlet, available either in your college's School of Education or by calling (609) 771-7395.

What is licensure?

Licensure in any area—medicine, law, architecture, accounting, cosmetology—is an assurance to the public that the person holding the license has demonstrated a certain level of competence. The phrase used in licensure is that the person holding the license *will do no harm*. In the case of teacher licensing, a license tells the public that the person holding the license can be trusted to educate children competently and professionally.

Because a license makes such a serious claim about its holder, licensure tests are usually quite demanding. In some fields licensure tests have more than one part and last for more than one day. Candidates for licensure in all fields plan intensive study as part of their professional preparation: some join study groups, others study alone. But preparing to take a licensure test is, in all cases, a professional activity. Because it assesses your entire body of knowledge or skill for the field you want to enter, preparing for a licensure exam takes planning, discipline, and sustained effort. Studying thoroughly is highly recommended.

Why does my state require The Praxis Series Assessments?

Your state chose The Praxis Series Assessments because the tests assess the breadth and depth of content—called the "domain" of the test—that your state wants its teachers to possess before they begin to teach. The level of content knowledge, reflected in the passing score, is based on recommendations of panels of teachers and teacher educators in each subject area in each state. The state licensing agency and, in some states, the state legislature ratify the passing scores that have been recommended by panels of teachers. You can find out the passing score required for The Praxis Series Assessments in your state by looking in the pamphlet *Understanding Your Praxis Scores,* which is free from ETS (see above). If you look through this pamphlet, you will see that not all states use the same test modules, and even when they do, the passing scores can differ from state to state.

What kinds of tests are The Praxis Series Subject Assessments?

Two kinds of tests comprise The Praxis Series Subject Assessments: multiple choice (for which you select your answer from a list of choices) and constructed response (for which you write a response of your own). Multiple-choice tests can survey a wider domain because they can ask more questions in a limited period of time. Constructed-response tests have far fewer questions, but the questions require you to demonstrate the depth of your knowledge in the area covered.

What do the tests measure?

The Praxis Series Subject Assessments are tests of content knowledge. They measure your understanding of the subject area you want to teach. The multiple-choice tests measure a broad range of knowledge across your content area. The constructed-response tests measure your ability to explain in depth a few essential topics in your subject area. The content-specific pedagogy tests, most of which are constructed-response, measure your understanding of how to teach certain fundamental concepts in your field. The tests do not measure your actual teaching ability, however. They measure your knowledge of your subject and of how to teach it. The teachers in your field who help us design and write these tests, and the states that require these tests, do so in the belief that knowledge of subject area is the first requirement for licensing. Your teaching ability is a skill that is measured in other ways: observation, videotaped teaching, or portfolios are typically used by states to measure teaching ability. Teaching combines many complex skills, only some of which can be measured by a single test. The Praxis Series Subject Assessments are designed to measure how thoroughly you understand the material in the subject areas in which you want to be licensed to teach.

How were these tests developed?

ETS began the development of The Praxis Series Subject Assessments with a survey. For each subject, teachers around the country in various teaching situations were asked to judge which knowledge and skills a beginning teacher in that subject needs to possess. Professors in schools of education who prepare teachers were asked the same questions. These responses were ranked in order of importance and sent out to hundreds of teachers for review. All of the responses to these surveys (called "job analysis surveys") were analyzed to summarize the judgments of these professionals. From their consensus, we developed the specifications for the multiple-choice and constructed-response tests. Each subject area had a committee of practicing teachers and teacher educators who wrote these specifications (guidelines). The specifications were reviewed and eventually approved by teachers. From the test specifications, groups of teachers and professional test developers created test questions.

When your state adopted The Praxis Series Subject Assessments, local panels of practicing teachers and teacher educators in each subject area met to examine the tests question by question and evaluate each question for its relevance to beginning teachers in your state. This is called a "validity study." A test is considered "valid" for a job if it measures what people must know and be able to do on that job. For the test to be adopted in your state, teachers in your state must judge that it is valid.

These teachers and teacher educators also performed a "standard-setting study"; that is, they went through the tests question by question and decided, through a rigorous process, how many questions a beginning teacher should be able to answer correctly. From this study emerged a recommended passing score. The final passing score was approved by your state's Department of Education.

In other words, throughout the development process, practitioners in the teaching field—teachers and teacher educators—have determined what the tests would contain. The practitioners in your state determined which tests would be used for licensure in your subject area and helped decide what score would be needed to achieve licensure. This is how professional licensure works in most fields: those who are already licensed oversee the licensing of new practitioners. When you pass The Praxis Series Subject Assessments, you and the practitioners in your state can be assured that you have the knowledge required to begin practicing your profession.

Chapter 3
Study Topics for the *Biology: Content Knowledge* Tests

► ► ► ► ► ► ► ► ► ► ► ►

Introduction to the tests

The *Biology: Content Knowledge* Tests are designed to assess the knowledge and understanding of the fundamental concepts, principles, phenomena, and interrelationships of the science of biology necessary for a beginning teacher in a secondary school. The topics for questions are typically those covered in introductory college-level biology and life science courses, although some questions of a more advanced nature are included, because secondary-school instructors must understand the subject matter from a more advanced viewpoint than that presented to their students. Also, since a major goal of science education is to have students develop an understanding of science and the impact of science and technology on the environment and human affairs, these areas are included in the assessment. The questions include definition of terms, comprehension of critical concepts, application, analysis, and problem solving.

The tests are designed to reflect current standards for knowledge, skills, and abilities in science education. Educational Testing Service (ETS) has aligned these tests closely with the National Science Education Standards and works in collaboration with teacher educators, higher education content specialists, and accomplished practicing teachers in the field of biology to keep the tests updated and representative of current standards.

This chapter is intended to help you organize your preparation for your test and to give you a clear indication about the depth and breadth of the knowledge required for success on the tests.

Using the topic lists that follow: You are not expected to be an expert on all aspects of the topics that follow. You should understand the major

characteristics of each topic, recognize the minor topics, and have some familiarity with the subtopics. Virtually all accredited undergraduate biology programs address the majority of these topics, subtopics, and even minor topics.

You are likely to find that the topics below are covered by most introductory biology textbooks, but a general survey textbook may not cover all of the subtopics. Consult materials and resources, including lecture and laboratory notes, from all your biology coursework. You should be able to match up specific topics and subtopics with what you have covered in your courses in cell biology, ecology, zoology, botany, and so on.

Try not to be overwhelmed by the volume and scope of content knowledge in this guide. An overview such as this that lists biology topics does not offer you a great deal of context. Although a specific term may not seem familiar as you see it here, you might find you could understand it when applied to a real-life situation. Many of the items on the actual PRAXIS test will provide you with a context to apply to these topics or terms, as you will see when you look at the practice questions in chapter 9.

Special questions marked with stars: Interspersed throughout the list of topics are questions that are outlined in boxes and preceded by stars (★). These questions are intended to help you test your knowledge of fundamental concepts and your ability to apply fundamental concepts to situations in the laboratory or the real world. Most of the questions require you to combine several pieces of knowledge in order to formulate an integrated understanding and response. If you spend time on these questions, you will gain increased understanding and facility with the subject matter covered on the test. You might want to discuss these questions and your answers with a teacher or mentor.

Note that the questions marked with stars are not short-answer or multiple-choice, and this study guide does not provide the answers. The questions marked with stars are intended as study questions, not practice questions. Thinking about the answers to them should improve your understanding of fundamental concepts and will probably help you answer a broad range of questions on the test. For example, the following box with a star appears in the list of study topics under "Molecular Basis of Heredity":

★ How has DNA technology been used to solve criminal cases? To treat diabetes?

If you think about this question, perhaps jotting down some notes on the important terminology involved, you will review your knowledge of recombinant DNA technology and its applications, and you will have probably prepared yourself to answer multiple-choice questions similar to the one below:

Which of the following is an application of recombinant DNA technology?

(A)   Detection of the presence of sickle cell anemia in an unborn fetus

(B)   Production of human insulin for a diabetic in large-scale batches

(C)   Matching DNA from a criminal suspect to a murder weapon

(D)   Determination of the DNA sequence of a human genome

(The correct answer is (B). Recombinant DNA technology has been used to insert the human insulin gene into bacterial expression vectors. This has allowed human insulin to be synthesized and purified in a laboratory, a great advantage over the previous method of purification of insulin from animal sources and thus a benefit in treating diabetes.)

History and Nature of Science

Nature of Scientific Knowledge, Inquiry, and Historical Perspectives

◗ Distinguish among facts, hypotheses, models, theories, and laws

◗ Scientific inquiry, the scientific method, and experimental design (i.e., making observations, formulating and testing hypotheses, drawing conclusions)

  • Different kinds of questions may be studied using different kinds of scientific investigations

---

★ Vegetable crops growing on a commercial farm are damaged by an unknown disease or pest with a 70 to 90 percent mortality rate. The farmer claims that he maintains the same practice for watering and applying fertilizers. Formulate a hypothesis about the causative agent given the observations above. What type of experiments would you use to help support or falsify your hypothesis?

◗ Scientific knowledge is subject to change and open to criticism

◗ Understand the unified, integrative nature of the various scientific disciplines and concepts in science

▶ Historical figures and landmark events in the field of biology (Mendel, Darwin, McClintock, germ theory, structure of DNA, radioisotope tagging, and so on.)

Mathematics, Measurement, and Data Manipulation

▶ Scientific measurement and notation systems

- Metric and U.S. standards for volume, mass, length, molarity, time, temperature, etc.

▶ Processes involved in scientific data collection, analysis, interpretation, and presentation and the critical analysis of sources of data

★ How would you compare information you obtain from the television, a newspaper article, a Web site, and a scientific journal for accuracy? For understandability? For use in the classroom setting?

▶ Interpret and draw conclusions from data, including those presented in tables, graphs, and charts

- Titles, legends, units, dependent and independent variables

▶ Analyze errors in data that are presented

- Statistical accuracy

- Source of error in procedure or process

Laboratory Procedures and Safety

▶ Safety procedures involved in the preparation, storage, use, and disposal of laboratory and field materials

- Acids, bases, toxins, microbiological samples, fire hazards, and so on.

▶ Appropriate use of laboratory techniques such as electrophoresis, chromatography, centrifugation, and the use of microscopes and their handling (calibration, maintenance)

▶ Ability to prepare reagents, materials, and apparatuses correctly for classroom use

★ How would you prepare 1 liter of a 300 mM NaCl solution? If you were going to use this solution to bathe live cells, would it be important to include a buffer in your solution? Explain.

▶ Knowledge of the teacher's legal responsibilities for safety and emergency procedures for the science classroom and laboratory

Molecular and Cellular Biology

Chemical Basis of Life

▶ Structure and characteristics of atoms, molecules, and chemical bonds

- Subatomic particles combine to form atoms
  — Neutrons, protons, electrons, atomic number

★ How do atoms of carbon and oxygen differ in structure and chemical behavior?

- Isotopes and radioactivity
  — Uses of radioactivity (such as medical treatment, energy sources)

- Formation of molecules by chemical bonding
  — Covalent, ionic, and hydrogen bonds

★ What are the four most abundant elements in the human body? What are some of the molecules they help form and why are these molecules important in terms of their biological function?

★ What are the relative strengths of the various types of bonds?

▶ Basic inorganic and organic molecular structures

• Features of carbon-containing molecules

• Functional groups allow for molecular diversity (e.g., carboxyl, amino, hydroxyl)

★ In an aqueous environment, many functional groups can exhibit a negative and/or positive charge. How does the charge influence their behavior? Which functional groups influence the pH of a solution?

▶ pH and its regulation

• Relative concentrations of $[H^+]$ and $[OH^-]$

• Classification of solutions as acidic, basic, or neutral

• pH scale ranges from 0 to 14

★ What are the physiological advantages of the stomach's high concentration of hydrochloric acid (HCl)?

★ What causes acid precipitation? Why is acid precipitation detrimental to the environment?

• Role of buffers

▶ Structure and function of biologically important molecules

• Water
— Unique features (e.g., cohesiveness, solvency, specific heat, density)

★ In a coastal environment, why does the air temperature increase much faster than the water temperature?

★ Explain why the density of water is important to a freshwater pond ecosystem in temperate regions.

• Organic molecules
— Amino acids, proteins
— Nucleotides, nucleic acids
— Glycerol, phosphates and other monomers, fats/lipids
— Monosaccharides (sugars), carbohydrates
— Covalent bonds link monomers together to form polymers
  – Peptide, phosphodiester, ester, and glycosidic bonds
— Polymers may take on higher order structures, as determined by their monomer sequences (e.g., the specific amino acid sequence determines the folding patterns of proteins), which gives them emergent properties and unique functions
— Identify the molecular structures of representative macromolecules

★ Why are fats insoluble in water?

★ What type of macromolecules are starch and glycogen? What are the differences between these two molecules?

★ Describe five important functions of proteins in the human body.

◆ Thermodynamics and free energy

- Anabolic versus catabolic pathways

- Endergonic versus exergonic reactions

- First and second laws of thermodynamics

★ ATP is the immediate source of cellular energy in most cases. How does ATP transfer usable energy to another molecule?

★ How would you classify the following reaction?
Amino acids + Energy $\xrightarrow{\text{(enzymes)}}$ Polypeptide

★ Is it an anabolic or catabolic reaction? Is the free energy change (ΔG) positive or negative for this reaction? Would this reaction occur spontaneously?

◆ Structure and function of enzymes and factors influencing their activity and regulation

- Features of enzymes (e.g., alter the activation energy (E_A) without changing overall ΔG)

- Function of coenzymes and cofactors

- Metabolic pathway regulation

★ How do temperature, pH, and the presence of chemical inhibitors influence enzyme activity?

★ In cellular respiration, ATP inhibits the activity of enzymes along the respiratory metabolic pathway when too much ATP is present in the cell. What benefit is this to the cell?

◆ Cellular bioenergetics: photosynthesis and cellular respiration

- Life processes and most cell functions involve chemical reactions

- Energy and carbon sources used by different life forms

- Photosynthesis
  - Overall chemical reaction for photosynthesis
  - Intracellular locations and functions of the light reactions and the Calvin cycle in eukaryotic cells

---

★ What are the sources of carbon dioxide, water, and oxygen used by a plant in the photosynthetic reaction? Through what structures and by what processes would they enter and/or exit a plant?

  - Pigments involved in photosynthesis
  - Wavelengths of light used in photosynthesis

- Cellular respiration
  - Overall chemical reaction for aerobic respiration
  - Intracellular locations and functions of glycolysis, the Kreb's cycle, electron transport chain, and oxidative phosphorylation in eukaryotic cells
  - Similarities and differences between aerobic and anaerobic (lactic acid and alcohol fermentation) pathways

---

★ At the cellular level, explain the benefit of producing ATP "aerobically." After excessive exercise your body is not able to continue strenuous activity and you may feel a burning sensation in your muscles. What accounts for the burning sensation?

★ Considering that sugars are carbohydrates and not fats, how can eating too much sugar lead to an increase in body fat content?

Cell Structure and Function

- Structure and function of organelles and other subcellular structures

  - Nucleus, nucleolus, ribosomes, smooth endoplasmic reticulum, rough endoplasmic reticulum, Golgi apparatus, lysosomes, vacuoles, mitochondria, chloroplasts, cytoskeletal elements (such as microtubules, microfilaments) extracellular matrix and intercellular junctions (such as gap junctions, plasmodesmata)

★ Plasma cells (B-lymphocytes) function to produce antibody proteins. What types of organelles would you find in high abundance within a plasma cell as compared to a skin cell? What organelles would be in high abundance in a cardiac muscle cell?

★ What structures would you expect to find in a typical plant cell but not in an animal cell?

  - Structural differences in cells leading to functional specialization (e.g., microvilli, flagella, and cilia)

  - Light and electron microscopic techniques used to identify cells and cell structures

- Membrane structure and function

  - Fluid-mosaic model of biological membranes

  - General membrane functions
    — Role of lipids in creating a semipermeable barrier, other factors controlling permeability of plasma membrane (e.g., molecular size change)
    — Role of proteins (e.g., transport, cell-cell recognition)

— Transport mechanisms
  – Passive transport: diffusion, facilitated diffusion, and osmosis
  – Active transport: ion pumps, endocytosis, and exocytosis

★ If you were stranded in a lifeboat on the ocean, why would drinking the ocean water be more harmful than not drinking the water?

★ What are the various mechanisms that organisms such as plants, protists, and bacteria have evolved to survive in water-rich environments?

★ Why must the human body digest large macromolecules into small monomers before it can use them as an energy source?

- Prokaryotic versus eukaryotic cells

  - Cellular level comparison such as DNA organization, presence of organelles, method of cell division

  - Origin of cells; cell theory

  - Endosymbiotic theory

★ A physician may prescribe an antibiotic, such as penicillin, to treat a bacterial infection. Why does penicillin kill bacteria without killing the human being?

★ What characteristics of mitochondria and chloroplasts provide evidence that they were once independent organisms?

- Homeostasis

  - Negative and positive feedback loops

★ Which hormones are involved in the feedback loops responsible for the homeostasis of blood glucose level? Blood calcium level? Are these examples of positive or negative feedback loops? Explain.

▶ The cell cycle

- Events of interphase (G_1, S, G_2)

- Events of the mitotic phase (prophase, metaphase, anaphase, and telophase)

- Cytokinesis (plant cell versus animal cell)

- Mitosis in prokaryotes - binary fission

- Cues for growth control (density, growth factors)

- Cancer cells undergo abnormal cell cycle control
  — Malignancy, metastasis

★ Chemotherapy is the use of chemicals to kill rapidly dividing cells. In addition to killing many types of cancer cells, why does chemotherapy treatment often cause side effects such as anemia, gastrointestinal distress, and hair loss?

★ New classes of drugs that inhibit angiogenesis (blood vessel growth) are being used to treat some forms of cancer. Why would this type of therapy have potential benefit?

▶ Meiosis

- Events of meiosis I and II

- Comparison of mitosis and meiosis in diploid cells (e.g., genetic makeup and size of daughter cells)

Molecular Basis of Heredity

▶ Structure and function of nucleic acids

- DNA and RNA comparison
  — Deoxyribonucleotides versus ribonucleotides
    – Sugar, base, and phosphate groups
    – A, C, G, T, and U bases, base pairing, and hydrogen bonding

★ Describe Watson and Crick's model of DNA.

▶ Mechanism of DNA replication

- Enzymes involved in replication (e.g., DNA polymerase, helicase, ligase)

★ Given the following strand of DNA, what would be the complementary (3'→ 5') strand's sequence? 5' ATTCCGTACGGC 3'

★ Describe the Meselson-Stahl experiment that supported the hypothesis that DNA replication is semiconservative.

▶ mRNA synthesis: Mechanism of Transcription

- Enzymes involved in RNA synthesis (e.g., RNA polymerase)

- Relationship between DNA and mRNA sequence

- Modification of mRNA transcript in eukaryotes

▶ Protein synthesis: Mechanism of Translation

- Functions of ribosomes, mRNA codons, tRNA anticodons

- Relationship between mRNA, tRNA, and protein sequence
  — One amino acid is coded for by a three-base mRNA codon

▶ Gene regulation controls cell growth, function, and differentiation
 — Genes give instructions for synthesis of specific proteins

★ If all the cells in the human body have the same DNA, why then are liver cells functionally and structurally different from muscle cells?

▶ Mutation and transposable elements generate genetic variability

 • Mutations may occur naturally (e.g., error in DNA replication)

 • Types of mutations (e.g., insertions, deletions, substitutions)

 • Mutations in germ cells (gametes) can be inherited; mutations in somatic cells are not inherited

▶ Mutations and their role in genetic diseases such as sickle-cell anemia, hemophilia, cancer

▶ Viral classification and their role in disease

 • Compare major viral classes (e.g., type of genetic material, life cycles)

★ What specific type of virus causes the common cold? The flu? Cold sores?

★ How does the HIV virus replicate in the human body? What techniques can be used to prevent the spread of HIV?

▶ Recombinant DNA in nature and in the laboratory

 • Cloning and gene splicing
  — Restriction enzymes, vectors (e.g., plasmids)

• Polymerase chain reaction (PCR)

• Gene therapy

• Diagnostic, forensic, and agricultural applications

★ How has DNA technology been used to solve criminal cases? To treat diabetes?

▶ Microbial genetics

 • Bacterial chromosomes are circular DNA

 • Mechanisms of transduction, conjugation, and transformation

▶ The significance of mapping the genome of organisms and the Human Genome Project

Genetics and Evolution

Genetics

▶ Mendelian inheritance

 • Dominant and recessive traits

 • Law of segregation, independent assortment

 • Use of Mendelian laws and prediction of genetic cross outcomes
  — Monohybrid cross
  — Dihybrid cross
  — Punnett square and probability analysis
  — Pedigree analysis to understand patterns of inheritance or history of traits in a family

▶ Non-Mendelian inheritance

 • Codominance

 • Epistasis

 • Incomplete dominance

 • Linkage and gene mapping

- Multiple allelism
- Polygenic inheritance
- Sex-linkage

★ What percentage of offspring will be expected to have blood type A if the parents have blood types AB and O? What percentage will have blood type O?

★ In an animal species, there are two alleles for fur color, black and white. These alleles exhibit incomplete dominance. If two animals are mated, one with black fur and one with white fur, what would be the predicted genotypes and phenotype ratios of their offspring?

★ A wild-type fruit fly (heterozygous for both body color and eye color) is mated with a fly exhibiting two recessive mutations, ebony body and sepia eye. The offspring distribution is 100 wild body/wild eye, 34 wild body/sepia eye, 30 ebony body/wild eye, and 94 ebony body/wild eye. Are the genes for these two mutations linked or not? Explain.

★ In humans, why are more males than females color-blind?

▶ Human Genetics

- Normal chromosome number (haploid versus diploid), karyotypes
- Autosomes versus sex chromosomes, sex determination

▶ Genetic aberrations may lead to common human disorders

- Chromosomal aberrations (e.g., Down syndrome, Klinefelter syndrome)
- Gene aberrations (e.g., cystic fibrosis, sickle cell disease, Tay-Sachs)

▶ Interactions between heredity and the environment

- Environmental factors influence gene expression (e.g., temperature changes, food sources)
- Chemical and radiation mutagenesis

★ What are the consequences of prolonged exposure to the Sun? How are these consequences related to changes in the DNA of skin cells?

★ Why do Siamese cats and Himalayan rabbits exhibit dark fur only in the regions of the nose, ears, and paws?

Evolution

▶ Scientific evidence supporting the theory of evolution

- Biogeography
- Comparative anatomy and embryology
- Fossil record
  — Mechanism of fossil formation
  — Stratigraphy
- Homology versus analogy
- Molecular evidence (DNA and protein comparisons)
- Historical figures (e.g., Cuvier, Darwin, Lamarck)

▶ The Hardy-Weinberg theorem and calculation of allelic frequencies in nonevolving populations

★ Cystic fibrosis is an autosomal recessive genetic disease. If one out of every 2,000 individuals has the disease, how many people in the population are expected carriers (heterozygotes)? What is the frequency of the "normal" allele?

★ What basic criteria must a population meet to be in Hardy-Weinberg equilibrium?

▶ Mechanisms altering allelic frequencies in a gene pool

- Genetic drift
  — Bottleneck effect
  — Founder's effect

- Gene flow

- Random mutation

- Non-random mating

- Natural selection

★ A radioactive meteorite falls to Earth and kills 90 percent of a secluded population of salamander. What processes are in action changing allelic frequencies in the gene pool of this population?

▶ Evolution, speciation, and phylogeny

- Mechanisms of evolution
  — Darwin's theory of natural selection

★ Explain the following concepts relative to Darwin's theory of natural selection to the environment: a) Descent with modification, b) Struggle for existence, and c) Adaptation.

★ A doctor prescribed the antibiotic tetracycline for treatment of an infection. The patient recovered. Several weeks later, the patient returned to the doctor with the same symptoms. Again the doctor prescribed tetracycline, but this time the infection was not cured. A prescription for vancomycin was given and treatment was successful. Use the concept of natural selection to explain what occurred in this case.

  — Gradualism versus punctuated equilibrium
  — Convergent versus divergent evolution

- Biological definition of species

★ Horses and donkeys can mate and produce offspring; why then are they not classified as the same species?

- Pre- and postzygotic barriers isolating gene pools, such as behavioral isolation, mechanical isolation, reduced hybrid viability

- Geographical barriers isolating populations
  — Allopatric speciation
  — Sympatric speciation
  — Adaptive radiation

- The basis for development of phylogenetic trees

- Mechanisms leading to the extinction of species

◆ Scientific theories of the origin of life on Earth

- Earth's age

- Abiotic synthesis

- Evidence for the appearance of different forms of life on Earth

★ Create a phylogenetic tree that includes the dates of the earliest evidence for the appearance of the following life forms on Earth: prokaryotes, multicellular organisms, fish, amphibians, plants, mammals, and reptiles

Organismal Biology and Diversity of Life

Diversity of Life

◆ Biological classification systems are based on how organisms are related

- Three-domain system: *Bacteria, Archaea, Eukarya*

- Five-kingdom system: *Monera, Protista, Fungi, Plantae, Animalia*

- Nomenclature schemes organize life from the most broad to the most specific relationships
  — Kingdom, Phylum/Division, Class, Order, Family, Genus, Species

★ Determine the proper nomenclature scheme (kingdom through species) for humans and understand why humans are placed into each of these categories (e.g., Humans are part of the kingdom *Animalia* because they are multicellular, eukaryotic, ingestive chemoheterotrophs).

◆ Characteristics and examples of bacteria, protists, fungi, plants, and animals

- The different species of life on Earth are related by descent from common ancestors

- Features shared by all forms of life (e.g., genetic material, energy requirements)

- Features not shared by all forms of life (e.g., cellular structure, reproductive strategies, food sources, unicellular versus multicellular organization)

★ Into which kingdom would you classify the following organisms and why? A green alga, a mushroom, *Planaria, Paramecium, E. coli,* an ocean sponge?

Plants

◆ Evolution

- Characteristics that facilitated the successful adaptation of plants to land
  — Root, stem and leaf specializations, seed formation

- Major plant divisions and the characteristics that determine placement of plants into these divisions (such as vascular versus avascular, seed forming versus seedless)
  — Bryophytes
  — Pterophytes (ferns)
  — Gymnosperms (conifers)
  — Angiosperms (flowering plants)
    – Understand the relationships between flowers, fruits, and seeds

★ What structural features and reproductive strategies have made angiosperms the most successful and diverse class of plants on Earth?

◗ Anatomy

- Structure and function of plant organs and tissues
  — Roots, stems, leaves
  — Reproductive organs
  — Vascular, ground, dermal, and meristematic tissues

◗ Physiology

- Nutrition (e.g., sources of carbon, nitrogen)

- Photosynthetic adaptations: C_3 versus C_4 versus CAM plants

- Regulation of growth and development using hormones (such as auxins, cytokinins), photoperiods, and tropisms (such as phototropism, gravitropism)

★ Consider a seed planted upside down in the soil. When the seed germinates, why does the root grow downward into the soil while the shoot grows upward?

- Nutrient uptake and distribution of materials within the plant, such as water, nitrates, minerals
  — Role of roots, stems, and leaves in transport
  — Role of xylem, phloem, and companion cells in transport and their locations within a plant
  — Transpiration

★ An experiment is set up to measure transpiration rates in geraniums. A control plant is placed in a growth chamber set up at 25°C, 50 percent relative humidity, and a cycle of 12 hours light and 12 hours dark. A second plant is placed in a different growth chamber with identical condition except that the relative humidity is set at 90 percent. A third plant is placed under identical conditions as the control except that it is kept in the dark. A fourth plant has identical conditions as the control except that the temperature is set to 35°C. For which plant would the transpiration rate be expected to be the highest? the lowest? Explain your predictions.

◗ Reproduction

- Alternation of generations
  — Compare gametophytes versus sporophytes, haploid versus diploid

- Fertilization and zygote formation

- Seed anatomy, dispersal, and germination

- Seedling growth, differentiation, and development

- Vegetative propagation (asexual reproduction)

Animals

◗ Evolution

- Classification based on phylogeny
  — *Porifera, Cnidaria, Platyhelminthes, Nematoda, Rotifera, Mollusca, Arthropoda, Annelida, Echinodermata, Chordata*

- Characteristics and examples of animals of the major phyla, including the presence of true tissues, radial versus bilateral symmetry, presence of a body cavity, protostomes versus deuterostomes

▶ Anatomy and physiology of structures associated with life functions of organisms in the animal kingdom:

- Digestion
  — Specialization of feeding/digestive structures on different animals
  — Structure and function of the human gastrointestinal tract and associated exocrine organs
  — Location and action of enzymes (e.g., trypsin, α-amylase) during digestion of food in the human digestive tract
  — Hormones controlling food digestion (e.g., cholecystokinin, gastrin)

★ How would you expect the digestive system of a rabbit (a herbivore) to differ from that of a lion (a carnivore)?

★ You have just finished a cheeseburger, potato chips, and an apple for lunch. For each major type of nutrient in this meal, describe the process of digestion from the mouth all the way to the large intestine. What hormones would be released into the bloodstream to help the body process this food more effectively and what would be the effects of these hormones?

- Circulation
  — Structure and function of the heart and major blood vessels (e.g., artery, vein, and capillary)

- Structure and function of blood components (e.g., erythrocytes, hemoglobin, leukocytes, platelets, plasma), role of bone marrow in cell formation

---

★ What are some noninherited and internal physiological factors that can lead to hypertension (high blood pressure)? If hypertension is uncontrolled, what health problems can occur?

★ What is an electrocardiogram (EKG) and what does it measure?

- Respiration
  — Compare the mechanisms of gills versus lungs for oxygen and carbon dioxide exchange (e.g., surface areas, environment, countercurrent exchange mechanism)

- Excretion
  — Control of osmotic balance and fluid volumes in different animals
  — Structure and function of the human kidney
  — Hormones controlling volume and composition of urine (e.g., antidiuretic hormone, angiotensin II)

- Nervous control
  — Brain and spinal cord structure and function
  — Sensory and motor systems, reflex actions
  — Neurotransmitters
  — Communication between cells using action potentials
  — Sense organs and interaction with the environment (vision, taste, etc.)

★ Some snakes and fish have a poisonous venom to help defend themselves and to kill prey. One such toxin, TTX, inhibits the activity of sodium channels in neuronal plasma membranes. How does the toxin cause paralysis and death in its victims?

- Contractile systems and movement
  — Skeletal, cardiac, and smooth muscle
  — Mechanism of contraction (e.g., roles of myosin, actin, Ca^{2+})

- Support systems (e.g., chitin exoskeleton, bony endoskeletons)

- Integument (skin)
  — Role in thermoregulation (vasodilation/constriction of skin blood vessels, sweating)
  — Role as a barrier to infection and fluid loss

- Immunity
  — Role of leukocytes (T-cells, B-cells, etc.), immunoglobulins, antibodies, antigens, inflammation, complement

- Endocrine control
  — Actions of major hormones (e.g., pituitary hormones, thyroid hormones)
  — Regulation by the hypothalamus
  — Regulation of cell activities by fat-soluble versus water-soluble hormones
  — Communication via pheromones

★ List the hormones involved in the human female menstrual cycle and describe how they regulate the cycle.

★ When a person is exercising, heart rate, breathing rate, and blood pressure elevate, glands in the skin begin to produce sweat, and digestion and urine formation slow. What types of hormones/neurotransmitters are most important in controlling this effect? Explain the physiological advantages of having each of these changes occur during exercise.

◗ Reproduction and Development

- Asexual strategies (e.g., parthenogenesis in *Daphnia*, budding in *Hydra*)

- Gametogenesis

- Fertilization and zygote formation
  — Internal versus external fertilization

★ Why do fish and frogs have different reproductive strategies than humans?

- Embryo development (cleavage, blastula formation, germ layers) growth, differentiation (e.g., induction, homeotic genes) and aging

- Metamorphosis (complete and incomplete)

◗ Behavior

- Taxes

- Innate/Instinctual behaviors (e.g., fixed action patterns)

- Learned behaviors (e.g., imprinting, classical and operant conditioning)

- Social behaviors (e.g., territoriality, altruism, dominance)

- Role of behavior in survival and reproductive success

- Understanding the biological basis of behavior helps our understanding of psychology, sociology, and anthropology

Ecology: Organisms and Environments

Populations

▶ Intraspecific competition

▶ Main concepts of population growth

- Exponential versus logistic growth, carrying capacity, S and J curves

- Features of r- versus K-selected populations

- Boom/bust cycling

- Density-dependent (e.g., habitat availability) and density-independent (e.g., weather) factors

- Human population growth: age-structure pyramids in developed and developing countries

- Life-history patterns
  — Survivorship curves
  — Reproductive strategies, birth rates, onset of sexual maturity, mortality rates, life span and factors that influence them

★ "The human population has been growing exponentially for the last three centuries and will continue to do so indefinitely." Is this statement accurate? Explain your answer.

▶ Patterns of dispersion (random, clumped, uniform)

Communities

▶ Species diversity

▶ Niche concepts (fundamental niche versus realized niche)

▶ Interspecific relationships and their effect on the community

- Impact on evolution, coevolution (e.g., evidence suggests that flowering plants and pollinating insects appeared on Earth during similar eras)

- Predation
  — Defense mechanisms against predation (e.g., mimicry)

- Parasitism

- Commensalism

- Mutualism

★ A lethal virus infects a large percentage of the mice population in a grassland ecosystem. What is the relationship between the virus and the mice? How will the virus ultimately influence other members of the ecosystem such as the grass and an owl?

▶ Succession

- Primary versus secondary (e.g., soil usage, vegetation succession)

Ecosystems

▶ Types, characteristics of and biological diversity within biomes

- Aquatic (e.g., wetland, estuary, lakes, oceanic pelagic)

> ★ Describe four abiotic factors that may be important to the life of a cactus in a desert. How might the cactus adjust on a daily basis to changes in these factors?

- Terrestrial (e.g., temperate deciduous, tundra, taiga, chaparral)

- Abiotic factors (e.g., temperature, moisture level, light)

▶ Energy flow

- Trophic levels
  — Producers, consumers, decomposers, autotrophs, and heterotrophs
  — Energy loss at trophic levels (10% rule)

- Food chains

- Food webs

- Productivity (gross, primary, net)

- Biomass, pyramids of biomass and numbers

- Biomagnification

> ★ Create a food web, with organisms placed at an appropriate trophic level, using the following organisms: zooplankton, eagle, freshwater shrimp, green algae, goose, mouse, beetle, bacteria, trout, bear, and mushroom. How would the presence of the pesticide DDT affect this food web?

▶ Biogeochemical cycles

- Nitrogen

- Carbon

- Water

- Phosphorus

▶ Concept of stability and the effects of disturbances on ecosystems

▶ Human impact on ecological systems (e.g., greenhouse effect, deforestation, ozone depletion, agriculture, pesticide use)

> ★ Describe the greenhouse effect. How have humans contributed to enhancing this effect? Why are environmental researchers concerned about its effect on the rising of sea level?
>
> ★ How could the use of fertilizer to increase crop yield on a farm be detrimental to a nearby lake ecosystem?

▶ Interrelationships among ecosystems

Science, Technology, and Social Perspectives

▶ The impact of science and technology on the environment and human affairs

- Personal and community health

- Population growth

- Natural resources

- Energy production and use

- Environmental quality

▶ Issues associated with human and nature-induced hazards (e.g., radioactive waste, flooding, volcanoes, smog, acid precipitation)

▶ Issues associated with the production, storage, use, management, and disposal of consumer products (e.g., recycling, logging, use of fossil fuels, landfills)

▶ Natural resource management (e.g., wetland conservation, soil erosion control, groundwater)

◆ The social, political, ethical, and economic issues arising from science, technology and health and medical advancements (e.g., genetic-property laws, cloning, prolonging life, stem cell research)

★ Give examples of how events such as the clear-cutting of the tropical rain forests and building of nuclear energy plants have had both positive and negative impacts on humans and the environment.

★ It what ways have humans contributed to depletion of the ozone layer? What effect would destruction of the ozone layer have on life on Earth, including humans?

Unifying Concepts in Science

Because conceptual and procedural schemes unify scientific disciplines, the understanding and abilities listed below can be found within any of the other specific content domains.

◆ Systems, order, and organization

◆ Evidence, models, and explanation

◆ Constancy, change, and measurement

◆ Evolution and equilibrium

◆ Form and function

★ Why is each of these ideas considered a crucial conceptual or procedural scheme and how is each one integrated throughout the study of biology?

Chapter 4

Study Topics for the *Chemistry: Content Knowledge* Tests

▶ ▶   ▶   ▶   ▶   ▶   ▶   ▶   ▶   ▶   ▶   ▶

Introduction to the tests

The *Chemistry: Content Knowledge* tests are designed to measure the subject-area knowledge and competencies necessary for a beginning teacher of chemistry in a secondary school. The topics for questions are typically those covered in introductory college-level chemistry and physical science courses, although some questions of a more advanced nature are included, because secondary-school instructors must understand the subject matter from a more advanced viewpoint than that presented to their students. In addition, since a major goal of science education is to have students develop an understanding of science and the impact of science and technology on the environment and human affairs, these areas are included in the assessment. The questions include definition of terms, comprehension of critical concepts, application, analysis, and problem solving.

Examinees will not need to use calculators in taking these tests. The test book contains a periodic table and a table of information that presents various physical constants and a few conversion factors among SI units. Whenever necessary, additional values of physical constants are printed within the text of a question.

The tests are designed to reflect current standards for knowledge, skills, and abilities in science education. Educational Testing Service (ETS) has aligned these tests closely with the National Science Education Standards and works in collaboration with teacher educators, higher education content specialists, and accomplished practicing teachers in the field of chemistry to keep the tests updated and representative of current standards.

You are likely to find that the topics below are covered by most introductory chemistry textbooks, but a general survey textbook may not cover all of the subtopics. Consult materials and resources, including lecture and laboratory notes, from all your chemistry coursework. You should be able to match up specific topics and subtopics with what you have covered in your courses in general chemistry, organic chemistry, chemical analysis, biochemistry, and so on.

Try not to be overwhelmed by the volume and scope of content knowledge in this guide. An overview such as this that lists chemistry topics does not offer you a great deal of context. Although a specific term may not seem familiar as you see it here, you might find you could understand it when applied to a real-life situation. Many of the items on the actual PRAXIS test will provide you with a context to apply to these topics or terms, as you will see when you look at the practice questions in chapter 11.

Special questions marked with stars:
Interspersed throughout the list of topics are questions that are outlined in boxes and preceded by stars (★). These questions are intended to help you test your knowledge of fundamental concepts and your ability to apply fundamental concepts to situations in the laboratory or the real world. Most of the questions require you to combine several pieces of knowledge in order to formulate an integrated understanding and response. If you spend time on these questions, you will gain increased understanding and facility with the subject matter covered on the test. You might want to discuss these questions and your answers with a teacher or mentor.

Note that the questions marked with stars are not short-answer or multiple-choice, and this study guide does not provide the answers. The questions marked with stars are intended as study questions, not practice questions. Thinking about the answers to them should improve your understanding of fundamental concepts and will probably help you answer a broad range of questions on the test. For example, the following box with a star appears in the list of study topics under Periodicity and Reactivity:

> ★ Know how atomic/ionic radii, ionization energy, and melting points and boiling points change across periods and down columns in the periodic table.

If you think about this question, perhaps jotting down some notes on the important terminology involved, you will review your knowledge of the periodic table that applies to atomic radii, ionization energy, melting points, and boiling points, and then you will have probably prepared yourself to answer multiple-choice questions similar to the one below:

Of the following, which has the smallest atomic radius?

(A) Sb
(B) I
(C) P
(D) Cl

The correct answer is D. As you proceed down the periodic table, atomic radius typically increases, and as you proceed across a row, the atomic radius typically decreases. Therefore, Cl is smaller than P.

Matter and Energy

◗ Particulate structure of matter

- Atomic, molecular, and ionic nature of matter

- Organization of molecules/atoms in solids, liquids, and gases

◗ Organization of matter

- Elements, compounds, solutions, mixtures

◗ Physical and chemical properties/changes of matter

- Difference between physical and chemical properties

- Difference between physical and chemical changes

- Basic physical properties of matter

> ★ Test tubes contain three colorless liquids: alcohol, water, and a weak solution of ammonia. What properties could be used to identify the liquids?

◗ Forms of energy

- Chemical, electrical, electromagnetic, heat, kinetic, light, magnetic, mechanical, nuclear, potential, sound, etc.

Atomic and Nuclear Structure

◗ Atomic models/structure

- Description of models
  — Thomson model, Bohr model, quantum mechanical model, etc.

- Atomic structure
  — Location and number of protons, neutrons, and electrons

— Atomic number and atomic mass

— Isotopes

— Experimental basis of atomic structure and subatomic particles; Rutherford's experiments, etc.

★ How are isotopes of the same element alike? How are they different?

◆ Electron configuration

- Aufbau principle

- Correlation of electron configuration to periodic table

- Relationship of electron configuration to chemical and physical properties

- Energy of electrons in various configurations

- Quantum numbers of electrons in various electron configurations

★ What are the electron configurations for atoms of the following elements: a) sodium, b) sulfur?

★ Based on their electron configurations, what is the formula of the compound that forms in the reaction of sodium and sulfur?

◆ Interaction of electromagnetic radiation with electrons

- Relationship between, energy, frequency, and wavelength of electromagnetic radiation and electron transition

- Emission spectrum of the hydrogen atom

- Photoelectric effect

★ List in order of increasing energy (or decreasing wavelength) the following forms of electromagnetic radiation: gamma rays, microwaves, x-rays, visible, ultraviolet, and infrared light.

★ What is the wavelength of the energy emitted when a hydrogen electron drops from the $n = 3$ to $n = 2$ electronic energy level?

◆ Radioactivity

- Characteristics and effects of various types of radioactive particles and decay
  — Alpha, beta, gamma, etc.
  — Symbols used to describe each

- Nuclear reactions
  — Fusion, fission, and transmutations
  — Symbols and balancing nuclear reactions

- Radioactive decay process
  — Half-life
  — Applications such as radiocarbon dating

★ Given that the half-life of carbon-14 is 5,730 years, estimate the age of a piece of charcoal that has a carbon-14 content equal to 12.5% of that in living matter.

Periodicity and Reactivity

◆ Periodic trends

- Atomic/ionic radii

- Electronegativity

- Ionization energy and electron affinity

- Physical properties such as melting point

★ Know how atomic/ionic radii, ionization energy, and melting points and boiling points change across periods and down columns in the periodic table.

◆ Chemical reactivity

• Bond types based on position of elements in the periodic table

• Periodic trends in reactivity

★ How do the chemical characteristics of the elements in a period change as you move from left to right across the periodic table?

★ How can the periodic table be used to identify ionic, covalent, or polar covalent bonds between atoms?

Heat, Thermodynamics, and Thermochemistry

◆ Heat and temperature

• Understand the terms "heat" and "temperature"

• Temperature scales such as Celsius and Kelvin

• Measurement of heat and units

◆ Phase equilibrium and thermal exchange

• Heat of vaporization, fusion, and sublimation

• Heat capacity and specific heat

• Phase diagrams

★ How much heat is needed to convert 10 grams of ice to 10 grams of water vapor?

★ Predict the boiling point of water at 2 bars pressure from a phase diagram.

◆ Kinetic molecular theory

• Description of an ideal gas

• Molecular speed and kinetic energy distribution

• Gas laws

• Real gases

★ If a gas expands from 5 liters to 10 liters and its temperature increases from 300K to 500K, what will happen to the pressure of the gas?

★ Will the volume of water vapor at room conditions be equal to, greater than, or less than that predicted for an ideal gas?

◆ Laws of thermodynamics

• First law and internal energy

• Second and third laws, and entropy

• Gibbs' energy, spontaneity, and equilibrium

★ Based on the first and second laws of thermodynamics, will the following exothermic reaction be spontaneous: $C(s) + O_2(g) \rightarrow CO_2(g)$?

◆ Thermochemistry

• Enthalpy of reaction (heat of reaction)

• Enthalpy of solution, lattice energy, etc.

• Hess's law

- Reaction coordinate energy diagrams
- Entropy changes and Gibbs' energy changes in chemical reactions

★ Given the heats of formation of H_2O, CO_2, and CH_4, calculate the heat of combustion of CH_4.

★ Given a reaction coordinate diagram, indicate the activation energy of a reaction.

Nomenclature

▶ Inorganic compounds

- Binary ionic compounds and compounds involving polyatomic ions
- Molecular compounds
- Acids/bases

★ Give the correct IUPAC name for each of the following compounds: $HClO_4$, $CaSO_4 \cdot 2H_2O$, and $CuCl_2$.

▶ Organic compounds

- Functional groups such as alkanes, alkenes, alkynes, alcohols, aldehydes, esters, ethers, ketones, carboxylic acids, amides, and amines, etc.

★ Give the correct IUPAC name for each of the following compounds: CH_3NH_2, CH_3OCH_3,

and $CH_3\overset{\displaystyle O}{\overset{\|}{C}}\!-\!X$, where

$X = H$, CH_3, OH, OCH_3, and NH_2.

- Common biological compounds, such as proteins, carbohydrates, etc.

The Mole, Chemical Bonding, and Molecular Geometry

▶ Chemical formulas

- Interpretation of formulas
- The mole concept
- Chemical composition
- Empirical and molecular formulas
- Calculations of numbers and masses of atoms and molecules, etc.

★ What is the number of moles of oxygen atoms in 5 moles of $CaSO_4 \cdot 2H_2O$?

★ What is the molecular formula of a compound that has the empirical formula C_2H_4O and a molar mass of 88 grams?

▶ Bond types

- Covalent
- Ionic
- Metallic
- Hybrid orbital bonding
- Sigma and pi bonding

★ How many sigma and pi bonds are in an ethyne, C_2H_2, molecule?

★ Determine the type of bonds found in $NaCl$, $NaSO_4$, and SO_2.

▶ Bond properties

- Bond angles
- Bond strength
- Bond length
- Bond energies

- Polarity/nonpolarity/degree of ionization and correlation with properties such as electrical conductivity
- Correlation with chemical reactivity

★ Compare the degree of ionization of HCl and H_2S in water.

★ Compare the bond lengths and bond strengths of the carbon oxygen bond in CH_3CH_2OH

and $CH_3\overset{\overset{\displaystyle O}{\|}}{C}CH_3$.

▶ Molecular structure
- Geometry and VSEPR theory
- Lewis dot structure and resonance structures
- Types of intermolecular forces: van der Waals, dipole-dipole, hydrogen bonding, etc.

★ Why is the shape of ammonia, NH_3, pyramidal?

★ What are both the Lewis dot and structural formulas for methane, CH_4?

★ What are the resonance structures for the carbonate ion, CO_3^{2-}?

- Correlation of intermolecular forces with physical properties such as boiling point, melting point, heat of vaporization, vapor pressure, etc.

★ Predict the relative boiling points of H_2O, Cl_2, Br_2, I_2, HCl, and H_2.

Solutions and Solubility

▶ Solution types and terminology
- Dilute and concentrated
- Ionic versus nonionic
- Supersaturated, saturated, and unsaturated

▶ Solubility and dissolution
- Factors affecting dissolution rate, such as temperature, stirring, surface area, etc.
- Factors affecting solubility, such as temperature, common ion effect, pH, nature of solvent, etc.

★ Why is ammonia gas very soluble in water while oxygen, O_2, is only slightly soluble?

- K_{sp} and solubility calculations
  — Calculation of K_{sp} from solubility data
  — Calculation of solubility from K_{sp}
  — Relative solubility of various compounds
- Electrical conductivity

▶ Concentration terms and calculations
- Calculation and interpretation of terms such as molar, molal, mole fraction, percent by mass or volume, parts per million, etc.
- Preparation of solutions and dilution calculations

★ How many grams of solute are present in 1.5 liters of 0.30 M KNO_3?

★ How do you prepare 200 mL of 0.5 M $CaSO_4$ from a stock solution of 2.0 M $CaSO_4$?

- Colligative properties

  - Freezing point depression and boiling point elevation
    — Understand phenomena
    — Calculate
    — Compare values for various substances

  - Vapor pressure effects

★ What will happen to vapor pressure, boiling point, and freezing point of water when a nonvolatile solute is added to water?

Acid/Base Chemistry

- Acid/base definitions and basic concepts

  - Brønsted-Lowry and Lewis definitions and identification of acids and bases

  - Conjugate acids and bases

  - Compare acid-base strength of various compounds

  - Weak and strong acids

  - Neutralization reactions

- Acid-base equilibrium

  - pH, [H$^+$], [OH$^-$] calculations

★ What is the [H$^+$] of a solution if pH = 5.5?

  - K_a and K_b for weak acids and bases

  - Percent ionization

  - Hydrolysis of salts of weak acids or bases

  - Buffer solutions

★ What is the pH of a solution of the salt NaCN, given the K_a for HCN?

- Acid-base titration

  - Titration curves involving strong and weak acids and bases

  - Indicators and end point detection

  - Calculations of pH, pKa from titration data

  - Analysis of species present at various points during a titration

★ Know the relationship between pK_a of indicator and its effective indicating range.

★ Based on a titration curve, determine the pK_a of the acid and the volume of base required to neutralize the acid.

Chemical Reactions

- Stoichiometry

  - Balancing chemical reaction equations, including redox reactions

  - Calculations of moles, masses, and volumes of reactants or products based on balanced reaction equations

- Types of reactions

  - Predict products
    — Single inorganic reactions
    — Family/group reactions

  - Single replacement, double replacement, combination, decomposition, and combustion reactions

  - Transition metal complexes

- Chemical kinetics

  - Rate laws and constants

  - Reaction mechanisms and rate law

- Half-lives
- Activation energy and temperature dependence of rate constants
- Catalysts
- Collision theory for simple bimolecular reactions

★ Be able to determine simple rate expressions based on experimental data and understand effect of temperature and catalysts on reaction rate.

◆ Chemical equilibrium
- Equilibrium constants and calculations
- Effects of temperature on equilibrium
- Gibbs' energy, enthalpy, and entropy of reactions
- Le Châtelier's principle

★ In general terms, what will happen to a chemical equilibrium if the temperature, pressure, or concentration of one of the reactants is changed?

◆ Redox chemistry
- Basic redox concepts
  — Oxidation and reduction
  — Oxidation number
  — Oxidizing and reducing agents
- Electrochemistry
  — Electrochemical cells' description and use
  — Reduction potentials and redox reactions/half reactions
  — Electrochemical reactivity series

  — Nernst equation
  — Faraday's law

★ Based on the reduction potentials, predict whether a particular electrochemical reaction will proceed spontaneously.

Biochemistry and Organic Chemistry

◆ Common biochemical compounds such as amino acids, proteins, sugars, carbohydrates, fatty acids, lipids, etc.
- Recognition of basic names and structures
- Well-known reactions such as hydrolysis and formation of peptide bonds

★ From a list of molecules, identify which is a protein, a carbohydrate, or lipid.

◆ Organic functional groups
- Names and structures of compounds such as alkanes, alkenes, alkynes, alcohols, aldehydes, ketones, esters, ethers, carboxylic acids, amides, and amines
- Common functional group reactions

★ Know the functional groups that distinguish alcohols, aldehydes, etc.

★ What is the product of the reaction of $CH_2=CH_2$ with HBr?

History and Nature of Science

- ◗ Methods and philosophy

  - Understand models, assumptions, hypotheses, theories, laws, etc.

  - Problem-solving methods
    — Making observations
    — Developing generalizations
    — Formulating problems
    — Forming and testing hypotheses
    — Making inferences
    — Categorizing, ordering, and comparing data
    — Applications

  - Experimental design
    — Data collection, interpretation, and presentation
    — Analysis of design and relationship to theory
    — Significance of controls

★ Compare and contrast scientific laws, hypotheses, theories, etc., and illustrate each with an example and support.

- ◗ Historical perspectives

  - Knowledge of major contributions made by well-known historical figures such as Boyle, Dalton, Lavoisier, Bohr, Lewis, etc.

  - Historical roots of current theory

  - Knowledge of how processes of science have affected historical development and changes (e.g., theories abandoned based on evidence; new theories arise)

  - Integration of the overarching concepts (e.g., conservation of energy in many contexts)

Scientific Procedures and Techniques

- ◗ Mathematics, measurement, and data manipulation

  - Measurements
    — Units
    — Scientific notation
    — Equipment

★ What is the mass in grams of a sample that has a mass of 20 mg?

★ What is the uncertainty in the measurements made when using various pieces of equipment such as a buret?

  - Data collection and processing
    — Significant figures
    — Organization of data
    — Interpret and draw conclusions from tables, charts, and graphs

---

★ How many significant figures are in each of the following measurements? a) 0.136 cm, b) 43.00 m, c) 7,000 g, d) 5.8×10^6 kg.

  - Data error analysis
    — Accuracy and precision
    — Mean, uncertainty, and standard deviation
    — Sources of error in procedure and process

★ Understand the general meaning of the concepts of accuracy, precision, uncertainty, and standard deviation.

◆ Laboratory Procedures and Safety

- Equipment
  — Calibration and maintenance
  — Proper use, safety procedures and precautions
  — Preparation for classroom use

- Chemicals and materials
  — Proper use and storage
  — Safe disposal and safety procedures or precautions
  — Preparation for classroom use

- Emergency procedures for the teaching laboratory

- Legal responsibility

- Proper procedures for carrying and basic tasks such as weighing, titration, etc.

★ Know all the procedures, precautions, and equipment used to prepare a 0.15 M HCl solution.

Science, Technology, and Social Perspectives

◆ Applications of chemistry in everyday life, such as radioisotope use in medicine

★ Would a gamma emitter with a half-life of 29 years be useful as a radioisotope used in medicine?

◆ Impact of chemistry

- The environment (acid rain, etc.)

- Human affairs (effect of changes in medicine, effect on lifestyle, etc.)

★ What are the major contributors of acid rain?

◆ Consumer products

- Production, storage, by-products, and waste disposal

- Use of products

- Economic, management, ethical, political, and social issues

★ Know the general chemical properties of some common consumer products, such as soap, vinegar, etc.

◆ Energy

- Production, transmission, and waste disposal

- Energy sources and resources

- Economic, management, ethical, political, and social issues

★ Compare the availability and limitations of the following sources of power: geothermal, nuclear, hydroelectric, solar, and fossil fuels.

◆ Management of natural resources

Chapter 5

Study Topics for the
Earth and Space Sciences: Content Knowledge Test

▶   ▶   ▶   ▶   ▶   ▶   ▶   ▶   ▶   ▶   ▶   ▶

Introduction to the test

The *Earth and Space Sciences* test is designed to assess whether an examinee has the knowledge and competencies necessary for a beginning teacher of secondary school Earth and space sciences. The 100 multiple-choice questions address the examinee's knowledge of fundamental scientific concepts, methods, principles, phenomena, and interrelationships. Questions are derived from topics typically covered in introductory college-level courses in Earth and space sciences, including geology, meteorology, oceanography, astronomy, and environmental science. The questions require a variety of abilities, including an emphasis on the comprehension of critical concepts, analysis to address and solve problems, and an understanding of important terms. Some questions may require the examinee to integrate concepts from more than one content area.

The test is designed to reflect current standards for knowledge, skills, and abilities in science education. Educational Testing Service (ETS) has aligned the test closely with the National Science Education Standards and works in collaboration with teacher educators, higher education content specialists, and accomplished practicing teachers in the field of Earth and space sciences to keep the test updated and representative of current standards.

You are likely to find that the topics below are covered by most introductory Earth and space sciences textbooks, but a general survey textbook may not cover all of the subtopics. Consult materials and resources, including lecture and laboratory notes, from all your Earth and space sciences coursework. You should be able to match up specific topics and subtopics with what you have covered in your courses in geology, oceanography, meteorology, astronomy, and so on.

Try not to be overwhelmed by the volume and scope of content knowledge in this guide. An overview such as this that lists Earth and space science topics does not offer you a great deal of context. Although a specific term may not seem familiar as you see it here, you might find you could understand it when applied to a real-life situation. Many of the items on the actual PRAXIS test will provide you with a context to apply to these topics or terms, as you will see when you look at the practice questions in chapter 13. Keep in mind that the subtopics and star questions below are used for study purposes only and don't include everything that could be on the test.

Special questions marked with stars:
Interspersed throughout the list of topics are questions that are outlined in boxes and preceded by stars (★). These questions are intended to help you test your knowledge of fundamental concepts and your ability to apply fundamental concepts to situations in the laboratory or the real world. Most of the questions require you to combine several pieces of knowledge in order to formulate an integrated understanding and response. If you spend time on these questions, you will gain increased understanding and facility with the subject matter covered on the test. You might want to discuss these questions and your answers with a teacher or mentor.

Note that the questions marked with stars are not short-answer or multiple-choice, and this study guide does not provide the answers. The questions marked with stars are intended as study questions, not practice questions. Thinking about the answers to them should improve your understanding of fundamental concepts and will probably help you answer a broad range of questions on the test. For example, the following box with a star appears in the list of study topics under the "Tectonics and Internal Earth Processes" topic:

> ★ How is paleomagnetism used to determine rates of seafloor spreading?

If you think about this question, perhaps jotting down some notes on the characteristics of midocean ridges, you will review your knowledge of the subject and you will probably be ready to answer multiple-choice questions similar to the one below:

Which of the following best explains why the magnetic bands recorded on isochron maps of a midocean ridge of the eastern Pacific Ocean are farther apart than similar bands on either side of the Mid-Atlantic Ridge?

(A) The magma formed at the eastern Pacific Ridge is less viscous than the magma formed at the Mid-Atlantic Ridge.

(B) The rate of spreading at the eastern Pacific Ridge is less than that at the Mid-Atlantic Ridge.

(C) The rate of spreading at the eastern Pacific Ridge is greater than that at the Mid-Atlantic Ridge.

(D) There are more subduction zones in the Pacific Ocean than in the Atlantic Ocean.

(The correct answer is (C). The magnetic anomalies found on each side of midocean ridges are associated with reversals of Earth's magnetic pole that are recorded in the basalts of the ocean floor. The bands are wider in the eastern Pacific Ocean because the rates of spreading are greater than those of the Mid-Atlantic Ridge.)

History and Nature of Science

▶ Scientific methods of problem solving

▶ The importance of the application of Earth and space sciences to everyday life

▶ Historical development of science and the contributions made by major historical figures, as well as members of cultural/ethnic groups (e.g., ancient Chinese and Greek astronomers, Galileo, Darwin, Curie, Hutton, etc.)

▶ The use of various measurement systems

▶ Compilation, evaluation, and interpretation of data, including analysis of errors

▶ Proper methods involved in using laboratory and field materials and equipment in a safe and appropriate manner, and in conducting safe field experiences

▶ Appropriate use of equipment/instruments for measurement and observation in Earth and space sciences

▶ The computer and related technologies as they apply to investigative activities

▶ Issues associated with the use and production of various energy sources (e.g., fossil fuels, nuclear, hydroelectric, geothermal)

Basic Scientific Principles of Earth and Space Sciences

▶ The role of energy in Earth systems

• Earth systems have internal and external sources of heat energy

— Earth's external source of energy is the Sun

— Internal sources of Earth's energy are the decay of radioactive isotopes and gravitational energy from the Earth's origin

★ What causes the motion of tectonic plates?

- The Sun's heating of the atmosphere and Earth's surface causes convection within the atmosphere and oceans.

★ How does the Sun influence global and local wind patterns?

★ What causes ocean waters to circulate?

- Global climate is related to the energy transfer from the Sun that occurs at or near Earth's surface.

★ What part does the angle of the Sun's rays as they strike Earth play in establishing climatic zones?

▶ The transfer and measurement of heat and the laws of thermodynamics as they relate to Earth systems

- Heat transfer by conduction, convection, and radiation

★ What is the greenhouse effect and how does it relate to the issue of global warming?

▶ The structure of atoms and compounds and their interrelationships in the solid, liquid, and gaseous components of Earth systems

- Isotopes

▶ Nuclear reactions and their products as they relate to Earth and space sciences

- Fusion, radioactive decay, radioactive dating

★ What is the source of the Sun's energy?

▶ Fundamental biological, chemical, and physical processes as they apply to the study of Earth and space sciences

- Evolution

- Biogeochemical cycles

- Chemical reactions

- Gravity

- Waves

▶ Patterns, interrelationships, and intrarelationships of matter and energy

Tectonics and Internal Earth Processes

▶ Plate tectonics, including the history of its development as a unifying theory

- The plates and their motions

- Convergent, divergent, and transform boundaries; subduction zones, trenches, rift valleys, seafloor spreading, and hot spots

★ Why do earthquakes occur much more frequently in some places than in others?

★ How are the locations of volcanoes related to plate tectonics?

★ How is paleomagnetism used to determine rates of seafloor spreading?

★ Have the continents always been where they are located today?

Praxis Sciences Content Knowledge Tests

▶ Processes by which the crust is deformed

• Extension, compression, and shear

★ What features on Earth's surface exhibit the influence of extension, compression, and shear?

• Mountain building, and folding and faulting of rock layers

★ Many mountains in the eastern United States consist of eroded anticlines and synclines. How did the original folds form and what is responsible for the appearance of the land surface today?

★ Mountain ranges in the western United States such as the Grand Teton Mountains of Wyoming and the Sierra Nevadas of California exhibit block faulting. Explain the origin of these structures.

• Isostasy

▶ Earthquakes and how they provide information about Earth

• Seismic waves

★ How do seismologists locate the epicenter of an earthquake?

★ How do seismic waves provide information about the structure and physical characteristics of the Earth?

★ How do oil companies use seismology to locate possible oil deposits prior to test drilling?

• The internal structure of Earth

★ What are the characteristics of Earth's internal layers?

▶ The origin and effects of Earth's magnetic field

★ Explain the role of Earth's magnetic field in the concept of paleomagnetism.

Earth Materials and Surface Processes

▶ The characteristics of minerals and the methods used to identify them

• Minerals: composition, structure, physical characteristics, use, and distribution

★ How are color, streak, hardness, cleavage, specific gravity, and luster used to identify minerals? What is the acid test? What mineral does it test for?

▶ The cycling of Earth materials

• The rock cycle

▶ Processes of weathering and soil formation

• Mechanical, chemical, and biological weathering

• Soil profiles

★ Why do we see horizons within Earth's regolith?

- Soil types

★ How are soil types related to climate?

▶ Sedimentary processes and how sedimentary rocks are formed

- Transportation and deposition of sediments
- Post-depositional processes
- Clastic, biological, and chemical origins of sedimentary rocks
- Identifying sedimentary rocks

▶ Igneous processes and how igneous rocks are formed

- Types of igneous rocks

★ Which silicate minerals are the first, next, and last to form as a magma chamber cools?

★ How are texture and composition used to identify an igneous rock?

▶ Metamorphic processes and how metamorphic rocks are formed

- Pressure and heat and their effect on rocks
- Types of metamorphic rocks
  — Foliated versus nonfoliated

★ What metamorphic steps lead to the formation of gneiss?

★ What is the origin of marble, and what is its composition? Would it fizz with the acid test? Why or why not?

★ What is regional metamorphism? How do the rocks of a given region indicate the intensity of the pressure?

▶ Interrelationships between civilization and Earth materials as resources

- Fossil fuels, minerals, and building stones

★ Would you consider resources removed from Earth renewable or nonrenewable? Why?

▶ Demonstrate understanding of the processes by which a landscape evolves

- Erosion
- Mass wasting

▶ Recognize and interpret geologic features as represented by photographs, and topographic and geologic maps

- Map interpretation: scale, direction, location, and recognition of natural and human-made features on a topographic map; rock ages and structures on a geologic map

★ How would you use a topographic map to lay out a trail of least difficulty when hiking from one place to another? How would you recognize steepness, direction, and distance?

▶ Analyze the interrelationships between civilization and natural hazards

- Living on a flood plain; seismic hazards; living on the slopes of a volcano

History of the Earth and its Life Forms

▶ The principle of uniformitarianism

▶ The basic assumptions behind stratigraphic correlation

- The law of superposition, the law of original horizontality, and the law of cross-cutting relationships

- Index fossils in correlation

★ Where are the oldest rock layers in the walls of the Grand Canyon? How do historical geologists know these are the oldest?

★ How might you correlate rock layers from the north wall of the Grand Canyon with rock layers from the south wall?

▶ How rocks provide a record of the history of Earth

- Unconformities

- Types of fossilization

- The fossil record

★ How is the fossil record used to infer the evolution of life forms?

- Paleogeography: positions of oceans and continents through time

- Paleoclimates

▶ The origin of Earth, including the formation of the atmosphere and hydrosphere

▶ Measurement of geologic time and the geologic time scale

- Relative age versus absolute age

★ What is radioactive dating and how is it used?

★ What time words are used to delineate the units of the geologic time scale?

▶ Paleontology, including the origin of life, development of life, and use of the fossil record

- Mass extinctions

Earth's Atmosphere and Hydrosphere

▶ The structure of the water molecule as it relates to its special properties (e.g., high specific heat, polarity, density changes)

▶ Understanding the paths that water follows as it moves through the water cycle and the energy transfers that accompany this movement

- Water in the atmosphere: water vapor, phase changes, and precipitation

- Runoff, infiltration, and transpiration

▶ Understanding the systematic development and movement of weather patterns and phenomena

- High- and low-pressure regions

★ What is the difference between the behavior of the air in a high and the air in a low? What kind of weather is associated with each?

- Air masses and fronts

★ What happens when a continental polar air mass meets with a maritime tropical air mass?

★ How do fronts form?

- Absolute and relative humidity

- Cloud formation

★ What is the relationship between dew point and cloud formation?

- Types of clouds and precipitation

- Hurricanes and tornadoes

- Weather prediction: short-term and long-term
  — Weather map interpretation
  — Symbols used on weather maps

★ How do weather satellites aid in weather forecasting? What kinds of images are available to a forecaster?

★ Why do weather systems generally move across the United States from west to east?

★ What kinds of weather precede and follow a passing cold front and warm front?

★ What weather would you predict for the next day if you observed a lowering sequence of stratiform clouds over a day or two?

◗ Understanding the origin, distribution, and variation of climate

- Structures and composition of the atmosphere

- Atmospheric circulation

- Coriolis effect

- Heat budgets

- Seasonal variations

- El Niño and La Niña

★ What influence do latitude, elevation, ocean currents, landforms, and world wind belts have on the climate of a region?

★ What are the causes and effects of El Niño?

- Climate modification, desertification, greenhouse effect, influence of volcanic eruptions

★ How do volcanic eruptions affect both regional and worldwide climate conditions?

◗ Interrelationships between civilization, and the atmosphere and hydrosphere

- Pollution

- Acid precipitation

- Urban climates

◗ The processes by which water moves on and beneath Earth's surface

- Groundwater

★ What characteristics make a soil or rock layer permeable or impermeable?

- Surface waters
- River systems; discharge, load, and gradient

★ How does a drainage system develop?

★ What are the stages in the life cycle of a river?

★ What influences stream velocity?

★ How deeply can a stream erode?

▶ Glaciers and ice ages
- The formation of glaciers (valley and continental)

★ Under what conditions do glaciers develop?

★ What conditions would be necessary for another ice age to occur?

▶ The physical and chemical characteristics and processes of the oceans
- Temperature, salinity, and density

★ How does the temperature of seawater vary with depth?

★ What is salinity? How is it measured?

★ How do oceanographers explain the difference in salinity of ocean water in different locations?

- Chemical cycles, nutrient cycles
- Oceanic circulation patterns and currents

★ What is a density current?

★ Explain the movement of ocean bottom currents.

- Upwelling

★ How is upwelling related to wind?

▶ The interrelationships between the waters of the oceans and the solid Earth
- Seafloor topography

★ What pattern of seafloor topography would you expect across the Atlantic or Pacific Ocean?

- Seafloor sediments

★ What types of sediments would you expect to find in different locations on the seafloor?

★ What do core samples of seafloor sediments reveal about the past?

- Waves and tides

★ How do ocean waves form? Why do these waves break at the shoreline?

★ What causes tides?

★ Are there two high tides and two low tides in all locations every day? Why or why not?

- Estuaries
- Erosional and depositional processes, and shore processes

★ What purpose does a groin along the shoreline serve?

- Sea-level changes

Astronomy

▶ The characteristics and consequences of Earth's rotation and revolution

• A day, seasons, a year

★ Why does the amount of daylight vary from day to day and from place to place?

★ Why were time zones invented? Why was the international date line established?

★ Why do seasons exist?

▶ The relationship between Earth, the Moon, and the Sun

• Moon phases

★ Why does the Moon appear to pass through phases as it completes one revolution around Earth?

• Eclipses

★ What are the conditions under which solar and lunar eclipses occur?

• Tides

★ How does the gravity of the Sun and Moon affect Earth's oceans?

▶ The components of the solar system in terms of composition, size, and motion

★ What makes a celestial object a member of the solar system?

• The Sun: structure, composition, and features

• Planets and moons

★ Why does the position of a planet as seen from Earth change in relation to the background of stars?

★ What is retrograde motion?

★ What are the laws of planetary motion?

★ Under what systems do astronomers classify the different planets?

• The asteroid belt

• Meteors, meteoroids, and meteorites

★ What is the difference between meteors, meteoroids, and meteorites? What is the origin of meteoroids?

• Comets

★ Why are comets referred to as "dirty snowballs"?

▶ The internal and surface processes of planetary bodies and their natural satellites

▶ The characteristics of stars and the processes that occur within them

- Temperature and color

★ How is a star's color related to its temperature?
★ How are dark line spectra used?

- Brightness

★ Why do astronomers use the terms apparent magnitude and absolute magnitude when describing the brightness of a star?

- The life cycle of stars

★ How do stars form? What stages does a star pass through?
★ How does the Hertzsprung-Russell diagram help summarize the life cycle of stars?
★ What are black holes?

- Composition of stars

★ How is spectroscopy used to determine the composition of a star?

- Distances in the universe

★ What is parallax?
★ How are Cepheid variable stars used to calculate distances in the universe?
★ Explain the different units of distance used in astronomy.

▶ The structure of the Milky Way and other galaxies in the universe

- Spiral, elliptical, and irregular galaxies
- Types of telescopes
- The Hubble space telescope
- Sensors on space probes
- The International Space Station
- The role of computers

▶ Hypotheses that relate to the origin and development of the universe

★ Why do most astronomers think that the big bang theory is the best explanation for the origin of the universe?

Chapter 6

Study Topics for the *General Science: Content Knowledge* Tests

▶   ▶   ▶   ▶   ▶   ▶   ▶   ▶   ▶   ▶   ▶   ▶

Introduction to the tests

The *General Science: Content Knowledge* tests are designed to assess the knowledge and understanding of fundamental scientific concepts, principles, processes, phenomena, and interrelationships of the sciences for a beginning teacher of general science. Teachers need to understand the subject matter from a more advanced viewpoint than is actually presented to students. Accordingly, some questions of a more advanced nature are included. Questions are derived from topics typically covered in introductory college-level courses in chemistry, physics, the life sciences, and earth sciences. The questions require a variety of abilities, including definition of terms, comprehension of critical concepts, and application and analysis, to address and solve problems.

The tests are designed to reflect current standards for knowledge, skills, and abilities in science education. Educational Testing Service (ETS) has aligned this tests closely with the National Science Education Standards and works in collaboration with teacher educators, higher education content specialists, and accomplished practicing teachers in science to keep the tests updated and representative of current standards.

You are likely to find that the topics below are covered by most introductory textbooks in the fields of biology, chemistry, physics, and earth and space sciences, but general survey textbooks may not cover all of the subtopics. Consult materials and resources, including lecture and laboratory notes, from all your science coursework. You should be able to match up specific topics and subtopics with what you have covered in your courses in chemistry, biology, physics, earth and space sciences, and so on.

Try not to be overwhelmed by the volume and scope of content knowledge in this guide. An overview such as this that lists science topics does not offer you a great deal of context. Although a specific term may not seem familiar as you see it here, you might find you could understand it when applied to a real-life situation. Many of the items on the actual PRAXIS test will provide you with a context to apply to these topics or terms, as you will see when you look at the practice questions in chapter 15.

Special questions marked with stars: Interspersed throughout the list of topics are questions that are outlined in boxes and preceded by stars (★). These questions are intended to help you test your knowledge of fundamental concepts and your ability to apply fundamental concepts to situations in the laboratory or the real world. Most of the questions require you to combine several pieces of knowledge in order to formulate an integrated understanding and response. If you spend time on these questions, you will gain increased understanding and facility with the subject matter covered on the test. You might want to discuss these questions and your answers with a teacher or mentor.

Note that the questions marked with stars are not short-answer or multiple-choice, and this study guide does not provide the answers. The questions marked with stars are intended as study questions, not practice questions. Thinking about the answers to them should improve your understanding of fundamental concepts and will probably help you answer a broad range of questions on the test. For example, the following box with a star appears in the list of study topics under the "Mechanics" topic within Physics:

> ★ What variables affect the period of a pendulum?

If you think about this question, perhaps jotting down some notes on the variables and how they relate to motion of a pendulum, you will review your knowledge of the subject and you will probably be ready to answer multiple-choice questions similar to the one below:

A simple pendulum has a period, T, on Earth. Which of the following would decrease the period of the pendulum if the pendulum were kept at the same location?

(A)   Increasing the length of the pendulum
(B)   Increasing the mass of the pendulum bob
(C)   Decreasing the length of the pendulum
(D)   Decreasing the mass of the pendulum bob

(The correct answer is (A). The period of a simple pendulum is dependent on the length and the acceleration due to gravity. The period of the pendulum does not depend on the mass of the pendulum bob. Acceleration due to gravity does not change because the location did not change. A long pendulum has a greater period than a short pendulum.)

History and Nature of Science

Nature of Scientific Knowledge, Inquiry and Historical Perspectives

- Scientific inquiry, the scientific method, and experimental design (i.e., making observations, formulating and testing hypotheses, drawing conclusions, communicating findings)
  - Different kinds of questions may be studied using different kinds of scientific investigations

- Scientific knowledge is consistent with evidence, subject to change and open to criticism

- Compare and contrast facts, hypotheses, models, theories, and laws

- Understanding of the unified, integrative nature of the various disciplines and concepts in science

- Historical figures and landmark events in Science (e.g., Curie, Mendel, Darwin, Newton, Galileo, Hutton, Mendeleev, Einstein, Dalton, DNA structure, big bang theory, atomic imaging, light bending in gravitation fields)

Mathematics, Measurement, and Data Manipulation

- Scientific measurement and notation systems
  - Metric and U.S. standards for volume, mass, length, molarity, time, and temperature
  - Estimation, significant figures
- Processes involved in scientific data collection, analysis, interpretation, manipulation, presentation, and the critical analysis of sources of data

★ How would you compare information obtained from the television, a newspaper article, a Web site, and a scientific journal for accuracy? For understandability? For use in the classroom setting?

◗ Interpret and draw conclusions from data, including that presented in tables, graphs, maps, and charts

- Titles, legends, units
- Dependent versus independent variables

◗ Analyze errors in data that are presented

- Statistical precision and accuracy
- Source of error in procedure or process

Laboratory/Field Activities Procedures and Safety

◗ Safety procedures involved in the preparation, storage, use, and disposal of laboratory and field materials

- Acids, bases, toxins, microbiological samples, fire hazards, etc.

◗ Identify, use, and maintain laboratory equipment appropriately in laboratory exercises

◗ Ability to prepare reagents, material, and apparatuses correctly for classroom use

★ How would you prepare 1 liter of a 300 mM NaCl solution? If you were going to use this solution to bathe live cells, would it be important to include a buffer in your solution? Explain.

◗ Knowledge of the teacher's legal responsibilities for safety and emergency procedures for the science classroom and laboratory

Physical Sciences

Basic Principles

◗ Matter and Energy

- Structure and properties of matter
  — Atomic, molecular, and ionic nature of matter
  — Physical and chemical properties of matter
    – Melting point, boiling point, color, density, etc.
    – Combustibility, oxidation potential, reactivity, etc.

★ What is the difference between the physical properties and the chemical properties of matter?

  — Organization of matter
    – Elements, compounds, solutions, mixtures
- Elements
  — Names and symbols
  — Factors that influence their occurrence and relative abundance
- Physical and chemical changes of matter
  — Change in form versus change in composition
  — Separation versus decomposition

★ How are physical and chemical changes related to the composition of matter, i.e., elements, compounds, and mixtures?

- Conservation of mass/energy
  — Conservation of energy
  — Relationship between conservation of matter and atomic theory

— Fusion and fission reactions

— Conversion of mass to energy

- Energy transformations
  — Kinetic-potential, electrical-mechanical, chemical-heat, etc.

★ How are kinetic energy and potential energy exhibited in terms of molecular behaviors and/or interactions within substances?

▶ Heat and Thermodynamics

- Distinguish between heat and temperature
  — Molecular behaviors and interactions
  — Heat as a form of energy
  — Temperature as a measure of the average kinetic energy of a sample of molecules

- Heat exchange
  — Heat lost equals heat gained
    – Measurement and transfer
    – Effects of thermal energy on matter: change in temperature and/or phase change
  — Quantitative problems
    – Change in temperature using specific heat capacity

- First and second laws of thermodynamics
  — Conservation of energy

★ How is the first law of thermodynamics related to the law of conservation of energy?

— Entropy

★ What is the relationship between the second law of thermodynamics and entropy?

▶ Atomic and Nuclear Structure

- Atomic models and related experiments
  — Cathode rays and electrons
  — Alpha-scattering experiment and the nuclear atom
  — Atomic spectra and electron orbitals

★ What was the major shortcoming of the Bohr model of the atom?

- Atomic and nuclear structure
  — Protons, neutrons, and electrons
  — Nuclear atom
  — Electron configuration

- Relationship of electron configuration to the chemical and physical properties of an atom
  — Loss or gain of electrons in bonds
  — Relative charges of ions formed from atoms
  — Chemical reactivity
  — Atomic size

★ Why is a helium atom smaller than a hydrogen atom?

- Radioisotopes and radioactivity
  — Types of radioactivity
    – Alpha, beta, and gamma radiation

★ How do the electrical charges of alpha, beta, and gamma particles differ?

— Properties
  – Half-life
  – Nuclear stability

★ Why is there lead, Pb, mixed in with all deposits of uranium, U, ores?

— Nuclear reactions
- Conservation of mass number and charge number in reactions
- Predicting products

Physics

⬧ Mechanics

- Motion in a straight line
  — Distance, speed, average speed and acceleration
  — Free fall

> ★ How does mass affect the acceleration of a falling object?
>
> ★ What is meant by the term "terminal velocity"?

- Motion in two dimensions

> ★ A ball is dropped and another ball of smaller mass is fired horizontally from the same height. Which ball has a greater acceleration when it hits the ground? Which ball hits the ground first?

- Circular and periodic motion
  — Frequency and period

> ★ What variables affect the period of a pendulum?

- Forces and Newton's laws of motion
  — Balanced and unbalanced forces

> ★ What forces act on a frictionless air puck as it moves across a table at constant speed in a straight line?

— Relate mass to inertia
— Action and reaction forces

- Distinguish between weight and mass
- Friction

> ★ Why is it more difficult to slide a crate starting from rest than it is to keep it moving once it is sliding?

- Work, energy, and power

> ★ Which requires more work: lifting a 100-kilogram sack a vertical distance of 2 meters or lifting a 50-kilogram sack a vertical distance of 4 meters?

- Simple machines and torque
  — Pulleys, levers, gears, and inclined planes
  — Mechanical advantage
- Momentum

> ★ When you ride your bicycle, which has greater momentum, you or your bike?

- Conservation of energy and momentum
  — Energy transformations
  — Collisions
- Force of gravity

> ★ Why is the force of gravity between a pair of objects reduced one-fourth when the distance between them is doubled?

- Fluids
  — Pressure
  — Archimedes' principle
  — Bernoulli's principle

> ★ Why does a dime on a table flip over when air is blown across the top of the dime?

◆ Electricity and Magnetism

• Conductors and insulators

★ Why are metals good conductors of heat and electricity?

— Charging by friction, conduction, and induction

• Repulsion and attraction of electric charges

• Characteristics of current electricity and simple circuits (e.g., resistance, electromotive force, potential difference, and current)
— Ohm's law in series and parallel circuits

★ If a current through each of the two branches of a parallel circuit is the same, what about the resistance of the two branches?

• Direct current and alternating current

• Sources of EMF (e.g., batteries, photocells, and generators)

• Magnets, magnetic fields, and magnetic forces
— Magnetic dipole and materials

• Transformers and motors

★ What is the basic difference between an electric motor and a generator? What is the basic similarity?

◆ Waves
• Wave characteristics, phenomena, models, and applications
— Speed, amplitude, wavelength, and frequency

— Reflection, refraction, absorption, transmission, and scattering

★ Why does the sky appear blue?

— Interference and diffraction
— Transverse and longitudinal waves and their properties
– Polarization

★ Why do polarized sunglasses reduce glare, while nonpolarized sunglasses simply reduce the total amount of light reaching the eyes?

– Doppler effect

• Sound
— Pitch and loudness
— Vibrations of air columns and strings

★ When you blow over a bottle, what happens to the frequency as you fill the bottle with water?

• Electromagnetic spectrum
— Transmission
— Color

★ What color light is transmitted through a piece of blue glass? Why?

• Geometric optics
— Plane and spherical mirrors, thin lenses, prisms, and fiber optics

★ Does the size of the image in a plane mirror change as the object moves away from the mirror?

Chemistry

♦ Periodicity

• The meaning of chemical periodicity
— The physical and chemical properties of the elements is a periodic function of the atomic number of the element

★ What is the relationship between the number of a period in the periodic table and the distribution of electrons in the atoms of the elements in that period?

• Periodic trends in chemical and physical properties (e.g., ionization energy, atomic size)

★ How do the chemical characteristics of the elements in a period change as you move from left to right across the periodic table?

♦ The Mole and Chemical Bonding

• The mole concept, chemical composition, and stoichiometry

★ What are the relationships between gram atomic mass, Avogadro's number, and a mole of carbon atoms?

• Chemical formulas

★ What information is provided in the formula for calcium hydroxide, $Ca(OH)_2$?

• Systematic nomenclature of inorganic and simple organic compounds

— Binary compounds
– Stock (Roman numeral) and classical systems for indicating oxidation states on multivalent cations

★ Name each of the following compounds, using the classic and stock systems: a) Cu_2O b) $Hg_2(NO_3)_2$

— Polyatomic ions and associated acids
– Prefix and suffix Utilization -ic, -ous, per-, hypo-, -ide, -ate, -ite
— IUPAC nomenclature of organic compounds according to their functional groups
– Alkanes, alkenes, alkynes, alcohols, carbohydrates, carboxylic acids, and amines

★ What are the molecular formulas of alkanes containing 7-, 8-, and 9-carbon atoms?

• Ionic, covalent, and metallic bonds
— The differences between these basic types of bonds
– Valence electron behavior
– Electron pairing, sharing, or transfer
• Electron dot and structural formulas
— Lewis dot structures
— Covalent bonds

★ What are both the electron dot and structural formulas for methane, CH_4?

♦ The Kinetic Theory and States of Matter

• Kinetic molecular theory
— Relationship among phases of matter, forces between particles, and particle energy

★ What are the arrangement and motions of molecules of substances in the solid phase? liquid phase? gaseous phase?

— Phase changes
  - The differences in intermolecular interactions among different states
  - Conversion between molecular potential energy and molecular kinetic energy
  - The special properties of water
— Relationships among temperature, pressure, volume, and number of molecules of an ideal gas

★ If a sample of gas is heated at a constant pressure, what will happen to the volume of the gas?

• Characteristics of crystals
  — Crystal lattice
  — Crystal systems with emphasis on the cubic system

★ What effect does the rate of evaporation have on the size of salt crystals that form when water evaporates from a saltwater solution?

◗ Chemical Reactions

• Chemical equations
  — Balancing

★ Why is it incorrect to balance an equation by changing subscripts in the chemical formulas of the reactants and the products?

• Types of chemical reactions
  — Single replacement, double replacement, combustion, combination (synthesis), and decomposition

• Endothermic and exothermic chemical reactions
  — Energy absorbed or released
  — Changes in the temperature of the surroundings

• Effects of temperature, pressure, concentration, and the presence of catalysts on chemical reactions
  — Reaction rates
  — Equilibrium shifts

★ In general terms, what will happen to a chemical equilibrium if the temperature, pressure, or concentration of one of the reactants is changed?

• Practical applications of electrochemistry
  — Oxidation-reduction processes, voltaic cells, and/or electroplating

★ In electroplating, which electrode is made of the object to be plated? Of what substance is the other electrode composed?

◗ Solutions and Solubility

• Solutions
  — Terminology and distinguishing among types of solutions
    - Solute, solvent, saturated, unsaturated, supersaturated, electrolytes, and nonelectrolytes

• Solubility
  — Selectivity of solvents

★ What type of solvent would be needed to dissolve fat, fingernail polish, sugar, and salt crystals, respectively?

— The dissolving process, and factors affecting the rate of dissolution

★ Why is ammonia gas very soluble in water while oxygen, O_2, is only slightly soluble?

— The effects of temperature and pressure on the solubility of a solute
  – Graphical interpretations

• Physical and chemical properties of acids, bases, and salts
— pH scale
— The effects of buffers

★ What is the general function of buffer mixtures?

★ Why are buffers essential in the bloodstream?

Life Sciences

◆ The Cell

• Biologically important inorganic and organic molecules
— Gases (carbon dioxide, oxygen, etc.)
— Water
— Macromolecules
  – Proteins . . . amino acids
  – Nucleic acids . . . nucleotides
  – Fats/lipids . . . glycerol and fatty acids
  – Carbohydrates (starch, cellulose, glycogen). . . monosaccharides (sugars)

• Structure and function of cells
— Organelles and other subcellular structures (e.g., Golgi apparatus, nucleus, mitochondria, endoplasmic reticulum, chloroplasts)

★ What structures would you expect to find in a typical plant cell but not in an animal cell? What functions do these unique structures carry out for the plant?

— Biological membranes
  – Fluid mosaic model
  – Transport mechanisms (e.g., diffusion, osmosis, passive transport, active transport, exocytosis, endocytosis)

★ If you were stranded in a lifeboat on the ocean, why would drinking the ocean water be more harmful than not drinking the water?

• Prokaryotic and eukaryotic cells
— Cellular level comparison (e.g., presence/absence of membrane-enclosed organelles, DNA organization, methods of cell division)
— Cell theory
— Endosymbiotic theory

• Cell cycle and cytokinesis
— Events of interphase and the mitotic phases
— Cytokinesis

★ What are the major differences between "normal" cells and cancerous cells? Chemotherapy is the use of chemicals to kill rapidly dividing cells. In addition to killing many types of cancer cells, why does chemotherapy treatment cause side effects such as anemia, gastrointestinal distress, and hair loss?

    — Events during meiosis I and meiosis II
    — Comparison of mechanisms (e.g., number of cell divisions, genetic makeup of daughter cells, cell types in which each event occurs)

- Bioenergetics
  — Metabolism
    – Anabolic versus catabolic pathways
    – Role of enzymes
  — Photosynthetic reactions (overall equation, light reaction, Calvin cycle)
    – Pigments, wavelengths of light, location within eukaryotic cells
  — Aerobic cellular respiration reactions (overall equation, glycolysis, Kreb's cycle, electron transport chain, oxidative phosphorylation)
    – Aerobic versus anaerobic reactions (fermentation)

★ At the cellular level, what is the benefit of exercising aerobically? Why do muscles become "sore" after excessive exercise?

★ What makes bread "rise" before it is baked?

- Homeostasis
  — Positive and negative feedback loops

★ Why are insulin and glucagon considered "antagonistic" hormones? Are there other such hormone pairs in the human body?

▸ Molecular Basis of Heredity and Classical Genetics

- DNA replication
  — Structure of DNA and RNA nucleotides (e.g., A, C, G, T, and U bases, ribose and deoxyribose sugars)

★ Describe Watson and Crick's model for DNA structure.

    — Mechanism of semiconservative, antiparallel replication, base pairing

- Protein synthesis
  — Transcription (DNA-directed mRNA synthesis)
  — Translation (mRNA-directed protein synthesis)
    – Functions of ribosomes, mRNA codons, tRNA anticodons

- Mutation and transposable elements generate genetic variability

- Mendel's laws and the use of his laws to predict the probable outcome of given genetic crosses
  — Dominant and recessive alleles
  — Law of segregation, independent assortment

★ How are Mendel's laws related to the behavior of chromosomes during the formation of gametes?

    — Monohybrid and dihybrid crosses, pedigree analysis, probability analysis

- Non-Mendelian inheritance
  — Complete dominance, epistasis, incomplete dominance, multiple alleles, polygenic inheritance

> ★ What percentage of offspring will have blood type A if the parents have blood types AB and O? What percentage will have blood type O?
>
> ★ Why are more males color-blind than females?

  — Linkage and crossing over
  — Sex-linkage

- Interaction between heredity and environment

- Chromosomal and gene aberrations lead to some common human genetic disorders (e.g., Down syndrome, sickle-cell disorder, cystic fibrosis)

> ★ A small percentage of individuals with Down syndrome possess a chromosomal translocation in which a copy of chromosome 21 becomes attached to chromosome 14. How does this translocation occur?

- Recombinant DNA in nature and in the laboratory
  — Cloning and gene splicing
    – Restriction enzymes, vectors
  — Diagnostic, medical, forensic and agricultural applications

> ★ How has recombinant DNA technology been used to solve criminal cases? To treat diabetes?

- The significance of mapping the human genome

◆ Evolution

- Scientific evidence supporting the theory of evolution
  — Biogeography, comparative anatomy and embryology, fossil record, molecular evidence
  — Key historical figures (e.g., Cuvier, Lyell, Darwin, Lamark)

- Mechanisms and rate of evolution
  — Natural selection
  — Gradualism versus punctuated equilibrium
  — Introduction of variation and changes in a gene pool's allele frequency
    – Gene flow (immigration, emigration), random mutation, nonrandom mating, genetic drift

> ★ A radioactive meteorite falls to Earth and kills 90 percent of a secluded population of salamander. What mechanisms are in action changing allelic frequency in this population's gene pool?

- Speciation
  — Biological definition of species
  — Pre- and postzygotic barriers isolating gene pools (e.g., behavioral isolation, mechanical isolation, reduced hybrid viability)
  — Geographical barriers isolating populations (e.g., allopatric speciation, sympatric speciation, adaptive radiation)
  — Darwin's theory of the origin of species

★ Explain the following concepts relative to Darwin's theory of the origin of species: a) Descent with modification, b) Struggle for existence, and c) Survival of the fittest.

- Scientific theories of the origin of life on Earth
  — Earth's age
  — Abiotic synthesis
  — Endosymbiotic theory

★ How would the presence of molecular oxygen, O_2, in the atmosphere affect early living things?

- ◗ Diversity of Life
  - Biological classification systems
    — Five-kingdom system (Monera, Protista, Fungi, Plantae, and Animalia)

★ What are the limitations of the five-kingdom system? Current debates about revising the five-kingdom system center mainly on which groups of organisms?

  — Nomenclature schemes organize life from the most broad to the most specific (Kingdom, Phylum/Division, Class, Order, Family, Genus, Species)
  - Characteristics of viruses, bacteria, protists, fungi, plants, and animals (e.g., unicellular versus multicellular, modes of nutrition, and energy sources)
    — Symbiotic and phylogenetic relationships

- ◗ Plants (Form and Function)
  - Major plant divisions and their characteristics (e.g., vascular versus avascular, seed bearing versus seedless)
    — Bryophytes
    — Pterophytes (ferns)
    — Gymnosperms (conifers)
    — Angiosperms (flowering plants)
  - Structure and function of roots, stems, and leaves
  - Hormones (e.g., auxin, cytokinins), photoperiods, and tropisms (e.g., phototropism, gravitropism/geotropism)

★ Consider a seed planted upside down three inches under the soil. When the seed germinates, why does the root grow downward into the soil while the shoot grows upward?

  - Water and nutrient uptake and transport systems
    — Role and location of xylem and phloem
    — Role of roots, stems, and leaves in transport
    — Transpiration

★ Under what environmental conditions would you expect the transpiration rate to be the highest in an average-sized oak tree? The lowest?

  - Sexual and asexual reproduction
    — Alternation of generations
    — Vegetative propagation
  - Growth
    — Seedling germination, differentiation, and development
    — Root and shoot meristems

◆ Animals (Form and Function)

- Anatomy and physiology of structures associated with life functions of organisms in the animal kingdom. Identify gross anatomical structures in humans and other major animal phyla. Know the functions, major physiological processes, and hormonal control mechanisms for each system.
  — Digestion
    – Nutritional requirements (e.g., food sources, calories)

★ Why must the human body digest large macromolecules into small monomers before it can use them? What enzymes does the human body use to digest these macromolecules?

★ Which type of nutrient has the highest caloric value per gram? (proteins, carbohydrates, fats, alcohols)

  — Circulation
  — Respiration
  — Excretion
  — Nervous control
  — Contractile systems and movement

★ What are the structural and functional differences between the three muscle types, i.e., skeletal, smooth, and cardiac?

  — Support (endo- and exoskeletons)
  — Immunity
  — Endocrine control
  — Reproduction and development
    – Sexual (gametogenesis, fertilization, zygote and embryo development)
    – Asexual (e.g., budding, parthenogenesis, self-fertilization)

- Changes in anatomy or physiology may lead to human disease
  — Mechanisms (e.g., heart disease, gastrointestinal ulcers, emphysema)

★ What are some genetic, lifestyle, and internal physiological factors that can lead to hypertension (high blood pressure)? If hypertension is uncontrolled, what health problems can occur? What types of treatments exist to help control hypertension?

- Animal behavior and response to stimuli (e.g., taxes, innate/instinctual behaviors, learned behaviors, behavior's role in survival and reproductive success)

◆ Ecology

- Population dynamics
  — Intraspecific competition
  — Population growth

★ Explain J-shaped and S-shaped population growth curves in terms of biotic potential and carrying capacity.

- Social behaviors (e.g., territoriality, dominance, altruism, threat display)
- Community structure and species diversity in communities
  — Niche concept
  — Competition

★ What is the principle of competitive exclusion?

- Interspecific relationships
  — Predation, parasitism, commensalism, mutualism

- The concepts of the ecosystem stability, the effects of disturbances, and succession
  — Human impact (e.g., acid precipitation, ozone depletion, deforestation, agriculture, cultural eutrophication, urbanization)

★ How have humans accelerated the process of the greenhouse effect? Why are environmental researchers concerned about what this accelerated greenhouse effect could have on sea level?

  — Succession
- Energy flow
  — Trophic levels and energy loss between levels (10% rule)
  — Food webs
  — Food chains
  — Productivity
  — Biomagnification

★ Create a food web, with organisms placed within an appropriate trophic level, with the following organisms: zooplankton, eagle, freshwater shrimp, green algae, goose, mouse, beetle, bacteria, trout, bear, and mushroom. What would the pyramids of number, biomass, and energy look like for this ecosystem? Describe the levels of DDT you would find in the tissues of the members of the community, if the pesticide DDT were introduced into this food web.

- Biogeochemical cycles (e.g., nitrogen, carbon, water)

- Types, characteristics of, and biological diversity within biomes
  — Aquatic (e.g., wetland, estuary, lake, oceanic pelagic)
  — Terrestrial (e.g., temperate deciduous, tundra, chaparral)

★ Compare the types of vegetation encountered with increasing altitude (e.g., traveling up a mountainside) and with increasing latitude (e.g., traveling toward the North Pole).

Earth & Space Sciences

▶ Physical Geology

★ What makes a topographic map different from any other map? Why is a topographic map useful to a geologist?

- Processes of mineral and rock formation

★ What are the source materials for the ingredients of sedimentary rocks?

- Methods used to identify and classify different types of minerals and rocks
- Earth's structure and the physical characteristics of Earth's various layers

★ What does the behavior of seismic waves reveal about the structure and physical characteristics of Earth's interior?

- Plate tectonic theory
- Internal processes and resulting features of Earth (e.g., folding, faulting, earthquakes, and volcanoes)

★ What evidence exists for "continental drift" and how is continental drift different from plate tectonics?

★ What processes occur at plate edges?

- Hydrologic cycle
- Processes of weathering, erosion, and deposition

★ What are the major agents of erosion?

▶ Historical Geology
- The principle of uniformitarianism and order of superposition
- Basic principles of stratigraphy
- Relative and absolute time (including dating techniques)

★ What is radioactive dating and how is it used to provide dates for the geologic time scale?

- Processes involved in the formation of fossils
- How fossils provide various types of information

★ How can fossils be useful to a geologist in correlating the north and south walls of the Grand Canyon?

- The geologic time scale and how it was developed
- Important events in Earth's history (e.g., formation of the atmosphere, formation of hydrosphere, mass extinction)

▶ Oceanography
- Physical and chemical properties of the ocean and seawater
- Processes involved in the formation and movement of ocean waves

★ Why do waves break as they approach the shore?

- Primary causes and factors that influence tides

★ How do the Sun and Moon influence tides? Why in general do two high tides occur every day even though the Moon is directly above any given portion of Earth's surface only once a day?

- Major surface and deep-water currents in the oceans and the causes of these currents

★ What is the Coriolis effect and how does it affect Earth's surface waters?

- Processes that influence the geology, biology, and topography of the ocean floor

★ What are black smokers and how do scientists explain their existence? What kinds of life are found in, on, and around black smokers?

★ What is the seafloor spreading? Explain the origin of the rift valley in the center of the mid-oceanic ridge.

- Nutrient cycles of the ocean
- Shore processes (e.g., formation of dunes, beach profiles, wave effects)

◆ Meteorology

• Structure of the atmosphere and physical, thermal, and chemical properties of atmospheric layers

★ List the layers of the atmosphere and discuss the temperature changes within each.

• Chemical composition of the atmosphere

• Factors influencing seasonal and latitudinal variation of solar radiation

• Causes of winds and of global wind belts

• Variations in small-scale (local and regional) atmospheric circulation (e.g., monsoons, land and sea breezes, desert winds)

★ How does the Sun influence global and local winds?

• Relative humidity versus absolute humidity

• Associated saturation processes (e.g., dew, frost, and fog)

• Cloud and precipitation types and their formation

• Major types of air masses in terms of temperature, moisture content, and source areas

• High- and low-pressure systems, including storms

★ Why do weather systems move across the United States from west to east?

★ Compare and contrast tornadoes and tropical cyclones (hurricanes).

• Structure and movement of frontal systems (e.g., cold, warm, stationary, occluded)

• Air circulation around and weather associated with frontal systems

★ What weather would you predict for the next day if you observed a lowering sequence of stratiform clouds over a day or two?

• Information on weather maps

• Short-term weather forecasting versus long-term weather forecasting

• Regional and local natural factors that affect climate (e.g., topography, latitude)

• How humans affect and are affected by climate (e.g., desertification, global warming, volcanic ash effect, El Niño)

★ What influence does one or more of the following have on the climate of a region: ocean currents, landforms, and world wind belts?

★ How does a volcanic eruption affect both regional and worldwide climate conditions?

◆ Astronomy

• Major theory of the origin and structure of the universe (e.g., galaxies, novas, black holes, quasars, and stars)

• Large units of distance (e.g., astronomical unit, light-year, parsec)

★ How far does light travel in a light-year?

• Origin and life cycle of stars

★ What information about stars and their life cycle can be obtained form a Hertzsprung-Russell (H-R) diagram?

- Major theories involving the origin of the solar system
- Features and characteristics of the Sun

★ How do the Sun and other stars generate their energy?

- Components of the solar system (planets, moons, asteroids, comets, and other solar system components) and their physical features
- Geometry of the Earth-Moon-Sun system
  — Phases of the Moon
  — Lunar eclipses
  — Solar eclipses

★ Why do a lunar and solar eclipses not occur every month?

- Causes of Earth's seasons

★ Describe the temperature and length of the day at the North Pole, the mid-latitudes, and the Equator on June 21 and on December 21.

- Units of time (e.g., year, day, hour)

★ Why does the length of daylight change from day to day?

- Time zones

★ What is the relationship between a time zone, longitude, and the Earth's rotation?

- Geosynchronous orbits
- Contributions of satellites
- Contributions of piloted and unpiloted space missions
- Scientific contributions of remote sensing
- Present limitations of space exploration

★ What limitation of Earth-based telescopes has been solved by the Hubble space telescope?

Science, Technology, and Social Perspectives

▶ The impact of science and technology on the environment and human affairs

▶ Issues associated with human and nature-induced hazards (e.g., radioactive waste, flooding, volcanoes, air pollution, global warming, agricultural pollutants)

★ Give examples of how events such as the clear-cutting of the tropical rain forests and building of nuclear energy plants have had both positive and negative impacts on humans and the environment.

▶ Issues associated with energy production, use, transmission, and management (including nuclear waste and removal)

★ Compare the availability and limitation of the following sources of power: geothermal, nuclear, hydroelectric, solar, and fossil fuel.

◗ Issues associated with the production, storage, use, management, and disposal of consumer products (e.g., logging, use of fossil fuels, CFCs and ozone depletion, energy production, air-conditioning, aerosol cans)

◗ Natural resource management (e.g., environmental quality, wetland conservation, soil erosion control, mining of industrial and economic minerals)

★ Compare and contrast the depletion of mineral resources with that of fossil fuels.

◗ The social, political, ethical, and economic issues arising from science, technology, and medical advancements (e.g., recycling, biotechnology, nutrition, evolutionary theory, corporate responsibility, miniaturization, nuclear power generation, piloted space missions)

Chapter 7

Study Topics for the *Physics: Content Knowledge* Tests

▶   ▶   ▶   ▶   ▶   ▶   ▶   ▶   ▶   ▶   ▶   ▶

Introduction to the tests

The *Physics: Content Knowledge* tests are designed to measure the subject-area knowledge and competencies necessary for a beginning teacher of physics in a secondary school. The topics for questions are typically those covered in introductory college-level physics and physical science courses, although some questions of a more advanced nature are included, because secondary-school instructors must understand the subject matter from a more advanced viewpoint than that presented to their students. Also, since a major goal of science education is to have students develop an understanding of science and the impact of science and technology on the environment and human affairs, these areas are included in the assessment. The questions include definition of terms, comprehension of critical concepts, application, analysis, and problem solving.

Examinees will not need to use a calculator in taking this test. The test book contains a periodic table and a table of information that presents various physical constants and a few conversion factors among SI units. When necessary, additional values of physical constants are printed with the text of a question.

The tests are designed to reflect current standards for knowledge, skills, and abilities in science education. Educational Testing Service (ETS) has aligned these tests closely with the National Science Education Standards and works in collaboration with teacher educators, higher education content specialists, and accomplished practicing teachers in the field of physics to keep the tests updated and representative of current standards.

This chapter is intended to help you organize your preparation for your test and to give you a clear indication about the depth and breadth of the knowledge required for success on the tests.

Using the topic lists that follow: You are not expected to be an expert on all aspects of the topics that follow. You should understand the major characteristics of each topic, recognize the minor topics, and have some familiarity with the subtopics. Virtually all accredited undergraduate physics programs address the majority of these topics, subtopics, and even minor topics.

You are likely to find that the topics below are covered by most introductory physics textbooks, but a general survey textbook may not cover all of the subtopics. Consult materials and resources, including lecture and laboratory notes, from all your physics coursework. You should be able to match up specific topics and subtopics with what you have covered in your courses in mechanics, electricity and magnetism, optics, modern physics, and so on.

Try not to be overwhelmed by the volume and scope of content knowledge in this guide. An overview such as this that lists physics topics does not offer you a great deal of context. Although a specific term may not seem familiar as you see it here, you might find you could understand it when applied to a real-life situation. Many of the items on the actual PRAXIS test will provide you with a context to apply to these topics or terms, as you will see when you look at the practice questions in chapter 17.

Special questions marked with stars:
Interspersed throughout the list of topics are questions that are outlined in boxes and preceded by stars (★). These questions are intended to help

you test your knowledge of fundamental concepts and your ability to apply fundamental concepts to situations in the laboratory or the real world. Most of the questions require you to combine several pieces of knowledge in order to formulate an integrated understanding and response. If you spend time on these questions, you will gain increased understanding and facility with the subject matter covered on the test. You might want to discuss these questions and your answers with a teacher or mentor.

Note that the questions marked with stars are not short-answer or multiple-choice, and this study guide does not provide the answers. The questions marked with stars are intended as study questions, not practice questions. Thinking about the answers to them should improve your understanding of fundamental concepts and will probably help you answer a broad range of questions on the test. For example, the following box with a star appears in the list of study topics under "Vectors":

> ★ Be able to determine, for example, distance, displacement, average speed, average velocity, and average acceleration for an object in motion.

If you think about this question, perhaps jotting down some notes on the common formulas involved, you will review your knowledge of how to calculate vectors, and you will have probably prepared yourself to answer multiple-choice questions similar to the one below:

A student walks 15 meters east and then turns and walks 20 meters north in a total time of 10 seconds. Which of the following gives the magnitude of the student's average velocity?

(A) 1.5 m/s
(B) 2.0 m/s
(C) 2.5 m/s
(D) 3.5 m/s

(The correct answer is (C). Velocity is the rate of change of position [$v = \Delta x \times \Delta t$]. Adding the displacement vectors geometrically, you find that the student changed position by 25 meters in a time of 10 seconds.)

Mechanics

Vectors

- ◆ Properties
- ◆ Addition and subtraction
- ◆ Multiplication
  - Scalar (dot) product
  - Vector (cross) product

> ★ Be able to determine, for example, distance, displacement, average speed, average velocity, and average acceleration for an object in motion.
>
> ★ Be able to calculate, for example, the magnitude and direction of the vector (cross) product **A** × **B** of two vectors **A** and **B**.

Kinematics

- ◆ Motion along a straight line
  - Displacement

- Velocity
- Acceleration

★ Be able to describe, for example, in graphical form the position, velocity, and acceleration of an object that is thrown vertically upward and returns to its starting point.

★ Be able to determine, for example, displacement, distance, velocity, and acceleration from graphs of position versus time, velocity versus time, and acceleration versus time.

- Motion in two dimensions
  - Uniform circular motion
  - Projectile motion

★ Be able to calculate, for example, the horizontal and vertical components of velocity for a projectile.

- Reference frames and relative motion
  - Relative velocity
  - Galilean relativity

Dynamics

- Force and Newton's laws of motion
  - Newton's first law
    — Inertia
    — Inertial reference frames
  - Newton's second law
    — Force and acceleration
    — Addition of forces (net force)
    — Balanced versus unbalanced forces

★ Be able to identify, compare, and sum, for example, the forces acting on a block that is accelerating or moving at constant velocity on a rough horizontal surface, including the reaction forces.

- Newton's third law
  — Action-reaction forces
- Weight and mass
- Friction
  - Static friction
  - Kinetic friction
  - Rolling friction

★ Be able to discern, for example, between the coefficients of static, kinetic, and rolling friction.

★ Be able to determine, for example, the coefficient of kinetic friction for a box sliding down an inclined plane at constant velocity.

- Equilibrium of forces
- Equilibrium of moments (torques)

★ Be able to explain, for example, why gymnasts performing on a balance beam raise their arms to regain their balance.

- Uniform circular motion

★ Be able to determine, for example, the forces acting on a toy cart of mass m moving at constant velocity v around a circular track of radius r.

◆ Work, energy, and power

  • Relationship between work and kinetic energy

> ★ Be able to explain, for example, how an adult pushing a child on a swing adds energy to the swinging motion.

  • Work done by a variable force

◆ Conservation of energy

  • Potential energy

  • Conservative and nonconservative forces

> ★ Be able to use, for example, the law of conservation of energy to predict the energy transformations of a bungee-cord jumper.

◆ Simple harmonic motion and oscillations

  • Hooke's law

  • Graphical and mathematical representations

  • Energy considerations

  • Pendulums

  • Springs

> ★ Be able to determine, for example, the variables that affect the period and/or frequency of an object in simple harmonic motion.
>
> ★ Be able to plot, for example, the potential energy, kinetic energy, and total mechanical energy of a linear harmonic oscillator as a function of position.

◆ Linear momentum and impulse

  • Momentum-impulse relationship

  • Conservation of linear momentum

> ★ Be able to explain, for example, why it is difficult to step out of a canoe.

◆ Elastic and inelastic collisions

> ★ Be able to apply, for example, the principles of conservation of momentum and energy to predict the results of collisions between objects in one or two dimensions.

◆ Rigid-body motion

  • Angular velocity and angular acceleration

  • Angular momentum, moment of inertia, torque, and center of mass

  • Conservation of angular momentum

  • Rotational kinetic energy

> ★ Be able to describe, for example, the changes that occur to the moment of inertia, angular momentum, and rotational kinetic energy of a student who extends his or her arms outward from an initial downward position while rotating about a vertical axis on a frictionless platform.

◆ Mass-energy relationships

  • Conservation of mass-energy

◆ Newton's law of universal gravitation and orbital motion

  • Motion of satellites

- Kepler's laws
  — Law of orbits (first law)
  — Law of areas (second law)
  — Law of periods (third law)

★ Be able to determine, for example, the acceleration and period of a satellite in circular orbit about Earth.

★ Be able to describe, for example, the relationship between a planet's period about the Sun and its mean distance from the Sun.

- Fluids
  - Density and pressure
  - Ideal fluids at rest
    — Pascal's law
    — Archimedes' principle
    – Buoyant forces
  - Ideal fluids in motion
    — Bernoulli's principle
    – Streamlines
    – Equation of continuity

★ Be able to compute, for example, the buoyant force acting on an object.

Electricity and Magnetism

Characteristics of static electricity, electric forces, and electric fields

- Electric forces and Coulomb's law
- Electric fields, Gauss's law, electric potential energy, electric potential, and potential difference

★ Be able to compute, for example, the electrostatic force between, and the potential energy of, two point charges q_1 and q_2 separated by a distance d.

★ Be able to determine, for example, the electric field and electric potential at a point midway between two point charges.

Electric and magnetic properties of materials

- Conductors, insulators, and semiconductors
  - Charging by friction, conduction, and induction
- Capacitance and dielectrics

★ Be able to compare, for example, the effect of adding a dielectric to a charged capacitor in an open circuit to the effect of adding a dielectric to a capacitor with a fixed voltage across it.

Electric circuits, components, and applications

- Conductors, insulators, and semiconductors as used in circuits
- Sources of EMF
  - Batteries, photocells, generators
- Current and resistance
  - Ohm's law
  - Resistivity

★ Be able to describe, for example, how the resistivity of a wire depends on its length and cross-sectional area.

◆ Capacitance and inductance

◆ Energy and power

★ Be able to compute, for example, the power dissipated by a resistor in a circuit.

◆ Analyzing circuits

• Series and parallel circuits using Ohm's law or Kirchhoff's rules

• Resistors and capacitors in series or parallel

★ Be able to compute, for example, the equivalent capacitance of two capacitors connected in series.

• Internal resistance

• RC circuits

◆ Power in alternating-current circuits

• Average power and energy transmission

◆ Measurement of potential difference, current, resistance, and capacitance

• Ammeter, galvanometer, voltmeter, and potentiometer

★ Be able to describe, for example, how to measure the resistance of a resistor using a voltmeter and an ammeter.

Magnetic fields: causes, effects, and applications

◆ Magnets, magnetic fields, and magnetic forces

• Magnetic dipoles and materials

• Forces on a charged particle moving in a magnetic and/or electric field

— Lorentz force law
— Cyclotron
— Mass spectrometer

★ Be able to determine, for example, the magnitude and direction of the electric field needed to allow an electron to travel eastward undeflected in Earth's magnetic field.

• Forces or torques on current-carrying conductors in magnetic fields

◆ Magnetic flux

• Gauss's law of magnetism

◆ Magnetic fields produced by currents

• Biot-Savart law

• Ampere's law
— Magnetic field of a wire
— Magnetic field of a solenoid
— Displacement current

★ Be able to determine, for example, the magnitude and direction of the resultant magnetic field at a point midway between two long, parallel wires carrying currents in opposite directions and separated by a distance d.

★ Be able to determine, for example, the magnitudes and directions of the magnetic forces on two long, parallel current-carrying wires.

◆ Electromagnetic Induction

• Magnetic flux

• Lenz's law

• Faraday's law

★ Be able to determine, for example, the current induced in a metal rod that is aligned east-west and is dropped in Earth's magnetic field.

• Transformers, generators, and motors

Optics and Waves

Wave characteristics, phenomena, models, and applications

▶ Speed, amplitude, wavelength, and frequency

▶ Inverse square law for intensity

▶ Reflection, refraction, absorption, transmission, and scattering

• Snell's law

• Rayleigh scattering

★ Be able to explain, for example, why the sky appears blue.

▶ Transverse and longitudinal waves and their properties

• Doppler effect

• Resonance and natural frequencies

• Polarization

▶ Sound

• Pitch and loudness

• Air columns and standing waves
— Open at both ends
— Closed at one end
— Harmonics

• Beats

★ Be able to calculate, for example, the fundamental frequency and harmonics of an organ pipe that is closed at one end.

▶ Electromagnetic spectrum

• Frequency regions

• Color

▶ Principle of linear superposition and interference

• Diffraction, dispersion, beats, and standing waves

• Interference in thin films and Young's double-slit experiment

★ Be able to explain, for example, why colors are observed when sunlight falls on a soap bubble or an oil slick.

Geometric Optics

▶ Reflection and refraction

• Snell's law

• Total internal reflection
— Fiber optics

▶ Thin lenses

▶ Plane and spherical mirrors

★ Be able to locate and describe, for example, the image formed when an object is placed 50 centimeters in front of a thin converging lens of focal length 20 centimeters.

▶ Prisms

▶ Optical instruments

- Simple magnifier
- Microscope
- Telescope

Heat and Thermodynamics

▶ Heat and temperature

- Measurement of heat and temperature
- Temperature scales
- Thermal expansion
- Thermocouples

★ Be able to describe, for example, the difference between heat and temperature.

- Heat capacity and specific heat
- Latent heat of phase change (heat of fusion, heat of vaporization)

★ Be able to determine, for example, the amount of thermal energy needed for a given amount of ice at 0°C to change to a gaseous state at 100°C.

▶ Transfer of heat: conduction, convection, and radiation

★ Be able to explain, for example, why metal feels cooler to the touch than wood at the same temperature.

▶ Kinetic molecular theory

- Ideal gas laws

▶ Laws of thermodynamics and thermodynamic processes

- First law
  — Internal energy
  — Energy conservation
- Second law
  — Entropy and disorder
  — Reversible and irreversible processes
  — Spontaneity
  — Heat engines
    – Carnot cycle
    – Efficiency
- Third law
  — Absolute zero of temperature
- Zeroth law
  — Law of equilibrium
- Thermal processes involving pressure, volume, and temperature

★ Be able to describe, for example, the relationship between entropy and the second law of thermodynamics.

★ Be able to compute, for example, the work done during the isothermal expansion of an ideal gas.

▶ Energy and energy transformations

- Kinetic, potential, mechanical, sound, magnetic, electrical, light, heat, nuclear, chemical

Modern Physics, Atomic and Nuclear Structure

▶ Nature of the atom

- Rutherford scattering
- Atomic models
  — Bohr model
- Atomic spectra

◗ Atomic and nuclear structure

- Electrons, protons, and neutrons

- Electron arrangement

- Isotopes

- Hydrogen atom energy levels

- Nuclear forces and binding energy

★ Be able to explain, for example, why energy is released when helium is formed from the fusion of two deuterium nuclei.

◗ Radioactivity

- Radioactive decay

- Half-life

- Isotopes

- Decay processes
  — Alpha decay
  — Beta decay
  — Gamma decay

- Artificial radioactivity

★ Be able to determine, for example, the amount of radioactive substance left after a specified number of half-lives have elapsed.

★ Be able to identify, for example, the daughter nucleus that results from the alpha decay of a uranium-238 nucleus.

◗ Elementary particles

- Ionizing radiation

◗ Organization of matter

- Elements, compounds, solutions, and mixtures

◗ Physical properties of matter (phase changes, states of matter)

◗ Nuclear energy

- Fission and fusion

- Nuclear reactions and their products

★ Be able to distinguish, for example, between nuclear fission and nuclear fusion.

◗ Special topics in modern physics

- Blackbody radiation

- Photoelectric effect

- De Broglie's hypothesis

- Wave-particle duality

- Special relativity
  — Michelson-Morley experiment (ether and the speed of light)
  — Simultaneity
  — Lorentz transformations
    – Time dilation
    – Length contraction
  — Velocity addition

★ Be able to describe, for example, the relationship between light frequency and the energy of ejected photoelectrons.

★ Be able to apply, for example, the Lorentz transformation equations to time dilation effects.

History and Nature of Science

Nature of Scientific Methodology, Inquiry, and Historical Perspectives

- Scientific method of inquiry
  - Formulating problems
  - Formulating and testing hypotheses
  - Making observations
  - Developing generalizations
- Science process skills
  - Observing
  - Hypothesizing
  - Ordering
  - Categorizing
  - Comparing
  - Inferring
  - Applying
  - Communicating

★ Be able to present, for example, a scientific argument with supporting data.

- Distinguish among hypotheses, assumptions, models, laws, and theories

★ Be able to explain, for example, the difference between a law and a theory.

- Experimental design
  - Data collection
  - Interpretation and presentation
  - Significance of controls

★ Be able to determine and control, for example, the parameters of measuring devices.

- Integrate the overarching concepts of science

★ Be able to explain, for example, how the concepts of mass and energy are integrated.

- Historical roots of the physical sciences and the contributions made by major historical figures to the physical sciences
- Scientific knowledge is subject to change.

Mathematics, Measurement, and Data Manipulation

- Scientific measurement and notation systems
- Processes involved in scientific data collection and manipulation
  - Organization of data
  - Significant figures
  - Linear regression

★ Be able to determine, for example, the number of significant digits from various measurement instruments.

- Interpret and draw conclusions from data, including those presented in tables, graphs, and charts

★ Be able to develop, for example, mathematical and graphical representations of experimental data.

◗ Analysis of errors in data that are presented

  • Sources of error

  • Accuracy

  • Precision

Laboratory Activities and Safety Procedures

◗ Safety procedures involved in the preparation, storage, use, and disposal of laboratory and field materials

◗ Identify appropriate use, calibration procedures, and maintenance procedures for laboratory and field equipment

◗ Preparation of reagents, materials, and apparatuses for classroom use

◗ Knowledge of safety and emergency procedures for the science classroom and laboratory

★ Be able to provide, for example, reasons for and against the use of alcohol- or mercury-filled thermometers in a laboratory.

★ Be able to identify, for example, the factors that should be taken into account when purchasing radioactive samples.

◗ Knowledge of the legal responsibilities of the teacher in the science classroom

Science, Technology, and Social Perspectives

◗ Impact of science and technology on the environment and human affairs

★ Be able to explain, for example, what is meant by the greenhouse effect.

★ Be able to identify, for example, the environmental reasons underlying the development of new refrigerants.

◗ Issues associated with energy production, transmission, management, and use (including nuclear waste removal and transportation)

★ Be able to identify, for example, the factors that must be taken into consideration when discarding nuclear waste.

◗ Issues associated with the production, storage, use, management, and disposal of consumer products

★ Be able to describe, for example, the procedures to be followed when discarding chemicals from a laboratory.

◗ Issues associated with the management of natural resources

◗ Applications of science and technology to daily life

◗ Social, political, ethical, and economic issues arising from science and technology

Chapter 8

Don't be Defeated by
Multiple-Choice Questions

► ► ► ► ► ► ► ► ► ► ► ►

Why the multiple-choice tests take time

When you take the practice questions, you will see that there are very few simple identification questions of the "Which of the following scientists wrote *The Origin of Species?*" sort. When The Praxis Series™ Assessments were first being developed by teachers and teacher educators across the country, it was almost universally agreed that prospective teachers should be able to analyze situations, synthesize material, and apply knowledge to specific examples. In short, they should be able to think as well as to recall specific facts, figures, or formulas. Consequently, you will find that you are being asked to think and to solve problems on your test. Such activity takes more time than simply answering identification questions.

In addition, questions that require you to analyze situations, synthesize material, and apply knowledge are usually longer than are simple identification questions. The Praxis Series test questions often present you with something to read (a case study, a sample of student work, a chart or graph) and ask you questions based on your reading. Strong reading skills are required, and you must read carefully. Both on this test and as a teacher, you will need to process and use what you read efficiently.

If you know your reading skills are not strong, you may want to take a reading course. College campuses have reading labs that can help you strengthen your reading skills.

Understanding multiple-choice questions

You will probably notice that the word order in multiple-choice questions (or syntax) is different from the word order you're used to seeing in ordinary things you read, like newspapers or textbooks. One of the reasons for this difference is that many such questions contain the phrase "which of the following."

The purpose of the phrase "which of the following" is to limit your choice of answers only to the list given. For example, look at this question:

> Which of the following is a flavor made from beans?
>
> (A) Strawberry
>
> (B) Cherry
>
> (C) Vanilla
>
> (D) Mint

You may know that chocolate and coffee are flavors made from beans also. But they are not listed, and the question asks you to select from among the list that follows ("which of the following"). So the answer has to be the only bean-derived flavor in the list: vanilla.

Notice that the answer can be submitted for the phrase "which of the following." In the question above, you could insert "vanilla" for "which of the following" and have the sentence "Vanilla is a flavor made from beans." Sometimes it helps to cross out "which of the following" and insert the various choices. You may want to give this technique a try as you answer various multiple-choice questions in the practice test.

Also, looking carefully at the "which of the following" phrase helps you to focus on what the question is asking you to find and on the answer choices. In the simple example above, all of the answer choices are flavors. Your job is to decide which of the flavors is the one made from beans.

The vanilla bean question is pretty straightforward. But the phrase "which of the following" can also be found in more challenging questions. Look at this question:

> The dominant vegetation of the taiga biome is best characterized by which of the following types of plants?
>
> (A) Grasses, sedges, and humus
>
> (B) Spruces, firs, and pines
>
> (C) Maples, oaks, and hickories
>
> (D) Lichens, mosses, and ferns

The placement of "which of the following" tells you that the list of choices is a list of "types of plants." What are you supposed to find as an answer? You are supposed to find the choice that characterizes the major vegetation found in the taiga biome.

Sometimes it helps to put the question in your own words. Here, you could paraphrase the question as "What are major types of plants in the taiga biome?" Since taigas are evergreen temperate forests composed mostly of conifers, such as spruces, firs, and pines, the correct answer is (B).

You may find that it helps you to circle or underline each of the critical details of the question in your test book so that you don't miss any of them. It's only by looking at all parts of the question carefully that you will have all of the information you need to answer the question.

Circle or underline the critical parts of what is being asked in this question:

> Which of the following statements is correct about any chemical reaction that is at equilibrium?
>
> (A) The molecules stop reacting.
>
> (B) Only side reactions continue; the main reaction stops.
>
> (C) Forward and backward reactions occur at equal rates.
>
> (D) There are as many molecules of reactant as there are molecules of product.

Here is one possible way you may have annotated the question:

> Which of the following statements is correct about any chemical reaction that is at equilibrium?
>
> (A) The molecules stop reacting.
>
> (B) Only side reactions continue; the main reaction stops.
>
> (C) Forward and backward reactions occur at equal rates.
>
> (D) There are as many molecules of reactant as there are molecules of product.

After spending a minute with the question, you can probably see that you are being asked to recognize what is the correct statement about equilibrium of a chemical reaction. The definition of an equilibrium is that the forward and backward reactions occur at equal rates. The answer is (C).

The important thing is understanding what the question is asking. With enough practice, you should be able to determine what any question is asking. Knowing the answer is, of course, a different matter, but you have to understand a question before you can answer it.

It takes more work to understand "which of the following" questions when there are even more words in a question. Questions that require application or interpretation invariably require extra reading.

Consider this question:

> In an attempt to compare the half-lives of two radioactive elements, X and Y, a student set aside 400 grams of each. After six months, the student found that 25 grams of X and 200 grams of Y remained.
>
> Which of the following statements is true?
>
> (A) The half-life of Y is twice the half-life of X.
>
> (B) The half-life of Y is four times the half-life of X.
>
> (C) The half-life of Y is eight times the half-life of X.
>
> (D) Unless the exact time interval is established, a comparison cannot be made.

Being able to select the right answer depends on your understanding of the statement given. Element Y decayed from 400 grams to 200 grams, a time period of one half-life. Element X decayed from 400 grams to 25 grams, a time period of four half-lives. Y decays more slowly than X, since the half-life of Y is four times that of X. The correct answer is (B).

Understanding questions containing "NOT," "LEAST," "EXCEPT"

In addition to "which of the following" and details that must be understood, the words "NOT," "EXCEPT," and "LEAST" often make comprehension of test questions more difficult. These words are always capitalized when they appear in The Praxis Series test questions, but they are easily (and frequently) overlooked.

For the following test question, determine what kind of answer you're looking for and what the details of the question are.

> All of the following represent primary consumers feeding on organisms in the first trophic level EXCEPT
>
> (A) paramecia feeding on green algae
>
> (B) mice feeding on dead grass
>
> (C) deer feeding on branches of trees
>
> (D) slugs feeding on mushrooms

You're looking for the type of organism that is NOT a primary consumer feeding on organisms in the first trophic level. The correct answer is (D), because all of the other choices are primary consumers that feed on producers. Neither slugs nor mushrooms are producers. In choices (A), (B), and (C), the producers are green algae, dead grass, and tree branches, and the primary consumers are paramecia, mice, and deer.

TIP It's easy to get confused while you're processing the information to answer a question with a LEAST, NOT, or EXCEPT in the question. If you treat the word "LEAST," "NOT," or "EXCEPT" as one of the details you must satisfy, you have a better chance of understanding what the question is asking. And when you check your answer, make "LEAST," "NOT," or "EXCEPT" one of the details you check for.

Understanding questions based on laboratory sets

Laboratory sets generally contain a body of introductory material followed by a group of related questions. The introduction to a set can be in one of many forms, for example, a summary of an experiment, an outline of a problem, a graph, a chart, or a table. Questions based on a laboratory or experimental situation require a careful strategy that balances time, efficiency, and critical understanding.

Since the laboratory or experimental situation can often be dense and complex, you should read through the description of the situation before reading the questions, but you should not spend time taking notes or reading the situation multiple times until you know what the questions are asking you to do.

For example, you might encounter a laboratory situation like this:

> A student in a laboratory is given 7 g of iron filings and 4 g of powdered sulfur. The two elements are thoroughly mixed together on a sheet of paper. (Molecular mass: iron = 55.85 g/mol, sulfur = 32.07 g/mol.)

In your first reading, you should make sure you understand the basics. In this example, you should grasp that the questions will probably focus on the two elements. In this first reading, you should also anticipate being asked questions about the purpose

of the experimental setup, factors that affect the experimental outcome, conclusions derived from the experiment, or calculations required to reach an end product. Once you have gained an overall understanding of the experimental situation, you should answer the first question.

> Which of the following is the best method for separating the iron from the sulfur?
>
> (A) Lifting out the iron particles by using a magnifying glass and tweezers
>
> (B) Adding water and filtering
>
> (C) Heating the mixture
>
> (D) Passing a magnet just above the mixture

For the second question, you may need to read the question carefully, with special attention to analyze the experimental situation and outcome. Pay attention to the word "If" that appears in the question.

> If the mixture of iron and sulfur is heated in a test tube, a red glow spreads throughout the tube. Heat energy is obviously released. After cooling, the test tube and its contents are weighed. If the empty test tube weighs 17 g and if it is assumed that no atmospheric gases were involved in the reaction, then the mass of the test tube and its contents should be approximately
>
> (A) 6 g
>
> (B) 17 g
>
> (C) 28 g
>
> (D) 54 g

The correct answers to these two questions are (D) and (C), respectively.

Be familiar with multiple-choice question types

Now that you have reviewed the basics of succeeding at multiple-choice questions, it should help to review the most common question formats you are likely to see.

1. Complete the statement

In this type of question, you are given an incomplete statement. You must select the choice that will make the completed statement correct.

> The purpose of generators in a power plant is to transform energy from
>
> (A) chemical to electrical
>
> (B) electrical to chemical
>
> (C) mechanical to chemical
>
> (D) mechanical to electrical

To check your answer, reread the question and add your answer choice at the end. Be sure that your choice best completes the sentence. The correct answer is (D).

2. Which of the Following

This question type is discussed in detail in a previous section. The question contains the details that must be satisfied for a correct answer, and it uses "which of the following" to limit the choices to the four choices shown, as this example demonstrates.

> Which of the following is an advantage of using wood, rather than fossil fuels, to heat or supplement the heating of homes?
>
> (A) Wood is a renewable natural resource.
>
> (B) Wood is easier for people to obtain, transport, and store than fossil fuels are.
>
> (C) Only wood contains compounds of hydrogen and carbon, which provide heating value.
>
> (D) Wood does not produce air pollution.

The correct answer is (A).

3. Roman numeral choices

This format is used when there can be more than one correct answer in the list. Consider the following example:

> Changes in which the entropy of the system increases include which of the following?
>
> I. Melting ice at room temperature
>
> II. Evaporating water at room temperature
>
> III. Dissolving NaCl in room-temperature water
>
> (A) I only
>
> (B) I and II only
>
> (C) II and III only
>
> (D) I, II, and III

One useful strategy in this type of question is to assess each possible answer before looking at the answer choices and then evaluate the answer choices. In the question above, entropy is a measure of disorder. In all three cases, the disorder of the system increases. Therefore, the correct answer is (D).

4. Questions containing LEAST, EXCEPT, NOT

This question type is discussed at length above. It asks you to select the choice that doesn't fit. You must be very careful with this question type, because it's easy to forget that you're selecting the negative. This question type is used in situations in which there are several good solutions, or ways to approach something, but also a clearly wrong way to do something.

5. Other formats

New formats are developed from time to time in order to find new ways of assessing knowledge with multiple-choice questions. If you see a format you are not familiar with, read the directions carefully. Then read and approach the question the way you would any other question, asking yourself what you are supposed to be looking for, and what details are given in the question that help you find the answer.

Useful facts about the test

1. **You can answer the questions in any order.** You can go through the questions from beginning to end, as many test takers do, or you can create your own path. Perhaps you will want to answer questions in your strongest field first and then move from your strengths to your weaker areas. There is no right or wrong way. Use the approach that works for you.

2. **There are no trick questions on the test.** You don't have to find any hidden meanings or worry about trick wording. All of the questions on the test ask about subject matter knowledge in a straightforward manner.

3. **Don't worry about answer patterns.** There is one myth that says that answers on multiple-choice tests follow patterns. There is another myth that there will never be more than two questions with the same lettered answer following each other. There is no truth to either of these myths. Select the answer you think is correct, based on your knowledge of the subject.

4. **There is no penalty for guessing.** Your test score is based on the number of correct answers you have, and incorrect answers are not counted against you. When you don't know the answer to a question, try to eliminate any obviously wrong answers and then guess at the correct one.

5. **It's OK to write in your test booklet.** You can work problems right on the pages of the booklet, make notes to yourself, mark questions you want to review later, or write anything at all. Your test booklet will be destroyed after you are finished with it, so use it in any way that is helpful to you.

Smart tips for taking the test

1. **Put your answers in the right "bubbles."** It seems obvious, but be sure that you are "bubbling in" the answer to the right question on your answer sheet. You would be surprised at how many candidates fill in a "bubble" without checking to see that the number matches the question they are answering.

2. **Skip the questions you find to be extremely difficult.** There are bound to be some questions that you think are hard. Rather than trying to answer these on your first pass through the test, leave them blank and mark them in your test booklet so that you can come

back to them. Pay attention to the time as you answer the rest of the questions on the test and try to finish with 10 or 15 minutes remaining so that you can go back over the questions you left blank. Even if you don't know the answer the second time you read the questions, see whether you can narrow down the possible answers, and then guess.

3. **Keep track of the time.** Bring a watch to the test, just in case the clock in the test room is difficult for you to see. Divide the total testing time available to you by the number of questions (see chapter 1) to determine the average amount of time you will have to answer each of the questions. This may not seem like much time, but you will be able to answer a number of questions in only a few seconds each. You will probably have plenty of time to answer all of the questions, but if you find yourself becoming bogged down in one section, you might decide to move on and come back to that section later.

4. **Read all of the possible answers before selecting one**—and then reread the question to be sure the answer you have selected really answers the question being asked. Remember that a question that contains a phrase like "Which of the following does NOT. . ." is asking for the one answer that is NOT a correct statement or conclusion.

5. **Check your answers.** If you have extra time left over at the end of the test, look over each question and make sure that you have filled in the "bubble" on the answer sheet as you intended. Many candidates make careless mistakes that could have been corrected if they had checked their answers.

6. **Don't worry about your score when you are taking the test.** No one is expected to get all of the questions correct. Your score on this test is not analogous to your score on the SAT, the GRE, or other similar tests. It doesn't matter on this test whether you score very high or barely pass. If you meet the minimum passing scores for your state, and you meet the other requirements of the state for obtaining a teaching license, you will receive a license. Your actual score doesn't matter, as long as it is above the minimum required score. With your score report you will receive a booklet entitled *Understanding Your Praxis Scores,* which lists the passing scores for your state.

Chapter 9

Practice Questions for the
Biology: Content Knowledge Tests

► ► ► ► ► ► ► ► ► ► ► ►

Practice Questions

Now that you have studied the content topics and have worked through strategies relating to multiple-choice questions, you should take the following practice test. You will probably find it helpful to simulate actual testing conditions, giving yourself about 60 minutes to work on the questions. You can cut out and use the answer sheet provided if you wish.

Keep in mind that the test you take at an actual administration will have different questions.

You should not expect the percentage of questions you answer correctly in these practice questions to be exactly the same as when you take the test at an actual administration, since numerous factors affect a person's performance in any given testing situation.

When you have finished the practice questions, you can score your answers and read the explanations of the best answer choices in chapter 10.

THE **PRAXIS**
S E R I E S
Professional Assessments for Beginning Teachers®

TEST CODE:

TEST NAME:
Biology: Content Knowledge

Practice Questions

Calculators Prohibited

Time—60 Minutes
75 Questions

(Note, at the official test administration, depending on which test you take, there will be either 150 questions, and you will be allowed 120 minutes to complete the test, or 75 questions, and you will be allowed 60 minutes to complete the test.)

Answer Sheet C

THE PRAXIS SERIES®
Professional Assessments for Beginning Teachers®

DO NOT USE INK

Use only a pencil with soft black lead (No. 2 or HB) to complete this answer sheet.
Be sure to fill in completely the oval that corresponds to the proper letter or number.
Completely erase any errors or stray marks.

1. NAME
Enter your last name and first initial.
Omit spaces, hyphens, apostrophes, etc.

Last Name (first 6 letters)   F I

(A)(B)(C)(D)(E)(F)(G)(H)(I)(J)(K)(L)(M)(N)(O)(P)(Q)(R)(S)(T)(U)(V)(W)(X)(Y)(Z)

2.

YOUR NAME: _____
(Print)

Last Name (Family or Surname) _____ First Name (Given) _____ M. I. ____

MAILING ADDRESS: _____
(Print)

P.O. Box or Street Address _____ Apt. # (If any) ____

City _____ State or Province ____

Country _____ Zip or Postal Code ____

TELEPHONE NUMBER: ( ) _____ Home   ( ) _____ Business

SIGNATURE: _____   TEST DATE: _____

3. DATE OF BIRTH

Month	Day
Jan.	
Feb.	
Mar.	
April	
May	
June	
July	
Aug.	
Sept.	
Oct.	
Nov.	
Dec.	

4. SOCIAL SECURITY NUMBER

(0)(1)(2)(3)(4)(5)(6)(7)(8)(9)

5. CANDIDATE ID NUMBER

(0)(1)(2)(3)(4)(5)(6)(7)(8)(9)

6. TEST CENTER / REPORTING LOCATION

Center Number _____ Room Number _____

Center Name _____

City _____ State or Province _____

Country _____

7. TEST CODE / FORM CODE

0
1

(0)(1)(2)(3)(4)(5)(6)(7)(8)(9)

8. TEST BOOK SERIAL NUMBER

9. TEST FORM

10. TEST NAME

51055 • 08920 • TF71M500   Q2573-06
MH01159

I.N. 202974   1 2 3 4

CERTIFICATION STATEMENT: (Please write the following statement below. DO NOT PRINT.)
"I hereby agree to the conditions set forth in the *Registration Bulletin* and certify that I am the person whose name and address appear on this answer sheet."

_____

_____

_____

SIGNATURE: _____   DATE: _____ / _____ / _____
                                                                                                    Month   Day   Year

BE SURE EACH MARK IS DARK AND COMPLETELY FILLS THE INTENDED SPACE AS ILLUSTRATED HERE: ● .

1 Ⓐ Ⓑ Ⓒ Ⓓ	41 Ⓐ Ⓑ Ⓒ Ⓓ	81 Ⓐ Ⓑ Ⓒ Ⓓ	121 Ⓐ Ⓑ Ⓒ Ⓓ
2 Ⓐ Ⓑ Ⓒ Ⓓ	42 Ⓐ Ⓑ Ⓒ Ⓓ	82 Ⓐ Ⓑ Ⓒ Ⓓ	122 Ⓐ Ⓑ Ⓒ Ⓓ
3 Ⓐ Ⓑ Ⓒ Ⓓ	43 Ⓐ Ⓑ Ⓒ Ⓓ	83 Ⓐ Ⓑ Ⓒ Ⓓ	123 Ⓐ Ⓑ Ⓒ Ⓓ
4 Ⓐ Ⓑ Ⓒ Ⓓ	44 Ⓐ Ⓑ Ⓒ Ⓓ	84 Ⓐ Ⓑ Ⓒ Ⓓ	124 Ⓐ Ⓑ Ⓒ Ⓓ
5 Ⓐ Ⓑ Ⓒ Ⓓ	45 Ⓐ Ⓑ Ⓒ Ⓓ	85 Ⓐ Ⓑ Ⓒ Ⓓ	125 Ⓐ Ⓑ Ⓒ Ⓓ
6 Ⓐ Ⓑ Ⓒ Ⓓ	46 Ⓐ Ⓑ Ⓒ Ⓓ	86 Ⓐ Ⓑ Ⓒ Ⓓ	126 Ⓐ Ⓑ Ⓒ Ⓓ
7 Ⓐ Ⓑ Ⓒ Ⓓ	47 Ⓐ Ⓑ Ⓒ Ⓓ	87 Ⓐ Ⓑ Ⓒ Ⓓ	127 Ⓐ Ⓑ Ⓒ Ⓓ
8 Ⓐ Ⓑ Ⓒ Ⓓ	48 Ⓐ Ⓑ Ⓒ Ⓓ	88 Ⓐ Ⓑ Ⓒ Ⓓ	128 Ⓐ Ⓑ Ⓒ Ⓓ
9 Ⓐ Ⓑ Ⓒ Ⓓ	49 Ⓐ Ⓑ Ⓒ Ⓓ	89 Ⓐ Ⓑ Ⓒ Ⓓ	129 Ⓐ Ⓑ Ⓒ Ⓓ
10 Ⓐ Ⓑ Ⓒ Ⓓ	50 Ⓐ Ⓑ Ⓒ Ⓓ	90 Ⓐ Ⓑ Ⓒ Ⓓ	130 Ⓐ Ⓑ Ⓒ Ⓓ
11 Ⓐ Ⓑ Ⓒ Ⓓ	51 Ⓐ Ⓑ Ⓒ Ⓓ	91 Ⓐ Ⓑ Ⓒ Ⓓ	131 Ⓐ Ⓑ Ⓒ Ⓓ
12 Ⓐ Ⓑ Ⓒ Ⓓ	52 Ⓐ Ⓑ Ⓒ Ⓓ	92 Ⓐ Ⓑ Ⓒ Ⓓ	132 Ⓐ Ⓑ Ⓒ Ⓓ
13 Ⓐ Ⓑ Ⓒ Ⓓ	53 Ⓐ Ⓑ Ⓒ Ⓓ	93 Ⓐ Ⓑ Ⓒ Ⓓ	133 Ⓐ Ⓑ Ⓒ Ⓓ
14 Ⓐ Ⓑ Ⓒ Ⓓ	54 Ⓐ Ⓑ Ⓒ Ⓓ	94 Ⓐ Ⓑ Ⓒ Ⓓ	134 Ⓐ Ⓑ Ⓒ Ⓓ
15 Ⓐ Ⓑ Ⓒ Ⓓ	55 Ⓐ Ⓑ Ⓒ Ⓓ	95 Ⓐ Ⓑ Ⓒ Ⓓ	135 Ⓐ Ⓑ Ⓒ Ⓓ
16 Ⓐ Ⓑ Ⓒ Ⓓ	56 Ⓐ Ⓑ Ⓒ Ⓓ	96 Ⓐ Ⓑ Ⓒ Ⓓ	136 Ⓐ Ⓑ Ⓒ Ⓓ
17 Ⓐ Ⓑ Ⓒ Ⓓ	57 Ⓐ Ⓑ Ⓒ Ⓓ	97 Ⓐ Ⓑ Ⓒ Ⓓ	137 Ⓐ Ⓑ Ⓒ Ⓓ
18 Ⓐ Ⓑ Ⓒ Ⓓ	58 Ⓐ Ⓑ Ⓒ Ⓓ	98 Ⓐ Ⓑ Ⓒ Ⓓ	138 Ⓐ Ⓑ Ⓒ Ⓓ
19 Ⓐ Ⓑ Ⓒ Ⓓ	59 Ⓐ Ⓑ Ⓒ Ⓓ	99 Ⓐ Ⓑ Ⓒ Ⓓ	139 Ⓐ Ⓑ Ⓒ Ⓓ
20 Ⓐ Ⓑ Ⓒ Ⓓ	60 Ⓐ Ⓑ Ⓒ Ⓓ	100 Ⓐ Ⓑ Ⓒ Ⓓ	140 Ⓐ Ⓑ Ⓒ Ⓓ
21 Ⓐ Ⓑ Ⓒ Ⓓ	61 Ⓐ Ⓑ Ⓒ Ⓓ	101 Ⓐ Ⓑ Ⓒ Ⓓ	141 Ⓐ Ⓑ Ⓒ Ⓓ
22 Ⓐ Ⓑ Ⓒ Ⓓ	62 Ⓐ Ⓑ Ⓒ Ⓓ	102 Ⓐ Ⓑ Ⓒ Ⓓ	142 Ⓐ Ⓑ Ⓒ Ⓓ
23 Ⓐ Ⓑ Ⓒ Ⓓ	63 Ⓐ Ⓑ Ⓒ Ⓓ	103 Ⓐ Ⓑ Ⓒ Ⓓ	143 Ⓐ Ⓑ Ⓒ Ⓓ
24 Ⓐ Ⓑ Ⓒ Ⓓ	64 Ⓐ Ⓑ Ⓒ Ⓓ	104 Ⓐ Ⓑ Ⓒ Ⓓ	144 Ⓐ Ⓑ Ⓒ Ⓓ
25 Ⓐ Ⓑ Ⓒ Ⓓ	65 Ⓐ Ⓑ Ⓒ Ⓓ	105 Ⓐ Ⓑ Ⓒ Ⓓ	145 Ⓐ Ⓑ Ⓒ Ⓓ
26 Ⓐ Ⓑ Ⓒ Ⓓ	66 Ⓐ Ⓑ Ⓒ Ⓓ	106 Ⓐ Ⓑ Ⓒ Ⓓ	146 Ⓐ Ⓑ Ⓒ Ⓓ
27 Ⓐ Ⓑ Ⓒ Ⓓ	67 Ⓐ Ⓑ Ⓒ Ⓓ	107 Ⓐ Ⓑ Ⓒ Ⓓ	147 Ⓐ Ⓑ Ⓒ Ⓓ
28 Ⓐ Ⓑ Ⓒ Ⓓ	68 Ⓐ Ⓑ Ⓒ Ⓓ	108 Ⓐ Ⓑ Ⓒ Ⓓ	148 Ⓐ Ⓑ Ⓒ Ⓓ
29 Ⓐ Ⓑ Ⓒ Ⓓ	69 Ⓐ Ⓑ Ⓒ Ⓓ	109 Ⓐ Ⓑ Ⓒ Ⓓ	149 Ⓐ Ⓑ Ⓒ Ⓓ
30 Ⓐ Ⓑ Ⓒ Ⓓ	70 Ⓐ Ⓑ Ⓒ Ⓓ	110 Ⓐ Ⓑ Ⓒ Ⓓ	150 Ⓐ Ⓑ Ⓒ Ⓓ
31 Ⓐ Ⓑ Ⓒ Ⓓ	71 Ⓐ Ⓑ Ⓒ Ⓓ	111 Ⓐ Ⓑ Ⓒ Ⓓ	151 Ⓐ Ⓑ Ⓒ Ⓓ
32 Ⓐ Ⓑ Ⓒ Ⓓ	72 Ⓐ Ⓑ Ⓒ Ⓓ	112 Ⓐ Ⓑ Ⓒ Ⓓ	152 Ⓐ Ⓑ Ⓒ Ⓓ
33 Ⓐ Ⓑ Ⓒ Ⓓ	73 Ⓐ Ⓑ Ⓒ Ⓓ	113 Ⓐ Ⓑ Ⓒ Ⓓ	153 Ⓐ Ⓑ Ⓒ Ⓓ
34 Ⓐ Ⓑ Ⓒ Ⓓ	74 Ⓐ Ⓑ Ⓒ Ⓓ	114 Ⓐ Ⓑ Ⓒ Ⓓ	154 Ⓐ Ⓑ Ⓒ Ⓓ
35 Ⓐ Ⓑ Ⓒ Ⓓ	75 Ⓐ Ⓑ Ⓒ Ⓓ	115 Ⓐ Ⓑ Ⓒ Ⓓ	155 Ⓐ Ⓑ Ⓒ Ⓓ
36 Ⓐ Ⓑ Ⓒ Ⓓ	76 Ⓐ Ⓑ Ⓒ Ⓓ	116 Ⓐ Ⓑ Ⓒ Ⓓ	156 Ⓐ Ⓑ Ⓒ Ⓓ
37 Ⓐ Ⓑ Ⓒ Ⓓ	77 Ⓐ Ⓑ Ⓒ Ⓓ	117 Ⓐ Ⓑ Ⓒ Ⓓ	157 Ⓐ Ⓑ Ⓒ Ⓓ
38 Ⓐ Ⓑ Ⓒ Ⓓ	78 Ⓐ Ⓑ Ⓒ Ⓓ	118 Ⓐ Ⓑ Ⓒ Ⓓ	158 Ⓐ Ⓑ Ⓒ Ⓓ
39 Ⓐ Ⓑ Ⓒ Ⓓ	79 Ⓐ Ⓑ Ⓒ Ⓓ	119 Ⓐ Ⓑ Ⓒ Ⓓ	159 Ⓐ Ⓑ Ⓒ Ⓓ
40 Ⓐ Ⓑ Ⓒ Ⓓ	80 Ⓐ Ⓑ Ⓒ Ⓓ	120 Ⓐ Ⓑ Ⓒ Ⓓ	160 Ⓐ Ⓑ Ⓒ Ⓓ

FOR ETS USE ONLY	R1	R2	R3	R4	R5	R6	R7	R8	TR	CS

BIOLOGY: CONTENT KNOWLEDGE

Questions 1-4 refer to the following information.

The onset of stomach ulcers and gastroesophageal reflux disease (GERD) has been directly linked to stomach hyperacidity in some cases. Data collected from an experiment measuring the effect of three new drugs, *X*, *Y* and *Z*, on stomach pH are shown below. The drugs were given at the same dosage.

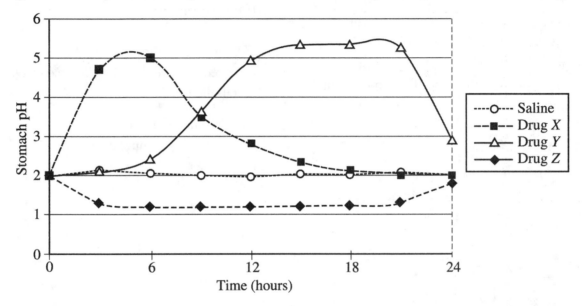

1. Treatment with which of the following was most effective in reducing stomach acid during the course of the experiment?

   (A) Saline
   (B) Drug *X*
   (C) Drug *Y*
   (D) Drug *Z*

2. The dependent variable in this experiment is

   (A) drug concentration
   (B) stomach pH
   (C) time
   (D) number of drugs tested

3. At 6 hours, drug *X* results in what percentage change in stomach pH over that of the control?

   (A) 300%
   (B) 250%
   (C) 150%
   (D) 35%

4. The gastric juice of the stomach is highly acidic as compared to fluids in the rest of the body. All of the following are functions of gastric juice in the stomach EXCEPT

   (A) destruction of microorganisms in ingested food
   (B) activation of pepsinogen to aid in protein digestion
   (C) hydrolysis of food polymers
   (D) inhibition of the release of cholecystokinin (CCK) during digestion

Questions 5-7 refer to the following information.

Metabolic studies were conducted to measure changes in dissolved oxygen levels over a 1-hour time period. A single goldfish was placed into each of four aquariums of identical size containing identical volumes of sterilized water. The aquariums were then sealed and measurements of the dissolved oxygen levels were taken. Variables in the experiment included goldfish mass, temperature, and presence of light. All other conditions remained constant. The experimental conditions are shown in the diagrams below.

O_2 electrode
25°C, lighted room
15-gram goldfish

Chamber *A*

25°C, lighted room
30-gram goldfish

Chamber *B*

25°C, dark room
15-gram goldfish

Chamber *C*

15°C, lighted room
15-gram goldfish

Chamber *D*

5. Which of the following metabolic processes is this study designed to measure?

(A) Aerobic respiration
(B) Fermentation
(C) Photosynthesis
(D) Transpiration

6. Which of the following variables would be expected to have the LEAST effect on metabolic rate?

(A) Presence of light
(B) Increasing temperature
(C) Decreasing temperature
(D) Size of the animal

7. Which graph most accurately represents the expected changes in oxygen levels in chambers *A* and *B*?

(A)

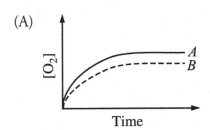

(B)

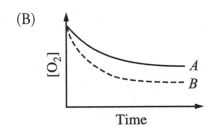

(C)

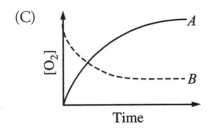

(D)

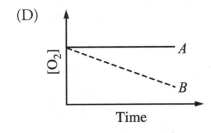

Questions 8-10 refer to the following food web. Each letter represents a different species, and the arrows show the flow of materials and energy.

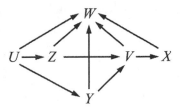

8. Species *U* most likely represents which part of a food web?

   (A) Decomposer
   (B) Primary consumer
   (C) Secondary consumer
   (D) Producer

9. Which of the following species most likely belongs to the kingdom Fungi?

   (A) Species *U*
   (B) Species *W*
   (C) Species *Y*
   (D) Species *Z*

10. Suppose that a toxic substance enters the ecosystem. The concentration of the toxic substance would most likely be highest in the tissues of which of the following species?

   (A) Species *V*
   (B) Species *X*
   (C) Species *Y*
   (D) Species *Z*

Questions 11-13 refer to the following information and diagram.

Samples of a circular plasmid were completely digested with either restriction enzyme *Eco*RI alone, *Bam*HI alone, or a combination of *Eco*RI and *Bam*HI. The resulting DNA fragments were separated by electrophoresis on an agarose gel. The gel was then stained with methylene blue and the results obtained are illustrated in the diagram below.

(−) Cathode

Fragment Size	Digests of Plasmid			Fragment Number
(wells) →	*Eco*RI —	*Bam*HI —	*Eco*RI + *Bam*HI —	
20 kb	—			I
18 kb				
16 kb				
14 kb				
12 kb		—		II
10 kb				
8 kb			—	III
6 kb		—	—	IV
4 kb			—	V
2 kb		—	—	VI
0 kb				

(+) Anode

11. At how many different sites did the restriction enzyme *Bam*HI cut the plasmid?

   (A) One
   (B) Two
   (C) Three
   (D) Four

12. From the information provided in the diagram, which of the following can be concluded?

   (A) The agarose pore size is smaller near the wells.
   (B) The DNA molecules are positively charged.
   (C) Smaller DNA fragments travel faster than larger DNA fragments.
   (D) Voltage levels control the direction of fragment movement.

13. If a gene for ampicillin resistance is located on fragment V and a gene for kanamycin resistance is located on fragment II, which of the following is a true statement about isolating both genes together?

   (A) A single digest using *Eco*RI would successfully isolate the gene for ampicillin resistance and the gene for kanamycin resistance.
   (B) A single digest using *Bam*HI would successfully isolate the gene for ampicillin resistance and the gene for kanamycin resistance.
   (C) A double digest using both *Eco*RI and *Bam*HI would successfully isolate the gene for ampicillin resistance and the gene for kanamycin resistance.
   (D) It would be impossible to isolate the gene for ampicillin resistance and the gene for kanamycin resistance using *Eco*RI and *Bam*HI.

14. Which of the following is an application of recombinant DNA technology?

    (A) Detection of the presence of sickle cell anemia in an unborn fetus
    (B) Production of human insulin for a diabetic in large-scale batches
    (C) Matching DNA from a criminal suspect to a murder weapon
    (D) Determination of the DNA sequence of a human genome

Questions 15-17 refer to the pedigree analysis below that follows the occurrence of β-thalassemia in two families. The disorder is caused by a mutation in hemoglobin. Circles represent females. Squares represent males. Affected individuals are indicated by darkened circles or squares.

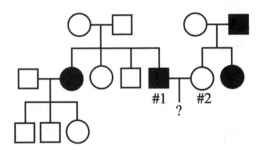

15. Based on the pedigree shown above, the most likely pattern of transmission for β-thalassemia is via an allele that is

    (A) autosomal dominant
    (B) autosomal recessive
    (C) codominant
    (D) X-linked

16. If individuals 1 and 2 have offspring, what is the probability that one of their offspring will exhibit the β-thalassemia trait?

    (A) 0
    (B) 1/4
    (C) 1/2
    (D) 1

17. Which of the following processes would be most directly affected in individuals expressing the β-thalassemia trait?

    (A) Oxygen transport by red blood cells
    (B) Formation of semen by the prostate gland
    (C) Absorption of iron in the digestive tract
    (D) Immune system function

18. Given the DNA sequence

    5' A T G C C C T C A 3',

    which of the following is the correct complementary sequence of messenger RNA?

    (A) 3' U A C G G G A G U 5'
    (B) 3' A C T C C C G T A 5'
    (C) 5' A U G C C C U C A 3'
    (D) 5' T A C G G G A G T 3'

19. Which of the following would be the most appropriate method for safely handling an acid spill in a laboratory?

    (A) Neutralize the acid with a 5 *M* sodium hydroxide (NaOH) solution.
    (B) Dilute the acid with water.
    (C) Wipe up the acid with paper towels.
    (D) Soak up the acid with an acid-neutralizing absorbent pad.

The graph below depicts the changes in free energy (ΔG) in a reaction without an enzyme.

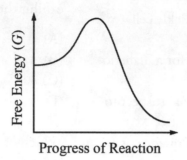

20. Which of the graphs shown below reflects the change in free energy that would occur when an enzyme specific for the reaction is added?

(A)

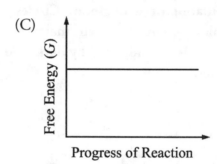

(C)

(B)

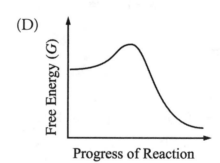

(D)

21. In a cancer patient, which of the following would LEAST likely be damaged by chemotherapy treatment?

    (A) Bone marrow
    (B) Skeletal muscle
    (C) Epidermis
    (D) Lining of the gastrointestinal tract

22. The presence of which molecule in the atmosphere, resulting from the burning of fossil fuels, is a major factor in the formation of acid precipitation (acid rain)?

    (A) Carbon dioxide
    (B) Carbon monoxide
    (C) Hydrochloric acid
    (D) Sulfur dioxide

23. Which of the following cellular structures would be expected to be found in high numbers within a phagocytic white blood cell as compared to a muscle cell?

    (A) Golgi apparatus
    (B) Lysosomes
    (C) Endoplasmic reticulum
    (D) Ribosome

24. If a patient is brought into the emergency room suffering from dehydration, should a healthcare worker select an IV (intravenous fluids) of isotonic Ringer's lactate solution or sterile, distilled water for treatment?

    (A) Ringer's solution should be used because water is hypertonic to the blood and would cause cell crenation.
    (B) Ringer's solution should be used because water is hypotonic to the blood and would cause cell hemolysis.
    (C) Water should be selected because the pH of the introduced fluid must be neutral.
    (D) Water should be selected to maintain a constant level of salts and nutrients in the blood.

25. Which of the following substances can cross a biological membrane by simple diffusion without the assistance of transport proteins or channels?

    (A) Oxygen (O_2)
    (B) Glucose
    (C) Sodium ions (Na^+)
    (D) Chloride ions (Cl^-)

26. Which of the following scientific theories is supported by the fact that mitochondria are enclosed by a double membrane and possess their own DNA?

    (A) Endosymbiotic theory
    (B) Lamarck's theory of evolution
    (C) Darwin's theory of natural selection
    (D) Pasteur's germ theory

27. Which of the following adaptations would be beneficial to a plant's survival in a hot, dry environment?

    I. Use of the C_3 pathway as the sole photosynthetic mechanism
    II. Thickening of the outer cuticle on the plant leaves and stems
    III. Placement of the stomata on the upper surface of the leaf

(A) I only
(B) II only
(C) I and II only
(D) I, II, and III

28. A researcher identifies a new species within the moist soil of a wooded area. The species exhibits bilateral symmetry, has internal body segmentation, and uses metanephridia to remove wastes from its blood and coelomic fluid. Based on these characteristics, this new species should be categorized in which of the following animal phylum?

(A) Mollusca
(B) Arthropoda
(C) Annelida
(D) Echinodermata

29. In a germinating seedling, the shoot grows upward toward the light, while the root grows downward into the soil. What responses explain these phenomena?

(A) The shoot exhibits positive phototropism; the root exhibits positive gravitropism.
(B) The shoot exhibits positive gravitropism; the root exhibits positive phototropism.
(C) The shoot and root both exhibit positive gravitropism.
(D) The shoot and root both exhibit positive phototropism.

30. Four percent of an isolated population suffers from an autosomal recessive genetic disease. Assuming the population is in Hardy-Weinberg equilibrium for the trait in question, what percentage of the population are carriers?

(A) 2%
(B) 16%
(C) 32%
(D) 68%

31. The DNA for the coding sequence of a gene that codes for a polypeptide containing 120 amino acids contains a minimum of how many nucleotide base pairs?

(A) 40
(B) 120
(C) 240
(D) 360

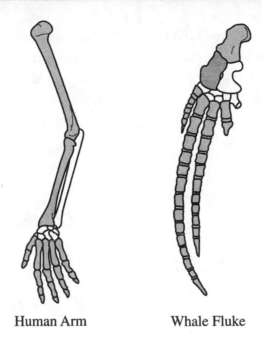

Human Arm   Whale Fluke

32. Compare the skeletal structure of the human arm and whale fluke shown above. The arm and fluke are examples of

(A) analogous structures
(B) homologous structures
(C) the results of convergent evolution
(D) the results of sympatric speciation

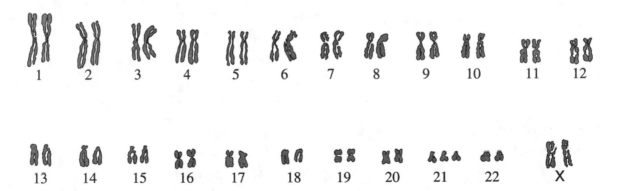

33. The karyotype shown above represents the chromosomal makeup from an individual with which of the following?

(A) Klinefelter syndrome
(B) Down syndrome
(C) Sickle cell disorder
(D) Turner syndrome

A wild-type fruit fly that is heterozygous for both body color and eye color is mated with a fly exhibiting two recessive mutations, ebony body color and sepia eye color. The offspring distribution is as follows:

Body Color	Eye Color	Sex	% Offspring
Wild	Wild	Female	18
Wild	Wild	Male	16
Wild	Sepia	Female	7
Wild	Sepia	Male	9
Ebony	Wild	Female	8
Ebony	Wild	Male	8
Ebony	Sepia	Female	18
Ebony	Sepia	Male	16

34. Based on the data presented above, genes for ebony body and sepia eye in fruit flies are most likely

   (A) sex-linked
   (B) unlinked
   (C) linked
   (D) codominant

A study was conducted to examine the growth patterns of bacteria. Three strains of bacteria were studied: 1) wild-type that can synthesize all amino acids, 2) mutant Y, which lacks the ability to synthesize methionine, and 3) mutant Z, which lacks the ability to synthesize tyrosine. Four experiments were conducted in which different strains of bacteria were incubated for one hour at 37°C in growth media containing all the essential amino acids, then plated onto a minimal-media agar plate and incubated overnight. (Minimal medium lacks amino acids but contains everything else that bacteria need to grow.) The results of the four experiments are shown in the table below.

Experiment Number	Strain Plated on Complete Medium	Colony Formation on Minimal Medium
1	Wild type	Positive
2	Mutant Y	Negative
3	Mutant Z	Negative
4	Mutant Y and Mutant Z	Positive

35. Which of the following mechanisms best explains the presence of colonies on the plates in experiment 4?

   (A) Mutation
   (B) Conjugation
   (C) Transformation
   (D) Transduction

36. Which of the following would be linked by a glycosidic bond?

    (A) Two amino acids in a peptide chain
    (B) Two glucose molecules in a starch molecule
    (C) A deoxyribose and a phosphate molecule in a strand of DNA
    (D) A glycerol and a fatty acid in a phospholipid

37. All of the following are characteristics of the human immunodeficiency virus (HIV) EXCEPT:

    (A) HIV causes acquired immunodeficiency syndrome (AIDS).
    (B) HIV may be spread by contact with body fluids, including blood and semen.
    (C) HIV binds to CD4 receptors on the surface of target cells within its host.
    (D) HIV is a retrovirus, having DNA as its genetic material.

38. Which of the following functions is carried out by DNA polymerase during DNA replication?

    (A) Adding nucleotides to the 3' end of the new DNA strand
    (B) Linking Okazaki fragments on the lagging DNA strand
    (C) Unwinding and denaturing the double-stranded DNA helix
    (D) Synthesizing RNA primers on the lagging strand

39. Which of the following mechanisms of inheritance is exhibited by the ABO blood groups, which have A, B, O, and AB blood types?

    I. Codominance
    II. Epistasis
    III. Multiple alleles

    (A) I only
    (B) II only
    (C) I and III
    (D) II and III

40. Which of the following is NOT an example of Darwin's concept of the mechanism of natural selection?

    (A) Selective breeding produces a variety of corn that will survive drought conditions.
    (B) Average beak size in a population of birds changes over time following their migration to an environment with larger seeds for food.
    (C) Bacteria develop resistance to antibiotics.
    (D) Infants tend to have birth weights between 3 and 4 kilograms, not higher or lower.

41. A volcano erupts, killing 87 percent of the members of a wildflower population. The original population had approximately equal numbers of pink and white flowering plants. Several generations after the eruption, only pink flowering plants are present in the population. Which of the following led to microevolution in this case?

    (A) Gene flow
    (B) Genetic drift
    (C) Geographic isolation
    (D) Polymorphism

42. In which of the following cell types would a mutation have the greatest possibility of having an impact on the gene pool of a population?

    (A) Liver
    (B) Neuron
    (C) Skin
    (D) Sperm

43. Which of the following hypothetical phylogenetic trees best represents the evolutionary relationship between species W and three other organisms, X, Y, and Z, based on the amino acid sequences shown in the table below for a region within a highly conserved protein found in all four species?

Amino acid #	1	2	3	4	5	6	7
Species W	Alanine	Arginine	Leucine	Proline	Valine	Isoleucine	Valine
Species X	Histidine	Asparagine	Leucine	Proline	Valine	Glutamine	Valine
Species Y	Histidine	Arginine	Isoleucine	Valine	Glycine	Glutamine	Valine
Species Z	Alanine	Asparagine	Leucine	Proline	Valine	Glutamine	Valine

(A)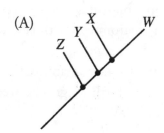

(C)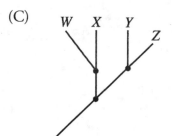

(B)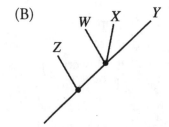

(D)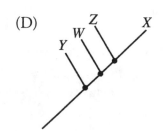

44. An insect species lays its eggs on a specific type of plant leaf. The leaves hide the insect eggs from predators and protect them from the environment. As the eggs hatch, the insect larvae feed on the leaves. Which of the following best describes the relationship between the insect and the plant?

    (A) Commensalism
    (B) Mimicry
    (C) Mutualism
    (D) Parasitism

45. Which of the following statements is accurate regarding global population growth?

    (A) The infant mortality rate exceeds the death rate.
    (B) Earth has reached its ultimate carrying capacity.
    (C) The human population is exhibiting exponential growth.
    (D) The human population exhibits characteristics of an r-selected population.

46. In many animal societies, a social hierarchy, or pecking order, controls the dominance behavior of its members. This pecking order generally serves to accomplish all of the following EXCEPT

    (A) providing a means whereby the weak members of the society are cared for and protected
    (B) influencing the way in which the members distribute themselves within the society's habitat
    (C) establishing a means by which the members of the society obtain mates
    (D) establishing a means by which food is distributed among the members of the society

47. Which of the following statements regarding the water cycle is correct?

    (A) On a global scale, there is a net movement of water vapor from the land to the oceans.
    (B) On a global scale, evaporation exceeds precipitation over the land.
    (C) The water cycle differs from other biogeochemical cycles because most water moves through ecosystems by physical rather than chemical processes.
    (D) Transpiration by terrestrial plants directly produces surface runoff and groundwater movement from the land to the oceans.

48. An isolated hillside of a temperate deciduous forest was used for an ecological study. The hillside was treated with defoliant and herbicides for one year. The dead organic matter was left to decay at the site. Which of the following statements most reflects what changes can be expected in this forest environment?

    (A) The hillside will have a decreased rate of water runoff and soil erosion.
    (B) Secondary succession will occur.
    (C) There will be a decrease in plant biodiversity, but animal biodiversity will remain unchanged.
    (D) The nutrient levels in the soil will remain constant because no plants were using the nutrient resources.

49. Which of the following biomes is correctly paired with the description of its characteristics?

   (A) Taiga: absence of tall plants and trees, low precipitation level, shallow topsoil, and permafrost
   (B) Tundra: presence of cone-bearing trees, high precipitation level, moderate to cool temperatures
   (C) Estuary: salt-marsh grasses, algae, and phytoplankton prevalent, variable water salinity
   (D) Chaparral: presence of grasses, scattered trees, and large herbivores, seasonal rains and droughts, equatorial latitude

50. When caribou migrate, the weaker ones often become the prey of wolves and other carnivores. If the vegetation eaten by caribou is sparse for several consecutive years, which of the following is most likely true about the wolf population during that same period?

   (A) The wolf population initially increases due to an increase in their food availability.
   (B) The wolf population initially decreases because they compete with the caribou for the same food.
   (C) The wolf population initially decreases because the stronger caribou begin to use wolves as a food source.
   (D) The wolf population does not change significantly; only the caribou population decreases.

51. Which of the following statements about the stratospheric ozone layer is accurate?

   (A) The ozone layer helps to absorb infrared radiation, preventing it from reaching Earth's surface.
   (B) Accumulation of chlorofluorocarbons (CFCs) in the atmosphere has led to depletion of the ozone layer.
   (C) Depletion of the ozone layer is most apparent in atmospheric regions above the equator.
   (D) Scientists believe that if the use of ozone-depleting agents is stopped, the damage to the ozone layer will repair itself within five to ten years.

52. Human beings, reptiles, birds, and fish all belong to the same

   (A) class
   (B) family
   (C) order
   (D) phylum

53. A researcher collects what she believes to be a new species of life in a freshwater stream. Microscopic analysis shows the presence of chloroplasts, mitochondria, a defined nucleus, and a cellulose-based cell wall. Individual cells cluster to form colonies, but the colony lacks any true tissue or organ formations. This new species would most likely be categorized in which of the following kingdoms?

   (A) Animalia
   (B) Fungi
   (C) Protista
   (D) Monera

54. Plants must obtain numerous molecules from their environment in order to synthesize macromolecules such as carbohydrates. Which of the following molecules is obtained by plants primarily from the atmosphere?

    (A) Carbon dioxide
    (B) Nitrogen
    (C) Oxygen
    (D) Water

55. Experiments were conducted to test the rate of transpiration in plants under different environmental conditions. The stem of a plant shoot was cut. Tubing, attached at one end to a water-filled pipette, was placed over the cut end of the shoot. The tubing and pipette were clamped as shown in the diagram below. Measurements of the water level in the pipette were recorded every 15 minutes. The experimental setup was placed in a room with partial sunlight at 25°C. Which of the following conditions would cause the most rapid lowering of the water level in the pipette?

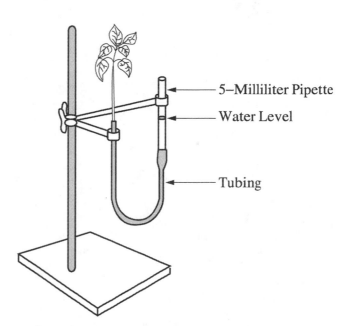

5–Milliliter Pipette

Water Level

Tubing

    (A) Increasing the light intensity
    (B) Misting the leaves with water
    (C) Removing half of the leaves
    (D) Placing the experimental setup inside a sealed, clear glass container

56. Molecular geneticists have created fruit varieties that will not ripen naturally, allowing the fruit to be shipped over long distances without being damaged. They do so by inactivating genes for the production of a hormone that causes the fruit to ripen. Which of the following would cause the fruit to ripen once it is received?

    (A) Introducing ethylene gas into shipping containers or storage rooms
    (B) Placing the fruit in complete darkness
    (C) Increasing the temperature to 40°C
    (D) Treating the fruit with the plant hormone auxin

57. Aphids are small insects that rest on the stems and leaves of plants and insert their needlelike mouthpiece directly into the phloem of the plants. Which of the following is the primary reason that an aphid infestation will kill a plant?

    (A) Aphids prevent normal water transport throughout the plant.
    (B) Aphids deplete the sugars normally available for the plant.
    (C) Damage to the phloem reduces transpiration levels.
    (D) Damage to the phloem prevents photosynthesis.

58. All of the following regions of a plant have active meristematic cells EXCEPT the

    (A) root tips
    (B) leaf tips
    (C) terminal bud
    (D) vascular cambium

59. The sciatic nerve from a frog was isolated and placed into a nerve chamber. A recording of an action potential was measured when the nerve was bathed in Ringer's solution (a bathing solution that mimics the extracellular fluid typically found surrounding a cell) and stimulated. The recording is shown below. If the toxin TTX, a potent sodium-channel blocker, is added to the bathing solution and the nerve is stimulated using a stimulus of the same strength, what will be the most likely change in the action potential?

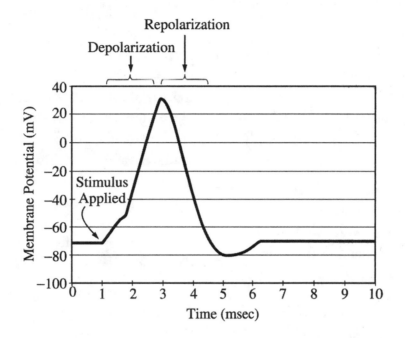

(A) The action potential will not occur because depolarization will not occur.

(B) The membrane will depolarize more quickly and the action potential will be of shorter duration.

(C) The membrane will repolarize more slowly and the action potential will last longer.

(D) Development of an action potential does not require sodium; therefore, the action potential will remain unchanged.

60. Male stickleback fish have a characteristic red belly coloration. A male stickleback fish will attack other male sticklebacks or any non-fishlike model with a red belly-sign stimulus to defend its territory. Attacking the non-fishlike model is an example of which of the following?

(A) Fixed action pattern
(B) Habituation
(C) Imprinting
(D) Operant conditioning

61. Which of the following physiological responses would be appropriate to help reduce body temperature?

(A) Contraction of skeletal muscle
(B) Release of thyroid hormone
(C) Activation of the sweat glands
(D) Release of prostaglandins from the hypothalamus

62. All of the following are believed to be factors that are involved in causing essential hypertension (persistent high blood pressure) EXCEPT

(A) atherosclerosis
(B) high cholesterol levels
(C) high dietary salt intake
(D) anemia

63. Which of the following molecules is an immunoglobulin secreted by B lymphocytes as a specific defense in response to a specific foreign invader?

(A) Antibody
(B) Antigen
(C) Complement protein
(D) Interferon

64. Which of the following structures would most likely be damaged if there were an injury to the cells of the endoderm during embryogenesis?

(A) Nervous system
(B) Skin
(C) Stomach lining
(D) Heart

Directions: Each group of questions below consists of four lettered headings followed by a list of numbered phrases or sentences. For each numbered phrase or sentence, select the one heading that is most closely related to it. One heading may be used once, more than once, or not at all in each group.

Questions 65-67 refer to the following hormones.

(A) Antidiuretic hormone (ADH)
(B) Estrogen
(C) Glucagon
(D) Prolactin

65. Hormone whose depletion is associated with the development of osteoporosis

66. Lipid-soluble hormone that is a cholesterol derivative

67. Hormone whose effects oppose those of insulin

Questions 68-69 refer to the following biotechnology issues and advancements.

    (A) Gene therapy

    (B) Cloning

    (C) Human Genome Project

    (D) In vitro fertilization

68. Insertion of a specific DNA sequence into a somatic cell genome to compensate for a gene that is functioning abnormally

69. Technique involving removal of genetic material from the ovum of an organism, inserting genetic material from a different organism's somatic cell into that ovum, followed by development of a new organism from the original ovum

Questions 70-71 refer to the following plant divisions.

    (A) Anthophyta (angiosperms)

    (B) Bryophyta

    (C) Coniferophyta (gymnosperms)

    (D) Pterophyta

70. Division with a dominant gametophyte life stage

71. Division characterized by the use of flowers, fruits, and seeds during the reproductive cycle

Questions 72-73 refer to the diagrams shown below, which depict chromosomes in phases of mitosis or meiosis in a cell where the diploid number is four ($2n = 4$).

(A)

(C)

(B)

(D)

72. Anaphase I

73. Event that will eventually result in the production of diploid, genetically identical daughter cells

Questions 74-75 refer to the following molecular structure.

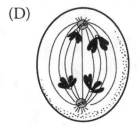

74. Region to which the oxygen end of a water molecule would most likely be attracted

75. Region that is most hydrophobic

Chapter 10

Right Answers and Explanations for the Practice
Questions for the *Biology: Content Knowledge* Tests

▶ ▶ ▶ ▶ ▶ ▶ ▶ ▶ ▶ ▶ ▶ ▶

Right Answers and Explanations for the Practice Questions

Question Number	Correct Answer	Content Category
1	C	History and Nature of Science (Mathematics, Measurement, and Data Manipulation)
2	B	History and Nature of Science (Mathematics, Measurement, and Data Manipulation)
3	C	History and Nature of Science (Mathematics, Measurement, and Data Manipulation)
4	D	Organismal Biology and Diversity of Life (Animals)
5	A	Molecular and Cellular Biology (Chemical Basis of Life)
6	A	Molecular and Cellular Biology (Chemical Basis of Life)
7	B	Molecular and Cellular Biology (Chemical Basis of Life)
8	D	Ecology (Ecosystems)
9	B	Ecology (Ecosystems)
10	B	Ecology (Ecosystems)
11	C	History and Nature of Science (Lab Procedures and Safety)
12	C	History and Nature of Science (Lab Procedures and Safety)
13	B	History and Nature of Science (Lab Procedures and Safety)
14	B	Science, Technology and Social Perspectives
15	B	Genetics and Evolution (Genetics)
16	C	Genetics and Evolution (Genetics)
17	A	Organismal Biology and Diversity of Life (Animals)
18	A	Molecular and Cellular Biology (Molecular Basis of Heredity)
19	D	History and Nature of Science (Lab Procedures and Safety)
20	D	Molecular and Cellular Biology (Chemical Basis of Life)
21	B	Molecular and Cellular Biology (Cell Structure and Function)
22	D	Science, Technology and Social Perspectives
23	B	Molecular and Cellular Biology (Cell Structure and Function)
24	B	Molecular and Cellular Biology (Cell Structure and Function)
25	A	Molecular and Cellular Biology (Cell Structure and Function)
26	A	Genetics and Evolution (Evolution)
27	B	Organismal Biology and Diversity of Life (Plants)
28	C	Organismal Biology and Diversity of Life (Animals)
29	A	Organismal Biology and Diversity of Life (Plants)
30	C	Genetics and Evolution (Evolution)
31	D	Molecular and Cellular Biology (Molecular Basis of Heredity)
32	B	Genetics and Evolution (Evolution)
33	B	Genetics and Evolution (Genetics)

Question Number	Correct Answer	Content Category
34	C	Genetics and Evolution (Genetics)
35	B	Molecular and Cellular Biology (Molecular Basis of Heredity)
36	B	Molecular and Cellular Biology (Chemical Basis of Life)
37	D	Molecular and Cellular Biology (Molecular Basis of Heredity)
38	A	Molecular and Cellular Biology (Molecular Basis of Heredity)
39	C	Genetics and Evolution (Genetics)
40	A	Genetics and Evolution (Evolution)
41	B	Genetics and Evolution (Evolution)
42	D	Genetics and Evolution (Evolution)
43	D	Genetics and Evolution (Evolution)
44	D	Ecology (Communities)
45	C	Ecology (Populations)
46	A	Ecosystems (Populations)
47	C	Ecology (Ecosystems)
48	B	Ecology (Communities and Ecosystems)
49	C	Ecology (Ecosystems)
50	A	Ecosystems (Communities)
51	B	Science, Technology and Society
52	D	Organismal Biology and Diversity of Life (Animals)
53	C	Organismal Biology and Diversity of Life (Diversity)
54	A	Organismal Biology and Diversity of Life (Plants)
55	A	Organismal Biology and Diversity of Life (Plants)
56	A	Organismal Biology and Diversity of Life (Plants)
57	B	Organismal Biology and Diversity of Life (Plants)
58	B	Organismal Biology and Diversity of Life (Plants)
59	A	Organismal Biology and Diversity of Life (Animals)
60	A	Organismal Biology and Diversity of Life (Animals)
61	C	Organismal Biology and Diversity of Life (Animals)
62	D	Organismal Biology and Diversity of Life (Animals)
63	A	Organismal Biology and Diversity of Life (Animals)
64	C	Organismal Biology and Diversity of Life (Animals)
65	B	Organismal Biology and Diversity of Life (Animals)
66	B	Organismal Biology and Diversity of Life (Animals)
67	C	Organismal Biology and Diversity of Life (Animals)
68	A	Science, Technology and Social Perspectives
69	B	Science, Technology and Social Perspectives
70	B	Organismal Biology and Diversity of Life (Plants)
71	A	Organismal Biology and Diversity of Life (Plants)
72	D	Molecular and Cellular Biology (Cellular Structure and Function)
73	A	Molecular and Cellular Biology (Cellular Structure and Function)
74	A	Molecular and Cellular Biology (Chemical Basis of Life)
75	D	Molecular and Cellular Biology (Chemical Basis of Life)

Explanations of Right Answers

1. This question requires a fundamental understanding of how to interpret graphic data. You must also understand the relationship between the numerical values on the pH scale and the classification of these values as acidic or basic. The data show that only drugs X and Y reduce acid (increase the pH value) as compared to the saline control. Drug Y's maximal effects last 9 to 10 hours, while drug X's effects last only 3 to 4 hours. The correct answer, therefore, is (C).

2. This question requires an understanding of dependent versus independent variables in experimental design. In this experiment, changes in the stomach pH depend on the presence of different drugs over a 24-hour time period. The correct answer, therefore, is (B).

3. This question requires you to quantitatively compare data presented in graphic form. After 6 hours have elapsed, the control pH is approximately 2.0, whereas treatment with drug X gives a pH value of 5.0. Drug X increases pH by 150 percent. The correct answer, therefore, is (C).

4. This question requires you to understand the roles of the acid environment in the stomach as well as several basic digestive processes. Acid does kill bacteria, activate pepsinogen, and act as a catalyst for the hydrolysis process, but it plays no significant role in the control of cholecystokinin (CCK) release. CCK's release is controlled primarily by the chemical composition of ingested food. The correct answer, therefore, is (D).

5. This question requires an understanding of fundamental metabolic processes. Aerobic respiration occurs in animals and requires the use of oxygen as the primary method of ATP synthesis. Although some level of anaerobic respiration may also be occurring, it would not be effectively measured in this experimental design. The correct answer, therefore, is (A).

6. This question requires you to know what factors influence metabolic rate. Overall, light would have very little influence on metabolism except when controlling sleep/wake cycles in animals. Temperature and animal size drastically influence metabolic rate at the cellular level in all cases. The correct answer, therefore, is (A).

7. This question requires you to predict how factors influence metabolic rate and how changes in aerobic respiration influence oxygen consumption. Both fish will be respiring, just at different rates. Since the animal in chamber B is larger than the one in chamber A, with all other conditions being identical, the larger fish will have higher metabolic demands and use more oxygen. The correct answer, therefore, is (B).

8. This question requires an understanding of food webs and trophic levels. Most producers in a food web are photosynthetic (i.e., plants, green algae) and gain energy from the Sun. This energy is used, directly or indirectly, by organisms in higher trophic levels. Species U is the only one that does not obtain its energy from another species in the food web. The correct answer, therefore, is (D).

9. This question requires an understanding of food webs, trophic levels, and classification of organisms. Decomposers gain energy from other organisms in the food web and break down complex organic molecules into their inorganic forms. Species *W* is the decomposer in this food web. Fungi are one of the major types of decomposers in an ecosystem. The correct answer, therefore, is (B).

10. This question requires an understanding of biomagnification within successive trophic levels. Toxins become more concentrated in the highest levels of consumers within the ecosystem and therefore are most likely to be affected by its presence. Species *X* is a tertiary consumer in this food web. The correct answer, therefore, is (B).

11. This question requires an understanding of restriction enzymes and their use in generating recombinant DNA. Since the plasmid is circular and cut by *Bam*HI at three different sites, the correct answer, therefore, is (C).

12. When placed in an electric field, DNA, which is negatively charged, will migrate through the gel matrix toward the positive electrode (anode). The DNA fragments will migrate at a different rate depending on their mass-to-charge ratio. Thus, smaller fragments will migrate faster than larger fragments. The correct answer, therefore, is (C).

13. From a cursory examination, it appears that a double digest would be necessary; however, only a single digest using *Bam*HI would be needed. The fragment labeled V in the double

digest is actually a component of fragment II, which is formed in the single digest using *Bam*HI. This is the only activity necessary to isolate the two genes together. The correct answer, therefore, is (B).

14. This question requires an understanding of the abilities and limitations of different biotechnology tools. Recombinant DNA is DNA in which genes from two different sources, even different species, are linked. This technology has been used to insert the human insulin gene into bacterial expression vectors. This has allowed human insulin to be synthesized and purified in a laboratory, a great advantage over the previous method of purification of insulin from animal sources. The correct answer, therefore, is (B).

15. This question requires you to analyze the path of inheritance for a genetic disorder and requires understanding of Mendelian genetics. Analysis shows that only individuals who have a homozygous genotype for the disease, e.g., individual #1, will express the trait, while heterozygotes, e.g., individual #2, will appear normal. The correct answer, therefore, is (B)

16. This question requires you to predict the outcome of a genetic cross. Using pedigree analysis, you can determine that individual #1 is homozygous recessive (*dd*) for the trait and that individual #2 is heterozygous, or a carrier, (*Dd*). When *dd* and *Dd* genotypes are crossed, half of the offspring will be expected to have a *Dd* genotype and half a *dd* genotype. Since β-thalassemia is a recessive trait, only the offspring with a *dd* genotype will exhibit the disease. The correct answer, therefore, is (C).

17. This question requires knowledge of the function of hemoglobin. Hemoglobin reversibly binds oxygen in red blood cells, aiding in the transport of oxygen throughout the body. The correct answer, therefore, is (A).

18. This question requires knowledge of DNA transcription, base pairing, and the difference in bases between DNA and RNA. A strand of messenger RNA would have bases complementary to the DNA strand (including the replacement of uracil for thymine), and the strand orientations would be antiparallel. The correct answer, therefore, is (A).

19. This question requires an understanding of basic safety protocols in the laboratory. The pH of the acid should be neutralized before handling, but never by increasing the volume of the spill with a strong base. Laboratory safety kits typically include absorbent pads or baking soda to help neutralize and absorb acid spills. The correct answer, therefore, is (D).

20. This question requires an understanding of the function of enzymes in a chemical reaction. Enzymes are biological catalysts that change the rates of chemical reactions without being consumed by the reactions. Enzymes reduce the free energy of activation, or activation energy (E_A), in a reaction without altering the free energy change for the reaction. The correct answer, therefore, is (D).

21. This question tests your knowledge of cell division and cancer. Chemotherapy generally targets rapidly dividing cells, whether they are cancerous or not. Muscle cells do not actively divide after their initial development. The correct answer, therefore, is (B).

22. This question requires an understanding of the ways in which humans impact the environment. The formation and acidity levels of precipitation have been greatly impacted by the release of nitrogen oxides and sulfur oxides during the burning of fossil fuels (coal, oil, and gas). The correct answer, therefore, is (D).

23. This question requires knowledge of cell structure and function. Phagocytic cells engulf large, particulate substances and degrade them (e.g., they destroy bacteria). Lysosomes are organelles that contain hydrolytic enzymes and function in intracellular digestion. The correct answer, therefore, is (B).

24. This question requires knowledge of osmosis and tonicity. Because animal cells do not have a cell wall they do not tolerate osmotic stress well. If distilled water (a hypotonic solution) were used, water would enter the cells due to the cell's high osmolarity, causing the cells to rupture. The correct answer, therefore, is (B).

25. This question requires knowledge of biological membrane structure, diffusion, and the role of molecular transport proteins. Substances that are small and uncharged (e.g., O_2) can cross the membrane most easily. Substances that are larger or that are charged cannot cross without the aid of a transporter protein or transport channel. The correct answer, therefore, is (A).

26. This question requires knowledge of the evolution of prokaryotic and eukaryotic life-forms on Earth. The endosymbiotic theory suggests that mitochondria and chloroplasts were once independent organisms that were engulfed by and entered into a symbiotic relationship with other cells. This accounts for the fact that both organelles have a double-membrane boundary while other organelles have only a single-membrane boundary, that they can replicate independently of the cell, and that they have their own genetic material. The correct answer, therefore, is (A).

27. This question requires an understanding of specific plant structures and physiological mechanisms that allow survival of plants in hot, dry environments. Thickening of the cuticle and the C_4 photosynthetic mechanism would help prevent excess transpiration, water evaporation, and photorespiration, whereas stomata on the upper surface and the C_3 photosynthetic mechanism would favor water loss. The correct answer, therefore, is (B).

28. This question requires knowledge of the characteristics of major animal phyla. Annelida (i.e., segmented worms) is the only phylum listed that possesses all the features listed. The correct answer, therefore, is (C).

29. This question requires an understanding of growth regulation in plants. Phototropism is the growth toward or away from light; gravitropism is growth toward or away from the force of gravity on Earth. Shoots exhibit positive phototropism, which allows the photosynthetic leaves and stems to gain access to the sunlight. Roots exhibit positive gravitropism, growing down into the soil to gain access to water and to provide anchoring for the plant. The correct answer, therefore, is (A).

30. This question requires you to apply the Hardy-Weinberg equations to determine allele and genotype frequencies in a nonevolving population. The equations used are $p + q = 1$ and $p^2 + 2pq + q^2 = 1$, where p equals the frequency of the dominant allele, q equals the frequency of the recessive allele, p^2 equals the frequency of individuals with a homozygous dominant genotype, q^2 equals the frequency of individuals with a homozygous recessive genotype, and $2pq$ equals the frequency of heterozygotes in the population. The problem gives the value of $q^2 = 0.04$. Using the equations, you can calculate that $q = 0.2$, $p = 0.8$, and therefore $2pq = 0.32$, or 32%. The correct answer, therefore, is (C).

31. This question requires an understanding of translation and the genetic code. Three adjacent nucleotides in a molecule of mRNA code for a specific amino acid. If there are 120 amino acids, then $120 \times 3 = 360$ nucleotide base pairs needed to code for the polypeptide. The correct answer, therefore, is (D).

32. This question tests knowledge of types of evidence for evolution. Descent with modification is evident between species within a taxonomic category. Comparative anatomy (e.g., comparing skeletal structures) provides evidence of this. Similarity in characteristics between species resulting from the species' having common ancestors is known as homology. The correct answer, therefore, is (B).

33. This question tests knowledge of the chromosomal basis of disease and genetic aberrations. Down syndrome occurs in individuals with trisomy 21 (three copies of the 21st chromosome rather than the normal two copies). The correct answer, therefore, is (B).

34. This question requires the ability to analyze the results of a genetic cross and to have an understanding of the concept of linkage. If the genes are on separate chromosomes (i.e., unlinked), random assortment during gamete formation would be expected to yield equal numbers of both parental type and recombinant type (one wild trait and one mutant trait) offspring. If the genes are in close proximity (i.e., linked), crossing-over events lead to the formation of a smaller number of recombinant offspring than expected for unlinked genes. The data shows that the frequency of recombinants is lower than that of the other parental type offspring, without a discrepancy between the occurrence of recombinants in males and females. The correct answer, therefore, is (C).

35. This question requires an understanding of bacterial reproduction and genetic recombination. Conjugation is the direct transfer of genetic material between bacteria cells. Genetic recombination in these cells can lead to new strains of bacteria. In this case, mutant *Y* and *Z* strains transferred genetic material that was lacking in the strains independently. The recipients of the transferred DNA can now synthesize both methionine and tyrosine and survive to form a colony on the minimal medium. The correct answer, therefore, is (B).

36. This question tests knowledge of covalent bond structures involved in macromolecular polymerization. Glycosidic bonds are formed between monosaccharides (sugars) by a dehydration reaction. The correct answer, therefore, is (B).

37. This question requires the knowledge of the general characteristics of viruses, viral replication, and HIV specifically. HIV is a retrovirus, but retroviruses carry RNA as their genetic material and then synthesize DNA, using reverse transcriptase, to incorporate their genetic material into the host's genome. The correct answer, therefore, is (D).

38. This question requires an understanding of events related to DNA synthesis. DNA polymerase functions to polymerize newly forming strands of complementary DNA in the $5' \rightarrow 3'$ direction, using an existing single strand of DNA as a template. DNA polymerase may also function to proofread for errors in the new DNA strand. The correct answer, therefore, is (A).

39. This question tests an understanding of common types of non-Mendelian modes of inheritance. The ABO blood groups exhibit both codominance and multiple alleles. Codominance is demonstrated by the fact the heterozygotes with one *A* allele and one *B* allele express traits from both genes; neither is dominant to the other. However, both the *A* allele and *B* allele are dominant to the *O* allele. Multiple allelism is demonstrated by the fact that there are more than two alleles (*A*, *B*, and *O*) for the gene. These three alleles are inherited in various combinations of two

alleles. In this way, four possible phenotypes for the ABO blood groups are produced. The correct answer, therefore, is (C).

40. This question tests an understanding of Darwin's concept of process of natural selection versus artificial selection. Artificial selection is employed when a farmer selectively breeds corn to produce a drought-resistant variety. In this case, the farmer, not nature, i.e., the environment, selects for particular traits. The correct answer, therefore, is (A).

41. This question requires that you understand microevolution and the causes of changes in allele frequency. When natural disasters (e.g., earthquakes, fires, and floods) kill large numbers of the population regardless of their fitness level, the surviving reduced population is likely to have a genetic makeup that is not representative of the original population. This situation is known as the bottleneck effect. Since, the allele frequencies in the remaining population are unlikely to be identical to that of the original population, microevolution occurs. The bottleneck effect is one type of genetic drift. The correct answer, therefore, is (B).

42. This question tests knowledge of the mechanisms of evolution. Mutations in DNA may result in changes in protein structure and expression. These changes may impact the fitness of the individual in its environment. If these changes occur in gametes, not somatic cells, then the changes can be inherited and influence the population's gene pool. The correct answer, therefore, is (D).

43. This question requires an understanding how molecular evidence is used to determine hypothetical evolutionary relationships between organisms and how phylogenetic trees are constructed. Cladistic analysis suggests that organisms that are closely related will have few differences between amino acid sequences, while organisms with little evolutionary relationship will have many. Species X and Z have one difference in sequence. Therefore, species X is most closely related to species Z. Species Y has a greater number of differences with species X and species Z than species W does. Therefore species X and Z are least related to species Y. The correct answer, therefore, is (D).

44. This question requires an understanding of interspecific relationships in a community. In the relationship between the insect and plant, the insect is protected and gains nutrients from the plant, but the plant is damaged by the insect. The correct answer, therefore, is (D).

45. This question requires knowledge of population ecology and the trend of human population growth. The human population has continued to grow exponentially since the mid-1600's. Earth's ultimate carrying capacity is debatable. Defining the carrying capacity for humans is difficult because it has been observed to change with the evolution of human culture, e.g., the advent of agriculture and the influence of industrial technology. The correct answer, therefore, is (C).

46. This question requires an understanding of social behaviors within animal populations. Pecking order, a type of dominance hierarchy, may be established when animals are kept together in a group over a period of time.

Once established, it allows higher-ranking individuals greater access to food, space, and mates, without regard for the success of lower-ranking individuals. The correct answer, therefore, is (A).

47. This question requires knowledge of biogeochemical cycling. On a global scale, net movement of water is from the oceans to the land. Evaporation exceeds precipitation over the oceans; precipitation exceeds evaporation over the land. In a land environment, precipitation returns water to the ground, where it either percolates through the soil to collect as groundwater or becomes surface runoff. The correct answer, therefore, is (C).

48. This question requires you to predict the outcome of environmental damage and requires understanding of the concepts of soil erosion and nutrients, succession and biodiversity. Although erosion and water runoff will deplete the soil of nutrients, once the defoliant and herbicide treatment cease, succession will occur. In this setting, succession will more than likely return the area to its original state. The correct answer, therefore, is (B).

49. This question tests knowledge of terrestrial and aquatic biomes and their characteristics. An estuary is an area where a freshwater stream or river merges with an ocean, causing variable salinity in the area. Major producers, including grasses, algae, and phytoplankton, support a wide variety of invertebrates and fish species. The correct answer, therefore, is (C).

50. This question requires you to understand interspecies relationships and predator–prey relationships within a community. In this scenario, the caribou population will weaken due to lack of food (caribou are herbivores), making the caribou easier prey for the wolves. With the increase in food, more wolves will survive and they will produce more offspring. The correct answer, therefore, is (A).

51. This question requires an understanding of the importance of the ozone layer and how its integrity has been influenced by humankind. Liberation of chlorine atoms from CFCs has been a major factor in formation of the "ozone hole" above Antarctica and thinning of the layer around the globe. Once there, chlorine atoms can remain in the atmosphere for decades, catalyzing the destruction of ozone molecules, thus causing an increase in the penetration of ultraviolet light through the atmosphere. The correct answer, therefore, is (B).

52. This question requires knowledge of taxonomic classification and animal characteristics. Human beings, reptiles, birds, and fish are all members of the phylum Chordata, but belong to unique classes, orders, and families. The correct answer, therefore, is (D).

53. This question requires knowledge of taxonomic classification and characteristics of the major forms of life. The characteristics described are those of green algae, which are protists. Although many of the features are also common to members of kingdom Plantae, plants all possess some level of tissue specialization and features that allow their adaptation to a terrestrial environment. The correct answer, therefore, is (C).

54. This question requires knowledge of plant nutrition. Plants gain many of their nutrients from the soil, but most carbon is obtained in the form of carbon dioxide, which enters the leaf stomata from the atmosphere. The correct answer, therefore, is (A).

55. This question requires an understanding of factors that regulate transpiration in plants. Transpiration is the evaporation of water through stomata in plant leaves, which creates a negative pressure and causes water to be absorbed into the plant through the roots. In this setup, an increase in transpiration rate will be indicated by a decrease in water level in the pipette. Of the choices, only increasing the light intensity will increase the transpiration rate. Additional light will allow photosynthesis to occur more rapidly, causing the stomata to open more fully and may possibly increase the temperature on the leaf surface. The correct answer, therefore, is (A).

56. This question tests knowledge of growth control and hormones in plants. Ripening in fruits and senescence (aging) are caused by the production and release of ethylene gas by the fruits. The reason that fruits ripen more quickly in a shipping container or a storage room is not because of the darkness, but because the container or the room prevents the escape of ethylene, concentrating it and speeding up the ripening process of the fruit. The correct answer, therefore, is (A).

57. This question requires knowledge of plant anatomy and transport mechanisms. Phloem transports the products of photosynthesis (sugars) to growing parts and storage areas of the plant. By removing the sap from the phloem, aphids reduce the nutrients available to carry out vital life processes. The correct answer, therefore, is (B).

58. This question requires an understanding of plant growth and development. Meristematic cells are mitotically active cells that produce new cells and tissues. Primary growth of the plant occurs from meristematic activity at the tips of roots and buds on the shoot. Secondary growth occurs in the vascular and cork cambiums located interior to the wood and bark, respectively. The correct answer, therefore, is (B).

59. This question requires an understanding of electrical signaling in neurons and the ability to predict the outcome of an experiment. When a neuron is given a threshold stimulus, an action potential will be generated. The initial depolarization of the membrane is caused by a rapid influx of sodium into the cell, making the intracellular charge positive. If the sodium channels in the neuronal membrane are blocked, sodium cannot enter the cell and the action potential cannot be generated. The correct answer, therefore, is (A).

60. This question requires an understanding of animal behavior. Fixed action patterns are a sequence of behaviors that are triggered by an external sensory stimulus and remain unchanged. Male sticklebacks will act aggressively towards anything that bears a red marking on its underside. The correct answer, therefore, is (A).

61. This question requires an understanding of thermoregulation in warm-blooded animals. Sweat gland activation will release sweat onto the surface of the skin and allow for evaporative cooling. All the other responses will lead to an increase in metabolic heat production and therefore raise the body temperature. The correct answer, therefore, is (C).

62. This question requires an understanding of the causes of a common health problem, high blood pressure. Blockage of the arteries, high cholesterol, and high salt intake (by causing an increase in blood volume) are all causes of hypertension. Anemia, or low blood cell and/or hemoglobin count, can result in hypotension (low blood pressure). The correct answer, therefore, is (D).

63. This question requires an understanding of the immune system. Antibodies are immunoglobulin proteins that are secreted in response to a foreign invader (antigens). Antibodies bind the invaders so that the host's immune system can recognize and destroy them. The correct answer, therefore, is (A).

64. This question requires an understanding of animal development and the fate of the germ layers in organogenesis. The endoderm layer becomes the epithelial lining of the digestive tract, respiratory system, liver, pancreas, thyroid gland, urinary bladder, reproductive system, and so on. The correct answer, therefore, is (C).

65. This question requires an understanding of human endocrinology and bone remodeling. Research has suggested that a low level of estrogen is one of the causes of osteoporosis. Statistics show that a high percentage of postmenopausal women (blood estrogen levels fall during and after menopause) develop this disorder and that estrogen therapy helps to reverse the problem. The correct answer, therefore, is (B).

66. This question requires an understanding of human endocrinology and hormone structure. Most hormones are chemical derivatives of either proteins, amino acids, or fats. Steroid hormones, such as estrogen, progesterone, cortisol, and testosterone are cholesterol derivatives. The correct answer, therefore, is (B).

67. This question requires an understanding of human endocrinology and glucose metabolism. Insulin is released in response to high blood glucose levels and causes cells to take up glucose for use in cellular respiration or for storage. Another pancreatic hormone, glucagon, is released in response to low blood glucose levels and is antagonistic to insulin. The correct answer, therefore, is (C).

68. This question tests your knowledge about current issues in biotechnology and the abilities and limitations of various techniques. Gene therapy is currently in an experimental phase for treatment of single-gene disorders, such as cystic fibrosis and muscular dystrophy. In gene therapy, a "normal" gene is placed into a specific delivery vector and introduced into defective somatic cells. The vector allows this

gene to be incorporated into the somatic cell genome and to be expressed as any other gene would be, returning normal function to the cells. The correct answer, therefore, is (A).

69. This question tests your knowledge about current issues in biotechnology and the abilities and limitations of various techniques. Techniques in cloning have been tested in different plants and animals. Making a genetic duplicate would involve removal of genetic material from an ovum and insertion of the genetic material from a somatic cell from the organism that is to be cloned. The correct answer, therefore, is (B).

70. This question requires the identification of the characteristics of the major plant divisions and an understanding of alternation of generations. Bryophyta (the mosses) is the only major division that has a dominant gametophyte life stage; most have a dominant sporophyte life stage. The correct answer, therefore, is (B).

71. This question requires the identification of characteristics in the major plant divisions. Anthophyta (the flowering plants) is the only major division that uses these adaptations for successful reproduction. The correct answer, therefore, is (A).

72. This question requires you to distinguish between the phases of mitosis and meiosis. Anaphase I is a stage of meiosis and is the event during which sister chromatids remain attached and move as a single unit toward one pole of the cell. The homologous pair of sister chromatids move as a single unit toward the opposite pole. The correct answer, therefore, is (D).

73. This question requires you to distinguish between the phases and resulting genetic makeup of cells in mitosis and meiosis. Mitosis results in the production of genetically identical cells, whereas meiosis results in genetically unique haploid daughter cells. The first diagram depicts a cell during the mitotic event of metaphase. The correct answer, therefore, is (A).

74. This question requires an understanding of the polar nature of water and the attraction between positively and negatively charged regions of molecules. Oxygen is more electronegative than hydrogen. In water, oxygen has hydrogen's electrons in its outermost shell more of the time, giving oxygen a partial negative charge. The negative charge on oxygen will be attracted to the positive charge on nitrogen in the phospholipid. The correct answer, therefore, is (A).

75. This question tests knowledge of common macromolecular structures and hydrophobicity. The hydrocarbon tails on the phospholipid, such as that in a biological membrane, will not interact with water. The correct answer, therefore, is (D).

Chapter 11
Practice Questions for the
Chemistry: Content Knowledge Tests

►   ►   ►   ►   ►   ►   ►   ►   ►   ►   ►   ►

Practice Questions

Now that you have studied the content topics and have worked through strategies relating to multiple-choice questions, you should take the following practice test. You will probably find it helpful to simulate actual testing conditions, giving yourself about 90 minutes to work on the questions. You can cut out and use the answer sheet provided if you wish.

Keep in mind that the test you take at an actual administration will have different questions.

You should not expect the percentage of questions you answer correctly in these practice questions to be exactly the same as when you take the test at an actual administration, since numerous factors affect a person's performance in any given testing situation.

When you have finished the practice questions, you can score your answers and read the explanations of the best answer choices in chapter 12.

THE PRAXIS SERIES
Professional Assessments for Beginning Teachers®

TEST CODE:

TEST NAME:
Chemistry: Content Knowledge

Practice Questions

Calculators Prohibited

Time—90 Minutes
75 Questions

(Note, at the official administration of test 0241, there will be 50 questions, and you will be allowed 60 minutes to complete the test; for test 0245, there will be 100 questions, and you will be allowed 120 minutes to complete the test.)

THE PRAXIS SERIES

Professional Assessments for Beginning Teachers®

DO NOT USE INK

Use only a pencil with soft black lead (No. 2 or HB) to complete this answer sheet.
Be sure to fill in completely the oval that corresponds to the proper letter or number.
Completely erase any errors or stray marks.

1. NAME

Enter your last name and first initial.
Omit spaces, hyphens, apostrophes, etc.

Last Name (first 6 letters)   F I

(grid of ovals A–Z for 6 letters plus first initial)

2.

YOUR NAME: (Print)

Last Name (Family or Surname) ____ First Name (Given) ____ M. I. ____

MAILING ADDRESS: (Print)

P.O. Box or Street Address ____ Apt. # (If any) ____

City ____ State or Province ____

Country ____ Zip or Postal Code ____

TELEPHONE NUMBER: ( ) ____ Home   ( ) ____ Business

SIGNATURE: ____   **TEST DATE:** ____

3. DATE OF BIRTH

Month	Day
Jan.	
Feb.	
Mar.	
April	
May	
June	
July	
Aug.	
Sept.	
Oct.	
Nov.	
Dec.	

(Day ovals 0–9)

4. SOCIAL SECURITY NUMBER

(grid of ovals 0–9)

5. CANDIDATE ID NUMBER

(grid of ovals 0–9)

6. TEST CENTER / REPORTING LOCATION

Center Number ____ Room Number ____

Center Name ____

City ____ State or Province ____

Country ____

7. TEST CODE / FORM CODE

0
1

(grid of ovals 0–9)

8. TEST BOOK SERIAL NUMBER

9. TEST FORM

10. TEST NAME

51055 • 08920 • TF71M500   Q2573-06
MH01159

I.N. 202974

1   2   3   4

CERTIFICATION STATEMENT: (Please write the following statement below. DO NOT PRINT.)
"I hereby agree to the conditions set forth in the *Registration Bulletin* and certify that I am the person whose name and address appear on this answer sheet."

_____

_____

_____

SIGNATURE: _____   DATE: _____/_____/_____
                                                                                           Month   Day   Year

BE SURE EACH MARK IS DARK AND COMPLETELY FILLS THE INTENDED SPACE AS ILLUSTRATED HERE: ● .

#					#					#					#				
1	Ⓐ	Ⓑ	Ⓒ	Ⓓ	41	Ⓐ	Ⓑ	Ⓒ	Ⓓ	81	Ⓐ	Ⓑ	Ⓒ	Ⓓ	121	Ⓐ	Ⓑ	Ⓒ	Ⓓ
2	Ⓐ	Ⓑ	Ⓒ	Ⓓ	42	Ⓐ	Ⓑ	Ⓒ	Ⓓ	82	Ⓐ	Ⓑ	Ⓒ	Ⓓ	122	Ⓐ	Ⓑ	Ⓒ	Ⓓ
3	Ⓐ	Ⓑ	Ⓒ	Ⓓ	43	Ⓐ	Ⓑ	Ⓒ	Ⓓ	83	Ⓐ	Ⓑ	Ⓒ	Ⓓ	123	Ⓐ	Ⓑ	Ⓒ	Ⓓ
4	Ⓐ	Ⓑ	Ⓒ	Ⓓ	44	Ⓐ	Ⓑ	Ⓒ	Ⓓ	84	Ⓐ	Ⓑ	Ⓒ	Ⓓ	124	Ⓐ	Ⓑ	Ⓒ	Ⓓ
5	Ⓐ	Ⓑ	Ⓒ	Ⓓ	45	Ⓐ	Ⓑ	Ⓒ	Ⓓ	85	Ⓐ	Ⓑ	Ⓒ	Ⓓ	125	Ⓐ	Ⓑ	Ⓒ	Ⓓ
6	Ⓐ	Ⓑ	Ⓒ	Ⓓ	46	Ⓐ	Ⓑ	Ⓒ	Ⓓ	86	Ⓐ	Ⓑ	Ⓒ	Ⓓ	126	Ⓐ	Ⓑ	Ⓒ	Ⓓ
7	Ⓐ	Ⓑ	Ⓒ	Ⓓ	47	Ⓐ	Ⓑ	Ⓒ	Ⓓ	87	Ⓐ	Ⓑ	Ⓒ	Ⓓ	127	Ⓐ	Ⓑ	Ⓒ	Ⓓ
8	Ⓐ	Ⓑ	Ⓒ	Ⓓ	48	Ⓐ	Ⓑ	Ⓒ	Ⓓ	88	Ⓐ	Ⓑ	Ⓒ	Ⓓ	128	Ⓐ	Ⓑ	Ⓒ	Ⓓ
9	Ⓐ	Ⓑ	Ⓒ	Ⓓ	49	Ⓐ	Ⓑ	Ⓒ	Ⓓ	89	Ⓐ	Ⓑ	Ⓒ	Ⓓ	129	Ⓐ	Ⓑ	Ⓒ	Ⓓ
10	Ⓐ	Ⓑ	Ⓒ	Ⓓ	50	Ⓐ	Ⓑ	Ⓒ	Ⓓ	90	Ⓐ	Ⓑ	Ⓒ	Ⓓ	130	Ⓐ	Ⓑ	Ⓒ	Ⓓ
11	Ⓐ	Ⓑ	Ⓒ	Ⓓ	51	Ⓐ	Ⓑ	Ⓒ	Ⓓ	91	Ⓐ	Ⓑ	Ⓒ	Ⓓ	131	Ⓐ	Ⓑ	Ⓒ	Ⓓ
12	Ⓐ	Ⓑ	Ⓒ	Ⓓ	52	Ⓐ	Ⓑ	Ⓒ	Ⓓ	92	Ⓐ	Ⓑ	Ⓒ	Ⓓ	132	Ⓐ	Ⓑ	Ⓒ	Ⓓ
13	Ⓐ	Ⓑ	Ⓒ	Ⓓ	53	Ⓐ	Ⓑ	Ⓒ	Ⓓ	93	Ⓐ	Ⓑ	Ⓒ	Ⓓ	133	Ⓐ	Ⓑ	Ⓒ	Ⓓ
14	Ⓐ	Ⓑ	Ⓒ	Ⓓ	54	Ⓐ	Ⓑ	Ⓒ	Ⓓ	94	Ⓐ	Ⓑ	Ⓒ	Ⓓ	134	Ⓐ	Ⓑ	Ⓒ	Ⓓ
15	Ⓐ	Ⓑ	Ⓒ	Ⓓ	55	Ⓐ	Ⓑ	Ⓒ	Ⓓ	95	Ⓐ	Ⓑ	Ⓒ	Ⓓ	135	Ⓐ	Ⓑ	Ⓒ	Ⓓ
16	Ⓐ	Ⓑ	Ⓒ	Ⓓ	56	Ⓐ	Ⓑ	Ⓒ	Ⓓ	96	Ⓐ	Ⓑ	Ⓒ	Ⓓ	136	Ⓐ	Ⓑ	Ⓒ	Ⓓ
17	Ⓐ	Ⓑ	Ⓒ	Ⓓ	57	Ⓐ	Ⓑ	Ⓒ	Ⓓ	97	Ⓐ	Ⓑ	Ⓒ	Ⓓ	137	Ⓐ	Ⓑ	Ⓒ	Ⓓ
18	Ⓐ	Ⓑ	Ⓒ	Ⓓ	58	Ⓐ	Ⓑ	Ⓒ	Ⓓ	98	Ⓐ	Ⓑ	Ⓒ	Ⓓ	138	Ⓐ	Ⓑ	Ⓒ	Ⓓ
19	Ⓐ	Ⓑ	Ⓒ	Ⓓ	59	Ⓐ	Ⓑ	Ⓒ	Ⓓ	99	Ⓐ	Ⓑ	Ⓒ	Ⓓ	139	Ⓐ	Ⓑ	Ⓒ	Ⓓ
20	Ⓐ	Ⓑ	Ⓒ	Ⓓ	60	Ⓐ	Ⓑ	Ⓒ	Ⓓ	100	Ⓐ	Ⓑ	Ⓒ	Ⓓ	140	Ⓐ	Ⓑ	Ⓒ	Ⓓ
21	Ⓐ	Ⓑ	Ⓒ	Ⓓ	61	Ⓐ	Ⓑ	Ⓒ	Ⓓ	101	Ⓐ	Ⓑ	Ⓒ	Ⓓ	141	Ⓐ	Ⓑ	Ⓒ	Ⓓ
22	Ⓐ	Ⓑ	Ⓒ	Ⓓ	62	Ⓐ	Ⓑ	Ⓒ	Ⓓ	102	Ⓐ	Ⓑ	Ⓒ	Ⓓ	142	Ⓐ	Ⓑ	Ⓒ	Ⓓ
23	Ⓐ	Ⓑ	Ⓒ	Ⓓ	63	Ⓐ	Ⓑ	Ⓒ	Ⓓ	103	Ⓐ	Ⓑ	Ⓒ	Ⓓ	143	Ⓐ	Ⓑ	Ⓒ	Ⓓ
24	Ⓐ	Ⓑ	Ⓒ	Ⓓ	64	Ⓐ	Ⓑ	Ⓒ	Ⓓ	104	Ⓐ	Ⓑ	Ⓒ	Ⓓ	144	Ⓐ	Ⓑ	Ⓒ	Ⓓ
25	Ⓐ	Ⓑ	Ⓒ	Ⓓ	65	Ⓐ	Ⓑ	Ⓒ	Ⓓ	105	Ⓐ	Ⓑ	Ⓒ	Ⓓ	145	Ⓐ	Ⓑ	Ⓒ	Ⓓ
26	Ⓐ	Ⓑ	Ⓒ	Ⓓ	66	Ⓐ	Ⓑ	Ⓒ	Ⓓ	106	Ⓐ	Ⓑ	Ⓒ	Ⓓ	146	Ⓐ	Ⓑ	Ⓒ	Ⓓ
27	Ⓐ	Ⓑ	Ⓒ	Ⓓ	67	Ⓐ	Ⓑ	Ⓒ	Ⓓ	107	Ⓐ	Ⓑ	Ⓒ	Ⓓ	147	Ⓐ	Ⓑ	Ⓒ	Ⓓ
28	Ⓐ	Ⓑ	Ⓒ	Ⓓ	68	Ⓐ	Ⓑ	Ⓒ	Ⓓ	108	Ⓐ	Ⓑ	Ⓒ	Ⓓ	148	Ⓐ	Ⓑ	Ⓒ	Ⓓ
29	Ⓐ	Ⓑ	Ⓒ	Ⓓ	69	Ⓐ	Ⓑ	Ⓒ	Ⓓ	109	Ⓐ	Ⓑ	Ⓒ	Ⓓ	149	Ⓐ	Ⓑ	Ⓒ	Ⓓ
30	Ⓐ	Ⓑ	Ⓒ	Ⓓ	70	Ⓐ	Ⓑ	Ⓒ	Ⓓ	110	Ⓐ	Ⓑ	Ⓒ	Ⓓ	150	Ⓐ	Ⓑ	Ⓒ	Ⓓ
31	Ⓐ	Ⓑ	Ⓒ	Ⓓ	71	Ⓐ	Ⓑ	Ⓒ	Ⓓ	111	Ⓐ	Ⓑ	Ⓒ	Ⓓ	151	Ⓐ	Ⓑ	Ⓒ	Ⓓ
32	Ⓐ	Ⓑ	Ⓒ	Ⓓ	72	Ⓐ	Ⓑ	Ⓒ	Ⓓ	112	Ⓐ	Ⓑ	Ⓒ	Ⓓ	152	Ⓐ	Ⓑ	Ⓒ	Ⓓ
33	Ⓐ	Ⓑ	Ⓒ	Ⓓ	73	Ⓐ	Ⓑ	Ⓒ	Ⓓ	113	Ⓐ	Ⓑ	Ⓒ	Ⓓ	153	Ⓐ	Ⓑ	Ⓒ	Ⓓ
34	Ⓐ	Ⓑ	Ⓒ	Ⓓ	74	Ⓐ	Ⓑ	Ⓒ	Ⓓ	114	Ⓐ	Ⓑ	Ⓒ	Ⓓ	154	Ⓐ	Ⓑ	Ⓒ	Ⓓ
35	Ⓐ	Ⓑ	Ⓒ	Ⓓ	75	Ⓐ	Ⓑ	Ⓒ	Ⓓ	115	Ⓐ	Ⓑ	Ⓒ	Ⓓ	155	Ⓐ	Ⓑ	Ⓒ	Ⓓ
36	Ⓐ	Ⓑ	Ⓒ	Ⓓ	76	Ⓐ	Ⓑ	Ⓒ	Ⓓ	116	Ⓐ	Ⓑ	Ⓒ	Ⓓ	156	Ⓐ	Ⓑ	Ⓒ	Ⓓ
37	Ⓐ	Ⓑ	Ⓒ	Ⓓ	77	Ⓐ	Ⓑ	Ⓒ	Ⓓ	117	Ⓐ	Ⓑ	Ⓒ	Ⓓ	157	Ⓐ	Ⓑ	Ⓒ	Ⓓ
38	Ⓐ	Ⓑ	Ⓒ	Ⓓ	78	Ⓐ	Ⓑ	Ⓒ	Ⓓ	118	Ⓐ	Ⓑ	Ⓒ	Ⓓ	158	Ⓐ	Ⓑ	Ⓒ	Ⓓ
39	Ⓐ	Ⓑ	Ⓒ	Ⓓ	79	Ⓐ	Ⓑ	Ⓒ	Ⓓ	119	Ⓐ	Ⓑ	Ⓒ	Ⓓ	159	Ⓐ	Ⓑ	Ⓒ	Ⓓ
40	Ⓐ	Ⓑ	Ⓒ	Ⓓ	80	Ⓐ	Ⓑ	Ⓒ	Ⓓ	120	Ⓐ	Ⓑ	Ⓒ	Ⓓ	160	Ⓐ	Ⓑ	Ⓒ	Ⓓ

PERIODIC TABLE OF THE ELEMENTS

DO NOT DETACH FROM BOOK.

1	2	3	4	5	6	7	8	9	10	11	12	13	14	15	16	17	18
1 **H** 1.0079																	2 **He** 4.0026
3 **Li** 6.941	4 **Be** 9.012											5 **B** 10.811	6 **C** 12.011	7 **N** 14.007	8 **O** 16.00	9 **F** 19.00	10 **Ne** 20.179
11 **Na** 22.99	12 **Mg** 24.30											13 **Al** 26.98	14 **Si** 28.09	15 **P** 30.974	16 **S** 32.06	17 **Cl** 35.453	18 **Ar** 39.948
19 **K** 39.10	20 **Ca** 40.08	21 **Sc** 44.96	22 **Ti** 47.90	23 **V** 50.94	24 **Cr** 52.00	25 **Mn** 54.938	26 **Fe** 55.85	27 **Co** 58.93	28 **Ni** 58.69	29 **Cu** 63.55	30 **Zn** 65.39	31 **Ga** 69.72	32 **Ge** 72.59	33 **As** 74.92	34 **Se** 78.96	35 **Br** 79.90	36 **Kr** 83.80
37 **Rb** 85.47	38 **Sr** 87.62	39 **Y** 88.91	40 **Zr** 91.22	41 **Nb** 92.91	42 **Mo** 95.94	43 **Tc** (98)	44 **Ru** 101.1	45 **Rh** 102.91	46 **Pd** 106.42	47 **Ag** 107.87	48 **Cd** 112.41	49 **In** 114.82	50 **Sn** 118.71	51 **Sb** 121.75	52 **Te** 127.60	53 **I** 126.91	54 **Xe** 131.29
55 **Cs** 132.91	56 **Ba** 137.33	57 *****La** 138.91	72 **Hf** 178.49	73 **Ta** 180.95	74 **W** 183.85	75 **Re** 186.21	76 **Os** 190.2	77 **Ir** 192.2	78 **Pt** 195.08	79 **Au** 196.97	80 **Hg** 200.59	81 **Tl** 204.38	82 **Pb** 207.2	83 **Bi** 208.98	84 **Po** (209)	85 **At** (210)	86 **Rn** (222)
87 **Fr** (223)	88 **Ra** 226.02	89 †**Ac** 227.03	104 **Rf** (261)	105 **Db** (262)	106 **Sg** (263)	107 **Bh** (262)	108 **Hs** (265)	109 **Mt** (266)	110 § (269)	111 § (272)	112 § (277)						

§Not yet named

*Lanthanide Series	58 **Ce** 140.12	59 **Pr** 140.91	60 **Nd** 144.24	61 **Pm** (145)	62 **Sm** 150.4	63 **Eu** 151.97	64 **Gd** 157.25	65 **Tb** 158.93	66 **Dy** 162.50	67 **Ho** 164.93	68 **Er** 167.26	69 **Tm** 168.93	70 **Yb** 173.04	71 **Lu** 174.97
†Actinide Series	90 **Th** 232.04	91 **Pa** 231.04	92 **U** 238.03	93 **Np** 237.05	94 **Pu** (244)	95 **Am** (243)	96 **Cm** (247)	97 **Bk** (247)	98 **Cf** (251)	99 **Es** (252)	100 **Fm** (257)	101 **Md** (258)	102 **No** (259)	103 **Lr** (260)

TABLE OF INFORMATION

Electron rest mass	m_e =	9.11×10^{-31} kilogram
Proton rest mass	m_p =	1.672×10^{-27} kilogram
Neutron rest mass	m_n =	1.675×10^{-27} kilogram
Magnitude of the electron charge	e =	1.60×10^{-19} coulomb
Bohr radius	a_0 =	5.29×10^{-11} meter
Avogadro's number	N_A =	6.02×10^{23} per mole
Universal gas constant	R =	8.314 joules/(mole $\cdot$ K)
	=	0.0821 L $\cdot$ atm/(mole $\cdot$ K)
Boltzmann constant	k =	1.38×10^{-23} joule/K
Planck constant	h =	6.63×10^{-34} joule $\cdot$ second
	=	4.14×10^{-15} eV $\cdot$ second
Speed of light	c =	3.00×10^8 meters/second
Vacuum permittivity	ϵ_0 =	8.85×10^{-12} coulomb^2/(newton $\cdot$ meter^2)
Vacuum permeability	μ_0 =	4×10^{-7} newton/ampere^2
Coulomb constant	$1/4\,\epsilon_0$ =	8.99×10^9 newtons $\cdot$ meter^2/coulomb^2
Universal gravitational constant	G =	6.67×10^{-11} newton $\cdot$ meter^2/kilogram^2
Acceleration due to gravity	g =	9.80 meters/second^2
1 atmosphere pressure	1 atm =	1.0×10^5 newtons/meter^2
	=	1.0×10^5 pascals (Pa)
Faraday constant	$\mathscr{F}$ =	9.65×10^4 coulombs/mole
1 atomic mass unit	1 amu =	1.66×10^{-27} kilogram
1 electron volt	1 eV =	1.602×10^{-19} joule

For H_2O:

heat of fusion	3.33×10^2 joules/gram
heat of vaporization	2.26×10^3 joules/gram
mean specific heat (liquid)	4.19 joules/(gram $\cdot$ K)
Volume of 1 mole of ideal gas at 0°C, 1 atmosphere	22.4 liters

CHEMISTRY: CONTENT KNOWLEDGE

1. Which of the following best accounts for the compressibility of gaseous substances?

   (A) High average kinetic energy of the molecules
   (B) Great average distance between the molecules relative to their size
   (C) Weak intermolecular attractions
   (D) The relatively low molecular mass of most gases

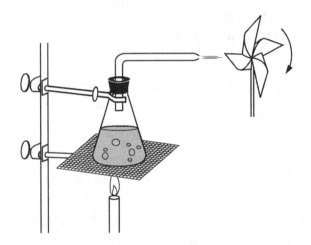

2. As shown above, when water is boiled in a flask over a Bunsen burner, steam is generated and directed through tubing, causing a pinwheel to turn. Of the following types of energy, which is (are) involved in these processes?

   I. Chemical
   II. Mechanical
   III. Electrical

   (A) II only
   (B) III only
   (C) I and II
   (D) II and III

Sample	Volume	Mass
I	2 mL	1 g
II	2 mL	2 g
III	4 mL	6 g
IV	4 mL	4 g

3. Which of the samples above has the greatest density?

   (A) I
   (B) II
   (C) III
   (D) IV

4. Which of the following elements is a liquid at room temperature and pressure?

   (A) Cs
   (B) Sn
   (C) Br
   (D) B

5. Which of the following correctly identifies the change given as either a physical change or a chemical change?

   (A) Formation of rust on a wrought-iron railing...physical change only
   (B) Boiling water in a teakettle...physical change only
   (C) A match burning...physical change only
   (D) Homogenizing milk at a dairy farm...chemical change only

6. What is the kinetic energy of a 10 kg ball moving at a velocity of 5 m/s?

   (A) 25 J
   (B) 50 J
   (C) 125 J
   (D) 250 J

7. A ground-state atom of which of the following elements has an electron with quantum numbers $n = 4$, $l = 1$, and $m_l = 1$?

   (A) Be
   (B) Cl
   (C) K
   (D) Se

8. Which of the following is the electron configuration of an alkaline earth metal?

   (A) $[Ar] 4s^2 3d^{10} 4p^2$
   (B) $[Ar] 4s^1$
   (C) $[Ne] 3s^2$
   (D) $[He] 2s^2 2p^1$

9. When $^{27}_{13}Al$ is bombarded with $^{1}_{0}n$, one of the products is $^{4}_{2}He$. Which of the following is the other product?

   (A) $^{24}_{10}Ne$

   (B) $^{24}_{11}Na$

   (C) $^{28}_{12}Mg$

   (D) $^{28}_{13}Mg$

10. Supporting evidence for the particle-like nature of light was provided by which of the following?

    (A) The photoelectric effect
    (B) The line spectrum of hydrogen
    (C) The emission of alpha particles from radioactive atoms
    (D) The diffraction of electrons

11. Which of the following pairs are isotopes?

    (A) Butane, isobutane
    (B) Carbon-13, carbon-14
    (C) Diamond, graphite
    (D) Ozone, oxygen

Isotope	Mass (amu)	Abundance (%)
^{30}X	30	15
^{32}X	32	70
^{34}X	34	10
^{35}X	35	5

12. Element X is composed of four common isotopes. The masses and respective relative abundances of its isotopes are as shown in the table above. The approximate atomic mass of element X in amu is closest to

    (A) 30
    (B) 32
    (C) 34
    (D) 35

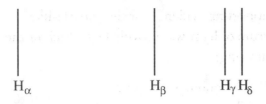

$H_\alpha \qquad H_\beta \qquad H_\gamma\, H_\delta$

H_α	$n = 3 \rightarrow n = 2$
H_β	$n = 4 \rightarrow n = 2$
H_γ	$n = 5 \rightarrow n = 2$
H_δ	$n = 6 \rightarrow n = 2$

13. The Balmer series of lines in the emission spectrum of atomic hydrogen includes the transitions shown above, where n is the principal quantum number. The reason that the spacing between the spectral lines becomes progressively closer as n increases is that

    (A) hydrogen has only one electron
    (B) hydrogen is readily ionized
    (C) the higher electronic energy levels for ground-state hydrogen are unoccupied
    (D) the electronic energy levels for hydrogen are progressively closer from $n = 1$ to $n = \infty$

14. Of the following, which has the smallest atomic radius?

    (A) Sb
    (B) I
    (C) P
    (D) Cl

15. Which of the following ranks the elements Na, Mg, K, Ba in order from least reactive to most reactive in distilled water?

    (A) Mg < Ba < Na < K
    (B) Ba < Mg < K < Na
    (C) Mg < Na < Ba < K
    (D) Mg < K < Ba < Na

Element	E_1	E_2	E_3
X_1	1,680	3,370	6,040
X_2	520	7,300	11,800
X_3	899	1,760	14,900
X_4	2,080	3,950	6,120

16. The table above shows the first three ionization energies for four elements from the same period on the periodic table as measured in kilojoules per mole. X_3 could be which of the following?

    (A) Li
    (B) Be
    (C) F
    (D) Ne

17. Which of the following properties increases as you proceed from left to right across the same period of the periodic table?

    I. Atomic Number
    II. Electronegativity
    III. Atomic radius

    (A) III only
    (B) I and II only
    (C) I and III only
    (D) I, II, and III

18. A metal M forms a compound with oxygen, having the chemical formula MO. What is the most likely chemical formula between M and phosphorus?

    (A) MP
    (B) M_2P
    (C) M_2P_3
    (D) M_3P_2

Questions 19 and 20 are based on the following energy diagram.

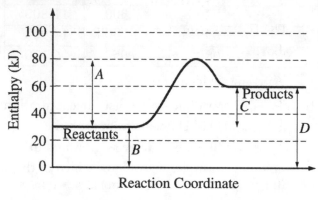

Reaction Coordinate

19. On the basis of the diagram above, what is the heat of reaction, ΔH_{rxn}?

(A) +50 kJ
(B) +30 kJ
(C) -30 kJ
(D) -50 kJ

20. Adding a catalyst would affect the diagram by shortening the length of arrow

(A) A
(B) B
(C) C
(D) D

$$2\ SO_2(g) + O_2(g) \rightarrow 2\ SO_3(g) \quad \Delta H^\circ = -196\ \text{kJ}$$
$$2\ S(s) + 3\ O_2(g) \rightarrow 2\ SO_3(g) \quad \Delta H^\circ = -790\ \text{kJ}$$

21. Given the data above, what is ΔH° for the reaction $S + O_2 \rightarrow SO_2$?

(A) +968 kJ
(B) +297 kJ
(C) -297 kJ
(D) -986 kJ

Sample	Volume	Temperature	Pressure
I	8 L	300 K	200 torr
II	8 L	900 K	300 torr
III	4 L	300 K	200 torr
IV	4 L	900 K	600 torr

22. On the basis of the ideal gas law, which of the samples of Ne gas described above has the largest number of molecules?

(A) I
(B) II
(C) III
(D) IV

WARMING CURVE

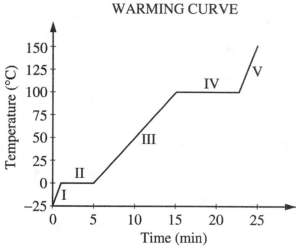

23. The warming curve above represents the data collected during an experiment using water. The initial temperature of the water was $-25°C$. Energy was added at a constant rate of 500 joules per minute. The temperature was recorded every 0.5 minute. The mass of water was constant throughout the experiment. The final temperature reading was made at 150°C. How much heat must be added to increase the temperature of water from 0°C to 100°C?

(A)   100 J
(B)   2,500 J
(C)   5,000 J
(D) 10,000 J

24. Of the reactions below, for which does the $\Delta H°_{rxn}$ represent the standard heat of combustion of ethane, $C_2H_6(g)$?

(A) $C_2H_6(g) \rightarrow 2\,C(s) + 2\,H_2(g)$

(B) $C_2H_6(g) + \frac{5}{2}\,O_2(g) \rightarrow 2\,CO(g) + 3\,H_2O(g)$

(C) $C_2H_6(g) + \frac{7}{2}\,O_2(g) \rightarrow 2\,CO_2(g) + 3\,H_2O(g)$

(D) $C_2H_6(g) + \frac{7}{2}\,O_2(g) \rightarrow 2\,CO_2(g) + 3\,H_2O(l)$

25. How much heat is absorbed by 10.0 g of water as the temperature is increased from 30°C to 50.0°C?

(A) 66,600 J

(B) 3,330 J

(C) 838 J

(D) 200 J

26. The formula for sulfurous acid is

(A) SO_2

(B) H_2S

(C) H_2SO_4

(D) H_2SO_3

27. The formula for tin(II) phosphate (stannous phosphate) is

(A) $SnPO_4$

(B) Sn_3PO_4

(C) $Sn_3(PO_4)_2$

(D) $Sn_3(PO_4)_4$

$$\overset{\displaystyle CH_3}{\underset{\displaystyle CH_3CHCH_2CH_2CH_2OH}{|}}$$

28. The IUPAC name for the compound shown above is

(A) 4–methylpentanol

(B) 2–methylpentanol

(C) 4,4–dimethylbutanol

(D) 1,1–dimethylbutanol

29. Which of the following chemical substances contains only ionic bonds?

(A) K_2O

(B) CO_2

(C) O_2

(D) $NaNO_3$

30. The bonding in the ethene molecule, C_2H_4, involves which of the following hybrid orbital types?

(A) sp

(B) sp^2

(C) sp^3

(D) dsp^3

31. A compound contains 53.3% C, 31.1% N, and 15.6% H. Which of the following could be the empirical formula of the compound?

(A) C_2H_3N

(B) C_2H_7N

(C) $C_4H_{16}N_2$

(D) $C_5N_3H_2$

32. With how many atoms does each nitrogen atom form a covalent bond in $Ca(NO_3)_2 \cdot 6\,H_2O$?

   (A) 2
   (B) 3
   (C) 4
   (D) 6

33. The number of moles of oxygen atoms in 0.50 mole of $Ba(NO_3)_2 \cdot 2\,H_2O$ is

   (A) 2
   (B) 3
   (C) 3.5
   (D) 4

34. Which of the following is considered the primary intermolecular attraction between molecules of butane, C_4H_{10}, in the liquid state?

   (A) Dispersion forces
   (B) Dipole-dipole interactions
   (C) Hydrogen bonding
   (D) Ion-dipole interactions

35. Which of the following is the correct geometry of the ammonia molecule, NH_3?

   (A) Linear
   (B) Trigonal planar
   (C) Trigonal pyramidal
   (D) Tetrahedral

36. What is the approximate sodium ion concentration in a solution that results from the addition of 50.0 mL of 0.10 M NaCl to 100. mL of 0.20 M Na_2SO_4 ?

   (A) 0.15 M
   (B) 0.20 M
   (C) 0.25 M
   (D) 0.30 M

37. A student needs to make 10 liters of 0.05 M glucose, $C_6H_{12}O_6$, to use in a science fair project. How many grams of $C_6H_{12}O_6$ does the student need?

   (A) 0.5 g
   (B) 90 g
   (C) 180 g
   (D) 360 g

38. If for $PbCl_2$ at 298 K, $K_{sp} = 1.6 \times 10^{-5}$, then the solubility of $PbCl_2$ is closest to

   (A) 4.1×10^{-15}
   (B) 4×10^{-6}
   (C) 1.6×10^{-5}
   (D) 1.6×10^{-2}

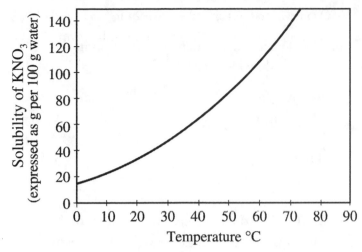

39. A saturated solution of potassium nitrate, KNO_3, dissolved in 25 g of water is cooled from 70°C to 10°C. Needle shaped crystals form as the solution is cooled. Based on the solubility curve above, what mass of potassium nitrate should crystallize from the solution?

    (A)   20 g
    (B)   30 g
    (C)   120 g
    (D)   140 g

40. Which of the following 0.5 M aqueous solutions would have the lowest freezing point?

    (A) $C_6H_{12}O_6$
    (B) $Al(NO_3)_3$
    (C) $AgCl_2$
    (D) KBr

41. A 0.20 M solution of a weak monoprotic acid is 3.0 percent ionized. What is the approximate pH of the solution?

    (A) 2.0 to 3.0
    (B) 4.0 to 5.0
    (C) 9.0 to 10.0
    (D) 11.0 to 12.0

42. The pH of a 0.002 M HCl solution is closest to

    (A) 2.7
    (B) 5.0
    (C) 9.0
    (D) 11.3

43. Which of the following solutions would exhibit a pH that is greater than 7 ?

    (A) 0.5 M HNO_3
    (B) 0.5 M NaCl
    (C) 0.5 M $(NH_4)_2SO_4$
    (D) 0.5 M K_3PO_4

44. Which of the following is the conjugate base of H_2SO_4?

    (A) H_2S
    (B) H_2SO_3
    (C) HSO_4^-
    (D) H^+

$$A(g) + B(g) \rightarrow C(g) + D(g)$$

45. Compound C is formed by a single-step reaction mechanism, as shown above. The rate law of the reaction is

    (A) $k\,[C]$
    (B) $k\,[A][B]$
    (C) $k\,[C][D]$
    (D) $k\,\dfrac{[C][D]}{[A][B]}$

$$\text{rate} = k\,[NO]^2[Br_2]$$

46. In the rate expression given above, the units of the rate constant, k , are

    (A) $mol \cdot L^{-1} \cdot s^{-1}$
    (B) $mol^{-1} \cdot L \cdot s$
    (C) $mol^{-1} \cdot L \cdot s^{-1}$
    (D) $mol^{-2} \cdot L^2 \cdot s^{-1}$

$$...Li_3N(s) + ...H_2O(l) \rightarrow ...Li^+(aq) + ...OH^-(aq) + ...NH_3(g)$$

47. When the equation above is balanced and all coefficients reduced to lowest whole-number terms, the coefficient for $OH^-(aq)$ is

    (A) 2
    (B) 3
    (C) 4
    (D) 6

    $$Cu^{2+}(aq) + 2e^- \rightarrow Cu(s) \qquad E° = 0.34 \text{ V}$$
    $$Co^{3+}(aq) + e^- \rightarrow Co^{2+}(aq) \qquad E° = 1.84 \text{ V}$$

48. Given the half reactions shown above, which of the following is the standard reduction potential, $E°$, for the reaction $Co^{3+}(aq) + Cu(s) \rightarrow Co^{2+}(aq) + Cu^{2+}(aq)$?

    (A) 4.02 V
    (B) 2.18 V
    (C) 1.50 V
    (D) 1.16 V

    $$4\,NH_3(g) + 5\,O_2(g) \rightarrow 4\,NO(g) + 6\,H_2O(l)$$

49. If 34.0 g of NH_3 reacts with 32.0 g of O_2 according to the reaction shown above, what is the maximum mass of H_2O that will form?

    (A) 54.0 g
    (B) 43.2 g
    (C) 21.6 g
    (D) 18.0 g

$$H_2SO_3(aq) + 2\,Mn(s) + 4\,H^+(aq) \rightarrow S(s) + 2\,Mn^{2+}(aq) + 3\,H_2O(l)$$

50. The element that undergoes oxidation in the reaction shown above is

    (A) oxygen
    (B) manganese
    (C) hydrogen
    (D) sulfur

51. When $Mg_3N_2(s)$ reacts with water, $NH_3(g)$ and $Mg(OH)_2(aq)$ are formed. If 2.0 moles of $Mg_3N_2(s)$ reacts with excess water, how many moles of $NH_3(g)$ will form?

    (A) 2.0
    (B) 3.0
    (C) 4.0
    (D) 6.0

    $$H_2(g) + Br_2(g) \rightleftharpoons 2\,HBr(g)$$

52. A 0.34 mol sample of $H_2(g)$ is added to a sealed 1.0 liter container that has 0.22 mole of $Br_2(g)$ in it. The mixture is allowed to come to equilibrium at 700 K, as represented by the equation above. When equilibrium is established and analyzed, it is found that 0.14 mole of $H_2(g)$ is present. How many moles of $HBr(g)$ would be present?

    (A) 0.68
    (B) 0.40
    (C) 0.34
    (D) 0.22

$$2\,SO_2(g) + O_2(g) \rightleftharpoons 2\,SO_3(g) \qquad \Delta H° < 0$$

53. Which of the following will cause an increase in the value of K_c for the reaction represented by the equation above?

    (A) Adding some SO_3 to the reaction vessel
    (B) Adding some SO_2 to the reaction vessel
    (C) Decreasing the size of the reaction vessel
    (D) Decreasing the temperature of the reaction vessel

54. Which of the following is the formula of a ketone?

    (A)
    $$CH_3CH_2\overset{\displaystyle O}{\overset{\displaystyle \|}{C}}CH_3$$

    (B) $CH_3CH_2OCH_2CH_3$

    (C)
    $$CH_3CH_2\overset{\displaystyle O}{\overset{\displaystyle \|}{C}}H$$

    (D)
    $$CH_3CH_2\overset{\displaystyle O}{\overset{\displaystyle \|}{C}}OH$$

55. An amine is an organic compound that has which of the following elements present?

    (A) Chlorine
    (B) Sulfur
    (C) Nitrogen
    (D) Oxygen

56. Proteins are composed of which of the following?

    (A) Carboxylic acids
    (B) Fatty acids
    (C) Nucleic acids
    (D) Amino acids

57. Dalton proposed that all matter is composed of indivisible particles called atoms. This proposal is

    (A) an observation
    (B) a theory
    (C) a law
    (D) a test of a hypothesis

58. Which of the following is a conclusion rather than an observation about the heating of an unknown solid cube?

    (A) The cube melts.
    (B) The temperature of the cube remains constant during melting.
    (C) The cube floats in the liquid that forms during melting.
    (D) The unknown solid is H_2O.

59. The law that involves the nature of the relationship between the pressure of a fixed gas and its relative volume under constant temperature conditions was confirmed by

    (A) Charles
    (B) Lavoisier
    (C) Mendeleev
    (D) Boyle

60. The process illustrated above is used when separating

    (A) a precipitate from an aqueous solution
    (B) dissolved salt from an aqueous solution
    (C) two miscible liquids
    (D) two solids of unequal density

61. Which of the following correctly expresses the number 0.003930 in scientific notation?

    (A) 0.393×10^{-2}
    (B) 3.93×10^{-3}
    (C) 3.930×10^{-3}
    (D) 3.93×10^{-4}

Sample	Initial Temperature	Mass
1	70°C	100 g
2	40°C	200 g

62. The two samples of water described above are mixed in a thermally insulated container. The temperature of the mixture at thermal equilibrium is

    (A) 60°C
    (B) 55°C
    (C) 50°C
    (D) 45°C

63. Which of the following substances is possibly explosive and should not be stored in a high school laboratory?

    (A) Acetone
    (B) Sulfuric acid
    (C) Methanol
    (D) Ethyl ether

64. Of the following, the smallest mass is

    (A) 1 kg
    (B) 1 μg
    (C) 1 mg
    (D) 1 g

65. In preparing diluted sulfuric acid, H_2SO_4, the concentrated acid should be added to the water during the dilution, not the other way around. Which of the following reasons accounts for this procedure?

    (A) The density of water is greater than that of the acid, so it is easier to add the acid to the water.
    (B) The diluting process is quite exothermic, so that the solution may splatter if diluted by adding the water.
    (C) Fewer fumes are given off when the concentrated acid is added to the water than when water is added to the acid.
    (D) Carbon dioxide from the air will dissolve into the acid while it is being poured, which tends to neutralize the acid.

66. A portion of a buret containing a liquid is shown above. The correct volume reading for this buret is

    (A) 20.7 mL
    (B) 20.68 mL
    (C) 21.3 mL
    (D) 21.32 mL

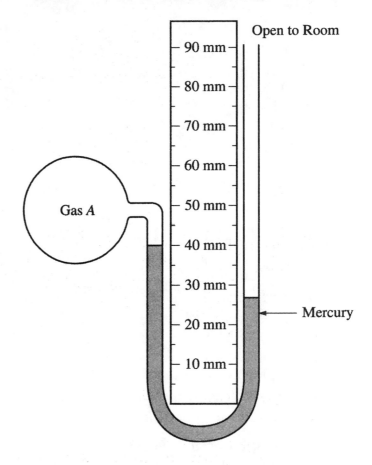

67. In the diagram above, gas *A* is trapped in a sealed container with an open-ended manometer attached. The ambient room pressure that day is 765 mm Hg. What is the pressure of gas *A* in this experiment?

    (A) 13 mm Hg
    (B) 752 mm Hg
    (C) 792 mm Hg
    (D) 805 mm Hg

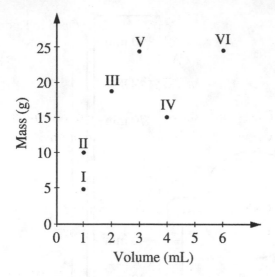

Trials	Mass (g)
1	11.50
2	11.20
3	10.90
4	10.60
5	10.30

68. A student measured the mass and volume of 6 metal objects labeled; I, II, III, IV, V, and VI. The metal objects were composed of homogenous materials. The data were collected and graphed as shown above. Which of the following statements represents a reasonable conclusion based on the data from the graph?

(A) The density of the substances tested cannot be determined.

(B) The density of item VI is greater than the density of the other items.

(C) The objects in this experiment did not all have the same composition.

(D) The objects in this experiment had different shapes.

69. All of the following correctly pair the quantity being measured with the appropriate unit used in the measurement EXCEPT

(A) enthalpy change during the combustion of gasoline . . . joule

(B) voltage of a car battery. . . volt

(C) surface area of a sphere. . . liter^2

(D) quantity of atoms present in a sample of sulfur. . . mol

70. A student measured the mass of an object five times and recorded the data in the table above. Having completed the required measurements, the student is informed that the accepted mass of the object is 10.91 g. Which of the following best describes the nature of the student's data?

(A) The student had good precision but poor accuracy.

(B) The student had good precision and good accuracy.

(C) The student had poor precision and poor accuracy.

(D) The student had poor precision but good accuracy.

71. Students are to prepare a solution of NaOH for use during an experiment. Students are instructed to determine the mass needed and weigh out the sample of NaOH. The teacher warns the students to perform their weight determinations as quickly as possible while still being precise and safe. Which of the following reasons should the teacher use to help motivate the students to work quickly?

(A) NaOH is deliquescent and will gain mass if left open to the room air for prolonged periods of time.
(B) NaOH is a volatile substance and will sublime if left open to the room air for prolonged periods of time.
(C) NaOH will react with oxygen from the air, forming Na_2O and H_2O, resulting in a solution of indeterminate concentration.
(D) NaOH will react with nitrogen from the air, forming $NaNO_2$, which has different chemical properties in solution than required.

72. Of the following common household products, which is most acidic?

(A) Rubbing alcohol
(B) Bottled water
(C) Orange juice
(D) Liquid soap

73. The symbol shown above is used in context with which of the following situations?

(A) Recycling of plastics
(B) Disposal of biomedical waste
(C) Radioactive materials warning
(D) Storage of flammable chemicals

74. Which of the following is true about hydrogen nuclear fusion as a potential energy source?

(A) The process produces polluting by-products.
(B) The fuel is not abundantly available.
(C) The technology for large-scale energy production is currently not available.
(D) The process results in a long-term radioactive-waste storage problem.

75. Which of the following is an outcome of both nuclear- and fossil-fuel electrical generation facilities?

(A) Thermal pollution of local streams
(B) Long term storage of toxic waste by-products
(C) Enlargement of the ozone hole on the South Pole
(D) Increased global warming

Chapter 12

Right Answers and Explanations for the Practice
Questions for the *Chemistry: Content Knowledge* Tests

▶   ▶   ▶   ▶   ▶   ▶   ▶   ▶   ▶   ▶   ▶   ▶   ▶

Right Answers and Explanations for the Practice Questions

Now that you have answered all of the practice questions, you can check your work.
Compare your answers with the correct answers in the table below.

Question Number	Correct Answer	Content Category
1	B	Matter and Energy
2	C	Matter and Energy
3	C	Matter and Energy
4	C	Matter and Energy
5	B	Matter and Energy
6	C	Matter and Energy
7	D	Atomic and Nuclear Structure
8	C	Atomic and Nuclear Structure
9	B	Atomic and Nuclear Structure
10	A	Atomic and Nuclear Structure
11	B	Atomic and Nuclear Structure
12	B	Atomic and Nuclear Structure
13	D	Atomic and Nuclear Structure
14	D	Periodicity and Reactivity
15	A	Periodicity and Reactivity
16	B	Periodicity and Reactivity
17	B	Periodicity and Reactivity
18	D	Periodicity and Reactivity
19	B	Heat, Thermodynamics, and Thermochemistry
20	A	Heat, Thermodynamics, and Thermochemistry
21	C	Heat, Thermodynamics, and Thermochemistry
22	A	Heat, Thermodynamics, and Thermochemistry
23	C	Heat, Thermodynamics, and Thermochemistry
24	D	Heat, Thermodynamics, and Thermochemistry
25	C	Heat, Thermodynamics, and Thermochemistry
26	D	Nomenclature
27	C	Nomenclature
28	A	Nomenclature
29	A	The Mole, Chemical Bonding, and Molecular Geometry
30	B	The Mole, Chemical Bonding, and Molecular Geometry
31	B	The Mole, Chemical Bonding, and Molecular Geometry
32	B	The Mole, Chemical Bonding, and Molecular Geometry
33	D	The Mole, Chemical Bonding, and Molecular Geometry
34	A	The Mole, Chemical Bonding, and Molecular Geometry
35	C	The Mole, Chemical Bonding, and Molecular Geometry
36	D	Solutions and Solubility
37	B	Solutions and Solubility
38	D	Solutions and Solubility

Question Number	Correct Answer	Content Category
39	B	Solutions and Solubility
40	B	Solutions and Solubility
41	A	Acid/Base Chemistry
42	A	Acid/Base Chemistry
43	D	Acid/Base Chemistry
44	C	Acid/Base Chemistry
45	B	Chemical Reactions
46	D	Chemical Reactions
47	B	Chemical Reactions
48	C	Chemical Reactions
49	C	Chemical Reactions
50	B	Chemical Reactions
51	C	Chemical Reactions
52	B	Chemical Reactions
53	D	Chemical Reactions
54	A	Biochemistry and Organic Chemistry
55	C	Biochemistry and Organic Chemistry
56	D	Biochemistry and Organic Chemistry
57	B	History and Nature of Science
58	D	History and Nature of Science
59	D	History and Nature of Science
60	A	Scientific Procedures and Techniques
61	C	Scientific Procedures and Techniques
62	C	Heat, Thermodynamics, and Thermochemistry
63	D	Scientific Procedures and Techniques
64	B	Scientific Procedures and Techniques
65	B	Scientific Procedures and Techniques
66	B	Scientific Procedures and Techniques
67	B	Scientific Procedures and Techniques
68	C	Scientific Procedures and Techniques
69	C	Scientific Procedures and Techniques
70	D	Scientific Procedures and Techniques
71	A	Scientific Procedures and Techniques
72	C	Science, Technology, and Social Perspectives
73	A	Science, Technology, and Social Perspectives
74	C	Science, Technology, and Social Perspectives
75	A	Science, Technology, and Social Perspectives

Explanations of Right Answers

1. Although all of the statements are accurate for gaseous substances, without a large distance between the molecules, gases would not be compressible. This average distance between the molecules is lessened in response to any additional external pressure, allowing for the compressibility of gases, as we know it. The correct answer, therefore, is (B).

2. The energy released during the combustion process in the Bunsen burner is first released as heat. The temperature rises and the liquid is converted to a gas. The steam is directed through a tube, causing the pinwheel to turn. This is mechanical energy. The correct answer, therefore, is (C).

3. The density of a sample is determined by dividing the mass of the object by its volume. The densities of I, II, III, and IV in g/mL are: 0.5, 1.0, 1.5, and 1.0, respectively. The correct answer, therefore, is (C).

4. At room temperature and pressure, bromine is a liquid and the others are solid. The correct answer, therefore, is (C).

5. A chemical change involves the production of new matter. A physical change results from a change in form but not composition. The physical properties of water do not change upon boiling. The matter is present in a new form due to the added energy to the system. No chemical bonds are destroyed or formed. The structure of the matter therefore is intact. The correct answer, therefore, is (B).

6. The kinetic energy of a moving particle is defined as $\frac{1}{2}$ times the mass of the particle times the velocity of the particle squared. The familiar formula is KE $= \frac{1}{2}mv^2$. One joule (J) is the kinetic energy of a 2-kilogram mass moving at a speed of 1 meter per second. The units in this question are appropriate, so that simply applying the formula will yield the units requested. Using these facts,

$$KE = \frac{1}{2} \cdot 10 kg \cdot \left(5\frac{m}{s}\right)^2 \cdot \frac{1 J \cdot s^2}{kg \cdot m^2} = 125 \text{ J}.$$

The correct answer, therefore, is (C).

7. Selenium has the electron configuration $1s^2 2s^2 2p^6 3s^2 3d^{10} 3p^6 4s^2 4p^4$. Thus, selenium has electrons in the fourth principal level, $n = 4$. The quantum number $l = 1$ designates the p orbital. The m_l designator of 1 is reasonable for any p sublevel. The correct answer, therefore, is (D).

8. Elements ending with a completed s sublevel (2 electrons) are found in the second group of the periodic table. This group is known, classically, as the alkaline earth metals. The correct answer, therefore, is (C).

9. Knowing that the sum of the mass numbers and atomic numbers on both sides of a balanced nuclear equation is constant makes a determination of the second product possible. On the reactant side, the mass numbers are 27 for the aluminum and 1 for the neutron. The total is 28. On the product side, the helium atom (alpha particle) has a mass number of 4. This means that the other product must have a mass number of 24. The sum of the atomic

numbers on the reactant side is 13. On the product side, the helium has an atomic number of 2. This means that the other product must have an atomic number of 11.

This yields $_{11}^{24}\text{Na}$. An alternative is to set up a nuclear equation. $_{13}^{27}\text{Al} + _{0}^{1}\text{n} \rightarrow _{2}^{4}\text{He} + \underline{\quad}$. Having organized the work in this fashion, you now can apply the concepts discussed earlier. The correct answer, therefore, is (B).

10. Einstein pointed out that the photoelectric effect can be explained if the energy of light is transferred to matter (the electrons) in concentrated bundles (particles), which later came to be called photons. The correct answer, therefore, is (A).

11. Isotopes are atoms with the same atomic number but different atomic mass numbers. The correct answer, therefore, is (B).

12. The atomic mass is determined by calculating the weighted average of all of the commonly occurring isotopes of an element. The formula is Atomic Mass = Σ (Iso. Mass)$_1$(Abundance)$_1$ + (Iso. Mass)$_2$(Abundance)$_2$ + . . . + (Iso. Mass)$_n$ (Abundance)$_n$.

In this formula, (Iso. Mass) represents the respective mass of each isotope and (Abundance) represents the relative abundance of each isotope. In this case, with four isotopes, four terms are needed.

Atomic Mass = (30 amu)(0.15) + (32 amu)(0.70) + (34 amu)(0.1) + (35 amu)(0.05) = 32.05 amu. The closest answer is 32.0 amu. The correct answer, therefore, is (B). But this answer could be estimated based on the rather large abundance (70%) of ^{32}X.

13. The electronic energy levels for hydrogen are progressively closer from $n = 1$ to $n = \infty$, resulting in the spectrum shown. The other statements cannot account for the spectrum. The correct answer, therefore, is (D).

14. As you proceed down the periodic table, atomic radius typically increases, and as you proceed across a row, the atomic radius typically decreases. Therefore, Cl is smaller than I, P is smaller than Sb, and Cl is smaller than P. The correct answer, therefore, is (D).

15. Metals become more active as you proceed down the periodic table and also as you proceed from right to left. The alkali metals (exemplified by potassium and sodium in this question) are the most active metals. Potassium is the most active of this group of four since it is lower than sodium in the group. Barium is more active than magnesium. The correct answer, therefore, is (A).

16. For Be, the greatest increase in ionization energies is between the second and third ionization energies. Having had a second electron removed, the original valence shell is stripped. Any further removal involves removing the electrons from much closer to the nucleus. The correct answer, therefore, is (B).

17. With increasing atomic number, the attraction for electrons increases. The electronegativity of the atoms increases and the size decreases simultaneously. The correct answer, therefore, is (B).

18. According to the oxidation number rule, the sum of all oxidation numbers on neutral compounds is 0. Therefore, the oxidation state of M must be $+2$, since the oxygen from column IV has the expected oxidation state of -2. With P from Group V commonly having an oxidation state of -3, three M atoms are needed for every two P atoms. The correct answer, therefore, is (D).

19. The heat of reaction reflects the difference in enthalpy between the products and the reactants. From the diagram, the enthalpy of the products can be seen to be $+60$ kJ, while the enthalpy of the reactants is $+30$ kJ. The difference (enthalpy of the products $-$ enthalpy of the reactants) is then $+30$ kJ. The correct answer, therefore, is (B).

20. A catalyst will speed up a chemical reaction by lowering the activation energy, E_a, of the overall reaction. The catalyst will not affect the enthalpy of either the reactants or the products, however. On this diagram, the activation energy is represented by arrow A. The correct answer, therefore, is (A).

21. In order to answer this question, the given equations must be rearranged and combined (added) so that the sum equals the desired equation. Rearranging and combining involves reversing the first reaction. This requires a change in sign for the $\Delta H°$. Both reactions must also be divided in half. This requires dividing their respective $\Delta H°$'s in half simultaneously. When combining the reactions, the $\Delta H°$'s are added as well. From the first reaction, $+98$ kJ, and from the second reaction, -395 kJ, add to give a net result of -297 kJ.

$$SO_3(g) \rightarrow SO_2(g) + \tfrac{1}{2}O_2(g) \quad \Delta H° = +98 \text{ kJ}$$
$$S(s) + \tfrac{3}{2}O_2(g) \rightarrow SO_3(g) \quad \Delta H° = -395 \text{ kJ}$$
$$\overline{S(s) + O_2(g) \rightarrow SO_2(g) \qquad \Delta H_{rxn} = -297 \text{ kJ}}$$

The correct answer, therefore, is (C).

22. The number of moles of molecules in sample I as compared to the number in samples II, III, and IV, respectively, is in the ratio 2:1, as determined by the equation $n = PV/RT$.

$$\frac{n_I}{n_{II}} = \frac{P_I}{P_{II}} \times \frac{T_{II}}{T_I} \times \frac{V_I}{V_{II}} = \frac{200}{300} \times \frac{900}{300} \times \frac{8}{8} = \frac{2}{1}$$

$$\frac{n_I}{n_{III}} = \frac{200}{200} \times \frac{300}{300} \times \frac{8}{4} = \frac{2}{1}$$

$$\frac{n_I}{n_{IV}} = \frac{200}{600} \times \frac{900}{300} \times \frac{8}{4} = \frac{2}{1}$$

The correct answer, therefore, is (A).

23. It took 10 minutes to heat the water from 0°C to 100°C. The amount of heat added was 10 min $\times$ 500 joules/min = 5,000 J. The correct answer, therefore, is (C).

24. The standard heat of combustion is defined as the energy released when one mole of $C_2H_6(g)$ reacts with $O_2(g)$ to form appropriate amounts of $CO_2(g)$ and $H_2O(l)$. Since the reaction occurs at standard conditions, the water should be a liquid in its standard state at 25°C. This reaction is represented by answer choice (D). The correct answer, therefore, is (D).

25. The amount of heat needed to raise the temperature of a substance over a specific temperature range is determined by multiplying the specific heat × the mass × the change in temperature.

$Q = C \times m \times \Delta t$
$Q = 4.19 \text{ J/g·°C} \times 10.0 \text{ g} \times (50.0°C - 30°C)$
$\quad = 838 \text{ J}$

The correct answer, therefore, is (C).

26. The names of oxy acids such as H_2SO_3 are based on the number of oxygen atoms in the formula. There is also a connection between the name of the anion and the acid: For any acid name ending with "ous," the anion ends in "-ite"; For any acid name ending with "ic," the anion ends in "-ate." In this example, sulfurous acid, H_2SO_3, has the sulfite anion SO_3^{2-}, and sulfuric acid H_2SO_4, has the sulfate anion SO_4^{2-}. The correct answer, therefore, is (D).

27. The charge of tin (Sn) is +2, as indicated by the (II) part of the name. The formula and charge of the phosphate polyatomic ion is PO_4^{3-}. In order to maintain charge neutrality, three tin(II) ions and two phosphate ions are required. This combination is indicated by the subscripts in answer choice (C). The correct answer, therefore, is (C).

28. Following IUPAC rules, choose the longest continuous chain and then number the chain from the end with the functional group. The chain has 5 carbons and is therefore referred to as pentanol. Locate the side groups on the chain using the assigned numbers and identify them correctly with the proper name; specifically, the side group on the 4-carbon is a methyl group. Separate the numbers from each other using commas and the numbers from the words using dashes. Use an appropriate prefix when describing more than one group. The correct answer, therefore, is (A).

29. Ions are present in compounds composed of elements with very low and very high electronegativities, i.e., metals and nonmetals. This large difference in electronegativity results in a transfer of one or more electrons from metal to nonmetal atoms. Transfer of electrons results in the formation of ions. When atoms of similar electronegativity combine, they tend to share the electrons and form covalent bonds. Electrons are shared and ions do not form. Potassium has a very low electronegativity as compared to oxygen. Potassium will release its valence electron to the oxygen atom. Potassium will therefore be present as potassium cations. The oxygen will accept two electrons from the two potassium atoms. The oxygen will then be present as oxide anions. In sodium nitrate, sodium gives up an electron to NO_3, forming NO_3^-, which contains covalent bonds between the nitrogen and the oxygen. The correct answer, therefore, is (A).

30. Ethene involves two carbon atoms linked to each other and to two of the hydrogen atoms. There are single bonds between the carbon atom and each of the two hydrogen atoms and a double bond between the two carbon atoms. With three bonding sites around each carbon atom, the s orbital and two of the three p orbitals on the valence shell hybridize to allow for the maximum displacement needed consistent with the VSEPR theory. The additional bond between the two carbon atoms is accomplished with the unhybridized "p" orbital from each atom. The correct answer, therefore, is (B).

31. The empirical formula is the smallest whole number ratio of atoms in the compound. In a 100 g sample of the compound, there is 53 g C, 31g N, and 16 g H. The number of moles of each is found from:

$$\frac{53.3 \text{ g}}{12 \text{ g/mol}} = 4.44 \text{ mol C};$$

$$\frac{31.1 \text{ g}}{14 \text{ g/mol}} = 2.22 \text{ mol N};$$

$$\frac{15.6 \text{ g}}{1 \text{ g/mol}} = 15.6 \text{ mol H}$$

Dividing each by 2.22 gives

$$\frac{4.44}{2.22} = 2.00 \text{ mol C}; \frac{2.22}{2.22} = 1.00 \text{ mol N};$$

$$\frac{15.6}{2.22} = 7.02 \text{ mol H};$$

The empirical formula is C_2H_7N. The correct answer, therefore, is (B).

32. In many polyatomic ions, a central atom is covalently bonded to a number of surrounding atoms. In the case of nitrate, NO_3^-, the nitrogen is covalently bonded to the three surrounding oxygen atoms. The structure involves resonance of one pair of electrons. The diagram below depicts the structure.

The correct answer, therefore, is (B).

33. There are 6 mol of oxygen atoms from the anhydrous portion of the compound. This can be seen by multiplying the subscripts 2 and 3. There are an additional 2 mol of oxygen atoms in the water portion of the compound. This can be seen from the coefficient in front of the H_2O. Thus, the sum of the number of mol of oxygen is 8. Since there are only 0.5 mol of the compound, the 8 is divided by 2, giving 4. The correct answer, therefore, is (D).

34. Butane is a nonpolar molecule. The electronegativity values of carbon (2.5) and hydrogen (2.1) are close enough that the bonds are considered nonpolar by most authorities. Any slight polarity of the bonds is symmetrically opposed about the center of the tetrahedral molecule. This results in a purely nonpolar molecule. Dispersion forces occur between nonpolar molecules due to temporary or instantaneous dipoles that form when the electrons move about the molecule. These dispersion forces are greater in more massive molecules and account for the fact that hydrocarbon molecules may form liquids or solids. The correct answer, therefore, is (A).

35. The bonding in the ammonia molecule can be represented using four sp^3 orbitals on the nitrogen atom. The four pairs of electrons arrange themselves into angles of approximately 107°. With one pair of electrons being unshared, the molecular shape is described based on the placement of the nitrogen and the three hydrogen atoms. The correct answer, therefore, is (C).

36. In order to determine the molarity (concentration) of the solution resulting from the mixture described, the total number of moles of the particle in question, in this case the sodium ion, must be divided by the total volume resulting from the mixture. Multiplying the molarity of each solution by its volume in liters (L) and adding the results can determine the total number of moles of sodium ion. Both $NaCl$ and Na_2SO_4 are strong electrolytes, so it can be assumed that there is 100 percent dissociation. The molarity is found as follows:

$$\frac{0.050\ L\ (0.10\ mol/L) + (0.100\ L)(0.20\ mol/L)}{(0.050\ L + 0.150\ L)}$$

$$= 0.30\ mol/L$$

The correct answer, therefore, is (D).

37. Multiplying the volume of 10.0 liters by the molarity of 0.05 mol/liter yields 0.5 mol of $C_6H_{12}O_6$. Multiplying 0.50 mol $C_6H_{12}O_6$ by 180 g/mol yields 90 g. The correct answer, therefore, is (B).

38. The solubility S is found as follows:

$$(S)(2S)^2 = 1.6 \times 10^{-5} = K_{sp}$$
$$S^3 = 4.0 \times 10^{-6}$$
$$S = 1.6 \times 10^{-2}$$

The correct answer, therefore, is (D).

39. Since crystals formed during cooling, it is known that the solution did not become supersaturated. The difference in solubility from 70°C to 10°C is 120 grams (140 grams minus 20 grams). Since the curve is based on 100 grams of water as the solvent and because we are dealing with only 25 grams of water as the solvent, we divide 120 grams by 4 to get 30 grams. The correct answer, therefore, is (B).

40. The freezing point of a solution depends on the concentration of the ions in solution as well as other factors. In this specific case, (A) forms no ions, (B) forms approximately four ions, (C) forms approximately three ions, and (D) forms approximately two ions. The correct answer, therefore, is (B).

41. Multiplying the molarity by the percent ionization will yield the approximate $[H^+]$.
$$0.20\ M \times 0.03 = 0.006\ M\ H^+$$
To find the pH, take the negative log of the $[H^+]$.
$$pH = -\log(6 \times 10^{-3}),$$
which is approximately 3. To choose the final answer without a calculator, remember that the pH of 0.01 (10^{-2}) $M\ H^+$ is 2 and the pH of 0.001 (10^{-3}) $M\ H^+$ is 3. Since 0.006 M falls between these limits, the correct answer is (A).

42. The pH is found as follows:
$$pH = -\log[H^+] = \log[2 \times 10^{-3}] = 2.7,$$
assuming 100 percent dissociation. The correct answer, therefore, is (A).

43. The K^+ ion from the salt will not hydrolyze in water, whereas the PO_4^{3-} ion will. The potassium ion is a spectator ion. The phosphate ion accepts a proton from a water molecule, changing the pH. The hydrolysis reaction forming a basic solution (pH > 7) is:

$$PO_4^{3-}(aq) + H_2O(l) \rightleftharpoons HPO_4^{2-}(aq) + OH^-(aq).$$

With the increase in OH^- concentration, the pH increases. The correct answer, therefore, is (D).

44. The relationship between conjugate acids and their respective conjugate bases is that the acid particle has an additional proton that the base particle does not. The correct answer, therefore, is (C).

45. For a single-step reaction, the rate law of the reaction can be found using the stoichiometric coefficients of the reactants as the order of each reactant in the rate expression. The correct answer, therefore, is (B).

46. The units for the rate are $mol \cdot L^{-1} \cdot s^{-1}$.
$mol \cdot L^{-1} \cdot s^{-1} = k(mol \cdot L^{-1})^2 (mol \cdot L^{-1})$.
The units for the rate constant, k, are
$k = (mol \cdot L^{-1} \cdot s^{-1}) \, mol^{-1} \cdot L^3$
$k = mol^{-2} \cdot L^2 \cdot s^{-1}$.
The correct answer, therefore, is (D).

47. This equation is tricky. An initial thought might be to balance the hydrogen atoms by using a coefficient of 2 before the H_2O. This process causes a conflict in the number of oxygen atoms. Keeping in mind that the ratio of hydrogen to oxygen atoms is 2 to 1, using a coefficient of 3 for OH^- will give 3 oxygen atoms and 6 hydrogen atoms on the product side. Using a coefficient of 3 for the water will balance these elements. The remaining elements can be balanced by using the concept that the subscripts on one side often suggest the coefficients on the other side. When the coefficients used are $Li_3N(s) + 3H_2O(l) \rightarrow 3Li^+(aq) + 3OH^-(aq) + NH_3(g)$, the number of atoms of each element is the same on both sides of the equation. The correct answer, therefore, is (B).

48. In order for the reaction to be spontaneous, the $E°$ must be positive. Reversing the Cu^{2+} half reaction would make Cu a reactant when the two half reactions are added. With reversal of a half reaction, the sign of $E°$ must be changed to negative. Doubling the second half reaction to get the same number of electrons in both half reactions does not affect the $E°$ of the half reactions. Add $1.84\,V + (-0.34\,V)$ to get the $E°$ of $1.50\,V$. The correct answer, therefore, is (C).

49. In this reaction, oxygen is the limiting reagent. Dividing the mass of each reactant by its respective molar mass gives the number of moles of each. If you compare the relative number of moles present to those in the balanced equation given, you find that oxygen is the limiting reagent.

Mol NH_3 = 34 g × 1 mol/17 g = 2 mol NH_3
Mol O_2 = 32 g × 1 mol/32 g = 1 mol O_2

The equation demands 5 mol of O_2 for every 4 mol of NH_3. Clearly, O_2 is the limiting reagent. To determine the mass of water formed, use the coefficients from the balanced equation and the number of moles of the limiting reagent.

$$1 \text{ mol } O_2 \times \frac{6 \text{ mol } H_2O}{5 \text{ mol } O_2} \times \frac{18 \text{ g } H_2O}{1 \text{ mol } H_2O}$$
$$= 21.6 \text{ g } H_2O$$

The correct answer, therefore, is (C).

50. The oxidation number of manganese in Mn(s) is 0. It is oxidized in the reaction to +2 in the Mn^{2+}(aq) ion. Oxidation involves the loss of electrons. This loss is accompanied by an increase in charge, as reflected in the change of the oxidation number of the manganese atoms. The sulfur atom undergoes an opposite change in this reaction. The correct answer, therefore, is (B).

51. Start by writing the correctly balanced equation: $Mg_3N_2 + 6 H_2O \rightarrow 3 Mg(OH)_2 + 2 NH_3$.

The coefficients represent the relative numbers of moles of each reactant and product. Since water is the excess reactant, all of the magnesium nitride will be used. We can therefore calculate the amount of product directly from the initial amount of Mg_3N_2. See the sample calculation below.

2.0 mol Mg_3N_2 × 2 mol NH_3/1mol Mg_3N_2
= 4.0 mol NH_3

The correct answer, therefore, is (C).

52. The number of moles of H_2 decreases by 0.20, since 0.34 − 0.20 = 0.14. Since the coefficient ratio between HBr and H_2 is 2:1, the number of moles of HBr would be equal to twice the decrease in the number of moles of H_2. The correct answer, therefore, is (B).

53. The equilibrium constant, K_c, is rather independent of pressure. So (A), (B), and (C) will not significantly affect the value of K_c. According to Le Châtelier's principle, when a system at equilibrium is subjected to a stress, the equilibrium will shift to reduce the stress. This reaction is exothermic in the forward direction, as can be seen by the negative value of ΔH (< 0). This negative value indicates that heat is released when the reactants are consumed and the product is formed. Lowering temperatures will favor the exothermic direction since the equilibrium shifts to replace the heat lost to the surroundings. The concentration of SO_3 will increase, while the concentrations of SO_2 and O_2 will decrease with decreasing temperature. Since the equilibrium constant is a ratio between the concentrations of the products and reactants, decreasing the temperature will therefore increase the value of the equilibrium constant, K_c. The correct answer, therefore, is (D).

54. Ketones are characterized by having a carbonyl,

$$\overset{\displaystyle |}{\underset{\displaystyle |}{C}} = O,$$

group attached to a nonterminal carbon atom on a hydrocarbon chain. (B) is an ether, (C) is an aldehyde, and (D) is a carboxylic acid. The correct answer, therefore, is (A).

55. In amines, a nitrogen atom is bonded to one carbon atom as well as to one or more hydrogen atoms in most cases. The correct answer, therefore, is (C).

56. Proteins are composed of amino acids bonded together by peptide bonds. The correct answer, therefore, is (D).

57. A proposal is a theory. The theory could be considered a law if it is supported by evidence collected and analyzed by many people over a period of time. However, Dalton's theory has been shown to be somewhat erroneous by evidence that suggests there are subatomic particles—i.e., the atom can be further divided. Dalton's proposal is not an observation, since he had no way of observing atoms and this proposal is not a test. The correct answer, therefore, is (B).

58. Options (A), (B), and (C) are observations. (D) involves evaluation of the observed data. Then based on these observations, a conclusion was made that the solid was H_2O. The correct answer, therefore, is (D).

59. Robert Boyle is credited with the famous Boyle's law. *The volume of a fixed quantity of gas maintained at constant temperature is inversely proportional to the pressure.* This can be represented mathematically as $P \times V = $ a constant, where P is pressure, V is volume, and the constant is indeterminate, but not varying, in this context. The correct answer, therefore, is (D).

60. The sizes of particles dissolved in an aqueous solution are small enough to fit through the tiny pores of the filter paper. The particles making up a precipitate are large enough in size to be caught by the paper. The correct answer, therefore, is (A).

61. In scientific notation, the number should be written with one figure to the left of the decimal point (in this case, 3) and all other significant figures to the right of the decimal point. The power of ten should be given unless it is zero. The total number of significant figures in this case is 4. The correct answer, therefore, is (C).

62. The heat gain by the cool water (sample 2) is equal to the heat loss by the warm water (sample 1). The final temperature (T_2) is found as follows:

Mass (1) × specific heat of water × (T_2 − 70) = − mass (2) × specific heat of water × (T_2 − 40) or

100 g (T_2 − 70) = − 200 g (T_2 − 40)

The first temperature of the mixture (T_2) is found as follows:

$$100\,T_2 - 7{,}000 = -200\,T_2 + 8{,}000$$
$$300\,T_2 = 15{,}000$$
$$T_2 = 50°C$$

The correct answer, therefore, is (C).

63. Ethyl ether is a potentially explosive compound. The other compounds listed, acetone, sulfuric acid, and methanol, are not explosive and can be used and stored in a high school laboratory. The correct answer, therefore, is (D).

64. 1 kg is 1,000 g, 1 mg is 1×10^{-3} g, and 1 μg is 1×10^{-6} g. The correct answer, therefore, is (B).

65. Water has a very high specific heat capacity. The excess water can absorb much of the heat released by the dissolving process when it is in greater amount. If water is added to acid, the water is in lesser amount and will boil. A boiling solution of concentrated sulfuric acid is quite dangerous. The correct answer, therefore, is (B).

66. Burets are read to the nearest 0.01 mL. Estimate one decimal beyond the calibration. The correct answer, therefore, is (B).

67. The manometer is open-ended. This means that the surrounding pressure must be accounted for in the observation. Since the level of mercury on the gas *A* side is higher than on the side open to the room, the pressure of gas *A* must be lower than that of the room. Subtracting the values at each side of the manometer gives the difference in the column heights. This difference is about 13 mm Hg. The final calculation is: 765 mm Hg − 13 mm Hg = 752 mm Hg. The correct answer, therefore, is (B).

68. (A) is not correct since the density of each object can be calculated from the data given on the mass per unit volume data. (B) is not correct since the density of VI is 25/6, which is less than that of all the others. (D) is not correct because the shape cannot be determined from the mass, volume, or density of objects. Since the objects do not all have the same density, they cannot all have the same composition. The correct answer, therefore, is (C).

69. (A), (B), and (D) are all correct matches. One liter is a unit of volume. Surface area in liters would be $L^{2/3}$. So (C) is not a correct match. The correct answer, therefore, is (C).

70. Good accuracy reflects data that are close to an accepted value, while good precision reflects a small range within the trials. In this data sequence, the range is 1.20 g. This is not very precise. The average mass would be 10.90 g. With the accepted value of 10.91 g, there is an error of 0.01 g. So this is very accurate. A balance reading to the nearest 0.01 g should obtain good results past the tenths place. The correct answer, therefore, is (D).

71. Since NaOH (which is deliquescent) absorbs water from the air, the mass of the NaOH will change and the solution will be less concentrated that expected. The correct answer, therefore, is (A).

72. Orange juice contains citric acid. Liquid soap is a base, bottled water is essentially neutral, and the acidity of the H in the rubbing alcohol is much less than that of citric acid. The correct answer, therefore, is (C).

73. The triangle made of circling arrows surrounding a number is used to symbolize the type of plastic of which the object is made. Generally speaking the lower the value of the number, the more easy the recycling of the plastic. The correct answer, therefore, is (A).

74. Hydrogen nuclear fusion does not produce polluting by-products. Its fuel is abundantly available, and it does not involve radioactive waste. But the technology for large-scale production is currently not available. The correct answer, therefore, is (C).

75. The production of electricity in both nuclear- and fossil-fuel generating plants involves the condensation of water after steam is generated and used to turn the turbine. Frequently, taking water from a stream and using it as a cooling source accomplishes this cooling process. But the water is too hot to be returned directly to the stream. This kind of thermal pollution has been known to be responsible for fish kills in the past. Power-generating stations often involve large cooling towers that release much of this excess heat before returning the water to the stream. These cooling towers are present at both nuclear and fossil-fuel facilities. The correct answer, therefore, is (A).

Chapter 13

Practice Questions for the
Earth and Space Sciences: Content Knowledge Test

▶　▶　▶　▶　▶　▶　▶　▶　▶　▶　▶　▶

Practice Questions

Now that you have studied the content topics and have worked through strategies relating to multiple-choice questions, you should take the following practice test. You will probably find it helpful to simulate actual testing conditions, giving yourself about 90 minutes to work on the questions. You can cut out and use the answer sheet provided if you wish.

Keep in mind that the test you take at an actual administration will have different questions.

You should not expect the percentage of questions you answer correctly in these practice questions to be exactly the same as when you take the test at an actual administration, since numerous factors affect a person's performance in any given testing situation.

When you have finished the practice questions, you can score your answers and read the explanations of the best answer choices in chapter 14.

TEST CODE:

TEST NAME:
Earth and Space Sciences:
Content Knowledge

Practice Questions

Calculators Prohibited

Time—90 Minutes
75 Questions

(Note, at the official administration of test 0571, there will be 100 questions;
you will be allowed 120 minutes to complete the test.)

Answer Sheet C

PAGE 1

DO NOT USE INK

Use only a pencil with soft black lead (No. 2 or HB) to complete this answer sheet.
Be sure to fill in completely the oval that corresponds to the proper letter or number.
Completely erase any errors or stray marks.

THE PRAXIS SERIES
Professional Assessments for Beginning Teachers®

1. NAME

Enter your last name and first initial.
Omit spaces, hyphens, apostrophes, etc.

Last Name (first 6 letters) | F.I.

(A) through (Z) ovals

2.

YOUR NAME: (Print)
Last Name (Family or Surname) — First Name (Given) — M.I.

MAILING ADDRESS: (Print)
P.O. Box or Street Address

Apt. # (If any)

City

State or Province

Country

Zip or Postal Code

TELEPHONE NUMBER:
( ) Home — ( ) Business

SIGNATURE:

TEST DATE:

3. DATE OF BIRTH

Month	Day
Jan.	
Feb.	
Mar.	
April	
May	
June	
July	
Aug.	
Sept.	
Oct.	
Nov.	
Dec.	

Day ovals: (0) (1) (2) (3) (4) (5) (6) (7) (8) (9)

4. SOCIAL SECURITY NUMBER

Ovals: (0) (1) (2) (3) (4) (5) (6) (7) (8) (9)

5. CANDIDATE ID NUMBER

Ovals: (0) (1) (2) (3) (4) (5) (6) (7) (8) (9)

6. TEST CENTER / REPORTING LOCATION

Center Number — Room Number

Center Name

City — State or Province

Country

7. TEST CODE / FORM CODE

Ovals: (0) (1) (2) (3) (4) (5) (6) (7) (8) (9)

0
1

8. TEST BOOK SERIAL NUMBER

9. TEST FORM

10. TEST NAME

Educational Testing Service, ETS, the ETS logo, and THE PRAXIS SERIES:PROFESSIONAL
ASSESSMENTS FOR BEGINNING TEACHERS and its logo are registered trademarks of
Educational Testing Service.

ETS Educational Testing Service

51055 • 08920 • TF71M500
MH01159   Q2573-06

I.N. 202974

1 2 3 4

CERTIFICATION STATEMENT: (Please write the following statement below. DO NOT PRINT.)

"I hereby agree to the conditions set forth in the *Registration Bulletin* and certify that I am the person whose name and address appear on this answer sheet."

_____

_____

_____

SIGNATURE: _____ DATE: _____ / _____ / _____

Month   Day   Year

BE SURE EACH MARK IS DARK AND COMPLETELY FILLS THE INTENDED SPACE AS ILLUSTRATED HERE: ● .

1 Ⓐ Ⓑ Ⓒ Ⓓ	41 Ⓐ Ⓑ Ⓒ Ⓓ	81 Ⓐ Ⓑ Ⓒ Ⓓ	121 Ⓐ Ⓑ Ⓒ Ⓓ
2 Ⓐ Ⓑ Ⓒ Ⓓ	42 Ⓐ Ⓑ Ⓒ Ⓓ	82 Ⓐ Ⓑ Ⓒ Ⓓ	122 Ⓐ Ⓑ Ⓒ Ⓓ
3 Ⓐ Ⓑ Ⓒ Ⓓ	43 Ⓐ Ⓑ Ⓒ Ⓓ	83 Ⓐ Ⓑ Ⓒ Ⓓ	123 Ⓐ Ⓑ Ⓒ Ⓓ
4 Ⓐ Ⓑ Ⓒ Ⓓ	44 Ⓐ Ⓑ Ⓒ Ⓓ	84 Ⓐ Ⓑ Ⓒ Ⓓ	124 Ⓐ Ⓑ Ⓒ Ⓓ
5 Ⓐ Ⓑ Ⓒ Ⓓ	45 Ⓐ Ⓑ Ⓒ Ⓓ	85 Ⓐ Ⓑ Ⓒ Ⓓ	125 Ⓐ Ⓑ Ⓒ Ⓓ
6 Ⓐ Ⓑ Ⓒ Ⓓ	46 Ⓐ Ⓑ Ⓒ Ⓓ	86 Ⓐ Ⓑ Ⓒ Ⓓ	126 Ⓐ Ⓑ Ⓒ Ⓓ
7 Ⓐ Ⓑ Ⓒ Ⓓ	47 Ⓐ Ⓑ Ⓒ Ⓓ	87 Ⓐ Ⓑ Ⓒ Ⓓ	127 Ⓐ Ⓑ Ⓒ Ⓓ
8 Ⓐ Ⓑ Ⓒ Ⓓ	48 Ⓐ Ⓑ Ⓒ Ⓓ	88 Ⓐ Ⓑ Ⓒ Ⓓ	128 Ⓐ Ⓑ Ⓒ Ⓓ
9 Ⓐ Ⓑ Ⓒ Ⓓ	49 Ⓐ Ⓑ Ⓒ Ⓓ	89 Ⓐ Ⓑ Ⓒ Ⓓ	129 Ⓐ Ⓑ Ⓒ Ⓓ
10 Ⓐ Ⓑ Ⓒ Ⓓ	50 Ⓐ Ⓑ Ⓒ Ⓓ	90 Ⓐ Ⓑ Ⓒ Ⓓ	130 Ⓐ Ⓑ Ⓒ Ⓓ
11 Ⓐ Ⓑ Ⓒ Ⓓ	51 Ⓐ Ⓑ Ⓒ Ⓓ	91 Ⓐ Ⓑ Ⓒ Ⓓ	131 Ⓐ Ⓑ Ⓒ Ⓓ
12 Ⓐ Ⓑ Ⓒ Ⓓ	52 Ⓐ Ⓑ Ⓒ Ⓓ	92 Ⓐ Ⓑ Ⓒ Ⓓ	132 Ⓐ Ⓑ Ⓒ Ⓓ
13 Ⓐ Ⓑ Ⓒ Ⓓ	53 Ⓐ Ⓑ Ⓒ Ⓓ	93 Ⓐ Ⓑ Ⓒ Ⓓ	133 Ⓐ Ⓑ Ⓒ Ⓓ
14 Ⓐ Ⓑ Ⓒ Ⓓ	54 Ⓐ Ⓑ Ⓒ Ⓓ	94 Ⓐ Ⓑ Ⓒ Ⓓ	134 Ⓐ Ⓑ Ⓒ Ⓓ
15 Ⓐ Ⓑ Ⓒ Ⓓ	55 Ⓐ Ⓑ Ⓒ Ⓓ	95 Ⓐ Ⓑ Ⓒ Ⓓ	135 Ⓐ Ⓑ Ⓒ Ⓓ
16 Ⓐ Ⓑ Ⓒ Ⓓ	56 Ⓐ Ⓑ Ⓒ Ⓓ	96 Ⓐ Ⓑ Ⓒ Ⓓ	136 Ⓐ Ⓑ Ⓒ Ⓓ
17 Ⓐ Ⓑ Ⓒ Ⓓ	57 Ⓐ Ⓑ Ⓒ Ⓓ	97 Ⓐ Ⓑ Ⓒ Ⓓ	137 Ⓐ Ⓑ Ⓒ Ⓓ
18 Ⓐ Ⓑ Ⓒ Ⓓ	58 Ⓐ Ⓑ Ⓒ Ⓓ	98 Ⓐ Ⓑ Ⓒ Ⓓ	138 Ⓐ Ⓑ Ⓒ Ⓓ
19 Ⓐ Ⓑ Ⓒ Ⓓ	59 Ⓐ Ⓑ Ⓒ Ⓓ	99 Ⓐ Ⓑ Ⓒ Ⓓ	139 Ⓐ Ⓑ Ⓒ Ⓓ
20 Ⓐ Ⓑ Ⓒ Ⓓ	60 Ⓐ Ⓑ Ⓒ Ⓓ	100 Ⓐ Ⓑ Ⓒ Ⓓ	140 Ⓐ Ⓑ Ⓒ Ⓓ
21 Ⓐ Ⓑ Ⓒ Ⓓ	61 Ⓐ Ⓑ Ⓒ Ⓓ	101 Ⓐ Ⓑ Ⓒ Ⓓ	141 Ⓐ Ⓑ Ⓒ Ⓓ
22 Ⓐ Ⓑ Ⓒ Ⓓ	62 Ⓐ Ⓑ Ⓒ Ⓓ	102 Ⓐ Ⓑ Ⓒ Ⓓ	142 Ⓐ Ⓑ Ⓒ Ⓓ
23 Ⓐ Ⓑ Ⓒ Ⓓ	63 Ⓐ Ⓑ Ⓒ Ⓓ	103 Ⓐ Ⓑ Ⓒ Ⓓ	143 Ⓐ Ⓑ Ⓒ Ⓓ
24 Ⓐ Ⓑ Ⓒ Ⓓ	64 Ⓐ Ⓑ Ⓒ Ⓓ	104 Ⓐ Ⓑ Ⓒ Ⓓ	144 Ⓐ Ⓑ Ⓒ Ⓓ
25 Ⓐ Ⓑ Ⓒ Ⓓ	65 Ⓐ Ⓑ Ⓒ Ⓓ	105 Ⓐ Ⓑ Ⓒ Ⓓ	145 Ⓐ Ⓑ Ⓒ Ⓓ
26 Ⓐ Ⓑ Ⓒ Ⓓ	66 Ⓐ Ⓑ Ⓒ Ⓓ	106 Ⓐ Ⓑ Ⓒ Ⓓ	146 Ⓐ Ⓑ Ⓒ Ⓓ
27 Ⓐ Ⓑ Ⓒ Ⓓ	67 Ⓐ Ⓑ Ⓒ Ⓓ	107 Ⓐ Ⓑ Ⓒ Ⓓ	147 Ⓐ Ⓑ Ⓒ Ⓓ
28 Ⓐ Ⓑ Ⓒ Ⓓ	68 Ⓐ Ⓑ Ⓒ Ⓓ	108 Ⓐ Ⓑ Ⓒ Ⓓ	148 Ⓐ Ⓑ Ⓒ Ⓓ
29 Ⓐ Ⓑ Ⓒ Ⓓ	69 Ⓐ Ⓑ Ⓒ Ⓓ	109 Ⓐ Ⓑ Ⓒ Ⓓ	149 Ⓐ Ⓑ Ⓒ Ⓓ
30 Ⓐ Ⓑ Ⓒ Ⓓ	70 Ⓐ Ⓑ Ⓒ Ⓓ	110 Ⓐ Ⓑ Ⓒ Ⓓ	150 Ⓐ Ⓑ Ⓒ Ⓓ
31 Ⓐ Ⓑ Ⓒ Ⓓ	71 Ⓐ Ⓑ Ⓒ Ⓓ	111 Ⓐ Ⓑ Ⓒ Ⓓ	151 Ⓐ Ⓑ Ⓒ Ⓓ
32 Ⓐ Ⓑ Ⓒ Ⓓ	72 Ⓐ Ⓑ Ⓒ Ⓓ	112 Ⓐ Ⓑ Ⓒ Ⓓ	152 Ⓐ Ⓑ Ⓒ Ⓓ
33 Ⓐ Ⓑ Ⓒ Ⓓ	73 Ⓐ Ⓑ Ⓒ Ⓓ	113 Ⓐ Ⓑ Ⓒ Ⓓ	153 Ⓐ Ⓑ Ⓒ Ⓓ
34 Ⓐ Ⓑ Ⓒ Ⓓ	74 Ⓐ Ⓑ Ⓒ Ⓓ	114 Ⓐ Ⓑ Ⓒ Ⓓ	154 Ⓐ Ⓑ Ⓒ Ⓓ
35 Ⓐ Ⓑ Ⓒ Ⓓ	75 Ⓐ Ⓑ Ⓒ Ⓓ	115 Ⓐ Ⓑ Ⓒ Ⓓ	155 Ⓐ Ⓑ Ⓒ Ⓓ
36 Ⓐ Ⓑ Ⓒ Ⓓ	76 Ⓐ Ⓑ Ⓒ Ⓓ	116 Ⓐ Ⓑ Ⓒ Ⓓ	156 Ⓐ Ⓑ Ⓒ Ⓓ
37 Ⓐ Ⓑ Ⓒ Ⓓ	77 Ⓐ Ⓑ Ⓒ Ⓓ	117 Ⓐ Ⓑ Ⓒ Ⓓ	157 Ⓐ Ⓑ Ⓒ Ⓓ
38 Ⓐ Ⓑ Ⓒ Ⓓ	78 Ⓐ Ⓑ Ⓒ Ⓓ	118 Ⓐ Ⓑ Ⓒ Ⓓ	158 Ⓐ Ⓑ Ⓒ Ⓓ
39 Ⓐ Ⓑ Ⓒ Ⓓ	79 Ⓐ Ⓑ Ⓒ Ⓓ	119 Ⓐ Ⓑ Ⓒ Ⓓ	159 Ⓐ Ⓑ Ⓒ Ⓓ
40 Ⓐ Ⓑ Ⓒ Ⓓ	80 Ⓐ Ⓑ Ⓒ Ⓓ	120 Ⓐ Ⓑ Ⓒ Ⓓ	160 Ⓐ Ⓑ Ⓒ Ⓓ

FOR ETS USE ONLY	R1	R2	R3	R4	R5	R6	R7	R8	TR	CS

PERIODIC TABLE OF THE ELEMENTS

1																	2
H 1.0079																	**He** 4.0026
3 **Li** 6.941	4 **Be** 9.012											5 **B** 10.811	6 **C** 12.011	7 **N** 14.007	8 **O** 16.00	9 **F** 19.00	10 **Ne** 20.179
11 **Na** 22.99	12 **Mg** 24.30											13 **Al** 26.98	14 **Si** 28.09	15 **P** 30.974	16 **S** 32.06	17 **Cl** 35.453	18 **Ar** 39.948
19 **K** 39.10	20 **Ca** 40.08	21 **Sc** 44.96	22 **Ti** 47.90	23 **V** 50.94	24 **Cr** 52.00	25 **Mn** 54.938	26 **Fe** 55.85	27 **Co** 58.93	28 **Ni** 58.69	29 **Cu** 63.55	30 **Zn** 65.39	31 **Ga** 69.72	32 **Ge** 72.59	33 **As** 74.92	34 **Se** 78.96	35 **Br** 79.90	36 **Kr** 83.80
37 **Rb** 85.47	38 **Sr** 87.62	39 **Y** 88.91	40 **Zr** 91.22	41 **Nb** 92.91	42 **Mo** 95.94	43 **Tc** (98)	44 **Ru** 101.1	45 **Rh** 102.91	46 **Pd** 106.42	47 **Ag** 107.87	48 **Cd** 112.41	49 **In** 114.82	50 **Sn** 118.71	51 **Sb** 121.75	52 **Te** 127.60	53 **I** 126.91	54 **Xe** 131.29
55 **Cs** 132.91	56 **Ba** 137.33	57 ***La** 138.91	72 **Hf** 178.49	73 **Ta** 180.95	74 **W** 183.85	75 **Re** 186.21	76 **Os** 190.2	77 **Ir** 192.2	78 **Pt** 195.08	79 **Au** 196.97	80 **Hg** 200.59	81 **Tl** 204.38	82 **Pb** 207.2	83 **Bi** 208.98	84 **Po** (209)	85 **At** (210)	86 **Rn** (222)
87 **Fr** (223)	88 **Ra** 226.02	89 **†Ac** 227.03	104 **Rf** (261)	105 **Db** (262)	106 **Sg** (263)	107 **Bh** (262)	108 **Hs** (265)	109 **Mt** (266)	110 § (269)	111 § (272)	112 § (277)						

§Not yet named

*Lanthanide Series

58 **Ce** 140.12	59 **Pr** 140.91	60 **Nd** 144.24	61 **Pm** (145)	62 **Sm** 150.4	63 **Eu** 151.97	64 **Gd** 157.25	65 **Tb** 158.93	66 **Dy** 162.50	67 **Ho** 164.93	68 **Er** 167.26	69 **Tm** 168.93	70 **Yb** 173.04	71 **Lu** 174.97

†Actinide Series

90 **Th** 232.04	91 **Pa** 231.04	92 **U** 238.03	93 **Np** 237.05	94 **Pu** (244)	95 **Am** (243)	96 **Cm** (247)	97 **Bk** (247)	98 **Cf** (251)	99 **Es** (252)	100 **Fm** (257)	101 **Md** (258)	102 **No** (259)	103 **Lr** (260)

TABLE OF INFORMATION

Electron rest mass	m_e	=	9.11×10^{-31} kilogram
Proton rest mass	m_p	=	1.673×10^{-27} kilogram
Neutron rest mass	m_n	=	1.675×10^{-27} kilogram
Avogadro's number	N_A	=	6.02×10^{23} per mole
Universal gas constant	R	=	8.31 joules/(mole • K)
		=	0.0821 L • atm/(mole • K)
Speed of light	c	=	3.00×10^8 meters/second
1 atmosphere pressure	1 atm	=	1.0×10^5 newtons/meter^2
		=	1.0×10^5 pascals (Pa)

For H_2O:

heat of fusion	3.33×10^2 joules/gram
heat of vaporization	2.26×10^3 joules/gram
mean specific heat (liquid)	4.19 joules/(gram • K)

Volume of 1 mole of ideal gas at 0°C, 1 atmosphere   22.4 liters

EARTH AND SPACE SCIENCES: CONTENT KNOWLEDGE

1. The phases of the Moon are caused by

   (A) the varying distance of the Moon from Earth
   (B) the varying distance of the Earth from the Sun
   (C) the rotation of Earth on its axis
   (D) changes in the relative positions of the Sun, Earth, and the Moon

2. The attractive force that most strongly influences the movement of astronomical bodies is the

   (A) cohesive force
   (B) magnetic force
   (C) gravitational force
   (D) frictional force

Time (hours)	Observed Counts per Minute
0	204
1	106
2	51
3	22
4	13

3. A sample of radioactive material is monitored for one minute at hourly intervals by use of a Geiger counter, yielding the data above. Which of the following statements is INCONSISTENT with these data?

   (A) Statistical fluctuations are present in the data.
   (B) Doubling the observation times to two minutes will approximately double the number of counts recorded.
   (C) The half-life of the radioactive material is approximately one hour.
   (D) The count rate will increase in the coming hours.

4. Approximately how many years does it take for the light from Sirius, the Dog Star, to reach Earth if Sirius is about 8.3×10^{13} kilometers from Earth? (1 light-year = 9.5×10^{12} kilometers.)

   (A) 0.87 yr
   (B) 1.1 yr
   (C) 8.7 yr
   (D) 11 yr

5. If the angle of tilt of the Earth's axis were 10 degrees greater than its actual present value, people at midlatitudes would most likely experience

   (A) hotter summers and warmer winters
   (B) hotter summers and colder winters
   (C) cooler summers and warmer winters
   (D) cooler summers and colder winters

6. Which of the following statements about dark absorption lines in the solar spectrum is correct?

   (A) They correspond to elements in the Sun's atmosphere.
   (B) They generally match the size and number of sunspots.
   (C) They are due to the fusion of iron and heavier elements in the Sun's interior.
   (D) They are identical and evenly spaced.

7. Which of the following statements comparing Uranus to Mars is correct?

   (A) Uranus has a higher average surface temperature than Mars.
   (B) Uranus has a shorter period of revolution than Mars.
   (C) Uranus is smaller than Mars.
   (D) Uranus is less dense than Mars.

8. Which of the following best helps explain why there are many more impact craters on the Moon than on Earth?

(A) The Moon shields Earth from meteoroids.
(B) Erosion and crustal movements eventually destroy craters on Earth.
(C) Earth has a much greater mass than the Moon.
(D) The Moon's surface is not as hard as Earth's surface and can thus be more easily deformed by meteorites.

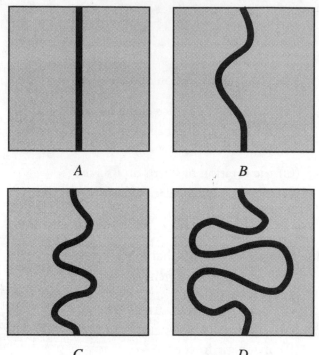

9. Which of the following best helps account for the differences in the slopes formed by different rock layers in the walls of the Grand Canyon, as shown above?

(A) Rock layers of the Grand Canyon weather and erode equally.
(B) Resistant rock layers form steep cliffs while less-resistant rock layers form gentler slopes.
(C) Glacial erosion during recent ice ages reached the Grand Canyon.
(D) The Grand Canyon is located on the Colorado Plateau.

10. The diagram above shows stages in the development of a stream. In which stage does this section of the stream most likely have the steepest gradient?

(A) A
(B) B
(C) C
(D) D

11. Which of the following best helps explain why quartz is a common mineral in sedimentary rocks?

(A) It is usually formed from the chemical weathering of other minerals.
(B) It is relatively stable in conditions found at Earth's surface.
(C) It is one of the densest minerals.
(D) Seawater contains a very high concentration of dissolved silica.

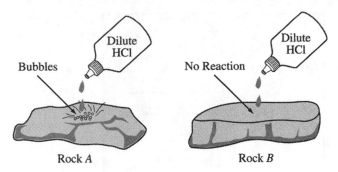

12. What can be inferred about the rock samples tested in the diagram above?

    (A) Rock A probably contains $CaCO_3$.

    (B) Rock B probably contains $CaCO_3$.

    (C) Rocks A and B are the same kind of rock.

    (D) Rocks A and B were found together.

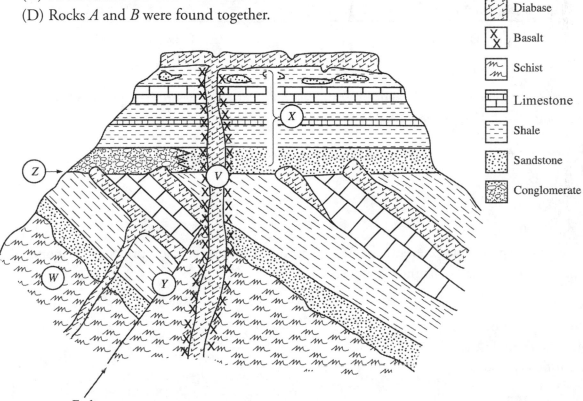

13. A geologic cross section is shown in the diagram above. Which of the following lists the features V-Z in order from oldest to youngest?

    (A) V, W, X, Y, Z

    (B) W, Y, Z, X, V

    (C) W, Z, Y, V, X

    (D) V, X, Z, Y, W

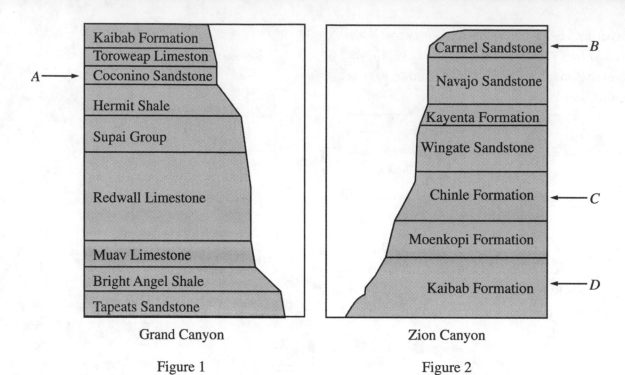

Figure 1 — Grand Canyon

Figure 2 — Zion Canyon

14. The figures shown above are rock columns from two different canyons on the Colorado Plateau. Of the following, which layer is the oldest?

(A) *A*
(B) *B*
(C) *C*
(D) *D*

15. The concept that past geologic events can be explained by the same physical principles that operate now, and in much the same manner, is known as

(A) evolution
(B) uniformitarianism
(C) catastrophism
(D) scientific method

Questions 16-17 are based on the graph below, which shows the average water level of a river in North America over a period of one year (September-August).

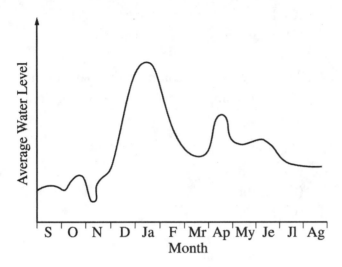

16. In what season did the watershed of the river probably receive the least amount of precipitation?

    (A) Summer
    (B) Fall
    (C) Winter
    (D) Spring

17. In what month did this river have the ability to carry the greatest load (bed load, suspended load, and dissolved load)?

    (A) January
    (B) February
    (C) May
    (D) November

18. In which of the following tectonic settings are the Hawaiian Islands located?

    (A) On a midocean ridge
    (B) At a convergent plate boundary
    (C) On the edge of a trench
    (D) Over a hot spot

19. Which of the following statements about earthquakes is correct?

    (A) Earthquakes occur only at plate boundaries.
    (B) During an earthquake, movement along the fault occurs only at Earth's surface.
    (C) Stored-up energy is released in the form of seismic waves.
    (D) An earthquake with a magnitude of 4 on the Richter scale releases approximately twice as much energy as an earthquake with a magnitude of 2.

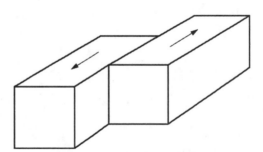

20. In the diagram above, which of the following types of faulting is being exhibited?

    (A) Normal
    (B) Reverse
    (C) Right-lateral strike slip
    (D) Left-lateral strike slip

21. Which of the following mineral properties would be most useful in distinguishing fluorite from quartz?

    (A) Color
    (B) Streak
    (C) Luster
    (D) Hardness

22. Which of the following pairs are clastic sedimentary rocks?

    (A) Conglomerate and shale
    (B) Granite and basalt
    (C) Rhyolite and gabbro
    (D) Travertine and geyserite

23. The rock sequence of shale → slate → phyllite → schist → gneiss illustrates a sequence of

    (A) sedimentation
    (B) weathering
    (C) metamorphism
    (D) lithification

24. In what regions of the world would aridisols most commonly be found?

    (A) Tropical
    (B) Humid temperate
    (C) Desert
    (D) Swamp

25. The lava flows that comprise the maria of the Moon are composed mostly of which of the following?

    (A) Rhyolite
    (B) Granite
    (C) Gabbro
    (D) Basalt

Questions 26-27 are based on the diagrams below, which show cylinders containing glass beads. The beads simulate clastic sediments. The cylinders containing the beads were filled with water, and the length of time it took for the water to drain out of each cylinder was recorded.

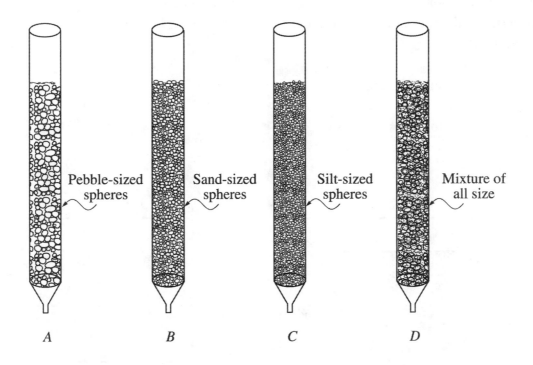

26. Which cylinder will the water drain out of at the fastest rate?

    (A) *A*
    (B) *B*
    (C) *C*
    (D) *D*

27. Which of the cylinders contains the most poorly sorted sediment?

    (A) *A*
    (B) *B*
    (C) *C*
    (D) *D*

28. A soil profile that includes a caliche zone would most likely form under which of the following climatic conditions?

    (A) Precipitation greater than potential evapotranspiration
    (B) Potential evapotranspiration greater than precipitation
    (C) Cold climate
    (D) Very warm and humid climate

29. Which of the following cross sections of the eastern equatorial Pacific Ocean best shows an El Niño event?

(A)
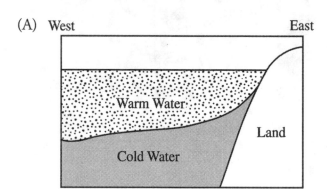

(B)
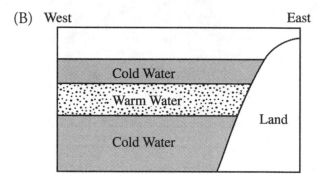

(C)
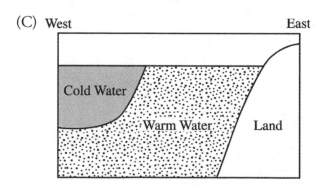

(D)
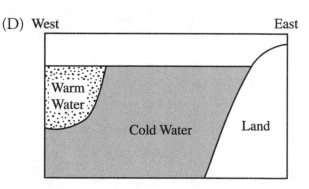

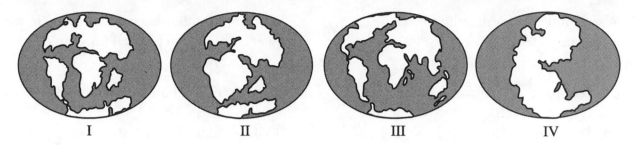

| I | II | III | IV |

30. The maps above show the orientation of Earth's landmasses at four different times. Which of the following gives the correct sequence, from first to last?

(A) I, II, III, IV
(B) I, III, IV, II
(C) IV, I, II, III
(D) IV, II, I, III

Temperature Regimes	Bowen's Reaction Series	Igneous Rock Types
High temperature First to crystallize	Olivine / Pyroxene / Amphibole / Biotite mica — Discontinuous Series of Crystallization; Calcium-rich / Sodium-rich — Plagioclase feldspar Continuous Series of Crystallization; Cooling magma	Komatiite/ Peridotite
		Basalt/ Gabbro
		Andesite/ Diorite
Low temperature Last to crystallize	Potassium feldspar / Muscovite mica / Quartz	Rhyolite/ Granite

31. Which of the rocks shown in the diagram above is classified as ultramafic?

(A) Peridotite
(B) Andesite
(C) Diorite
(D) Granite

32. Which of the following minerals is a carbonate?

   (A) Quartz
   (B) Feldspar
   (C) Gypsum
   (D) Dolomite

33. Which of the following elements makes up the largest percentage, by mass, of Earth's core?

   (A) Aluminum
   (B) Iron
   (C) Magnesium
   (D) Silicon

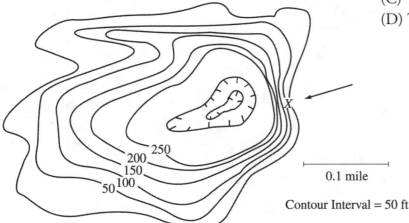

0.1 mile

Contour Interval = 50 ft

34. Which of the following land features is represented at location *X*?

   (A) Valley
   (B) Depression
   (C) Cliff
   (D) Hilltop

35. Which of the following best helps explain why water is an agent in physical (mechanical) weathering?

   (A) It absorbs carbon dioxide from the air and becomes acidic.
   (B) It expands when it freezes.
   (C) It dissolves many nonsilicate minerals.
   (D) It exists in the crystal structures of hydrous minerals.

36. Which of the following statements about the large rock fragments found in a sedimentary breccia is most likely true?

   (A) They were loosened during an earthquake.
   (B) They did not travel far from their source.
   (C) The are composed primarily of calcite.
   (D) They were formed during a drought.

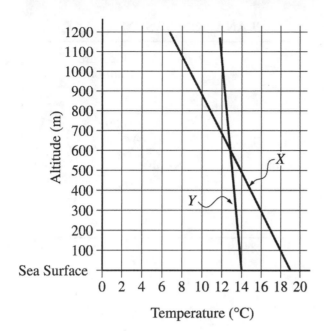

Altitude (m)

Temperature (°C)

Table of Dew Points

Dry-Bulb Temperature	Dry-Bulb Temperature Minus Wet-Bulb Temperature					
	3	4	5	6	7	8
65	60	59	57	55	53	51
70	65	64	62	61	59	57
75	71	69	68	66	64	63

38. On the basis of the table above, if the dry-bulb temperature is 73°F and the wet-bulb temperature is 67°F, the dew point is closest to

(A) 68°F

(B) 66°F

(C) 64°F

(D) 61°F

37. The graph above depicts the conditions for a rising parcel of air. Line *X* shows how the temperature of the parcel of air changes with altitude. If a cloud forms at the intersection of *X* and *Y*, what does line *Y* represent?

(A) Dew point

(B) Air Pressure

(C) Relative humidity

(D) Absolute humidity

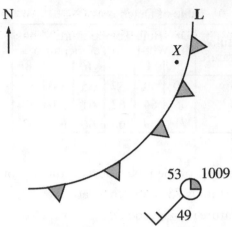

EXPLANATION OF SYMBOLS

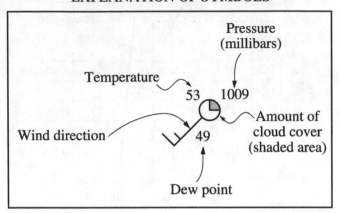

39. The map above shows a cold front and a low-pressure region in the midlatitudes of the Northern Hemisphere. Which of the following weather symbols shows the conditions that most likely exist at point X on the map?

(A)

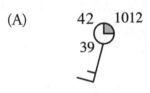

(B)

(C)

(D)

40. When it is Tuesday in the United States and midnight on the international date line, what day is it in Japan?

(A) Sunday
(B) Monday
(C) Tuesday
(D) Wednesday

41. What is the airflow pattern near the center of a high-pressure system as it moves across the United States?

(A) Downward and outward in clockwise spiral

(B) Downward and inward in a counterclockwise spiral

(C) Upward and outward in a clockwise spiral

(D) Upward and inward in a counterclockwise spiral

42. What is the airflow pattern near the center of a low-pressure system as it moves across the United States?

(A) Downward and outward in clockwise spiral

(B) Downward and inward in a counterclockwise spiral

(C) Upward and outward in a clockwise spiral

(D) Upward and inward in a counterclockwise spiral

43. Which of the following graphs best shows how the temperature of the atmosphere varies with altitude?

(A)
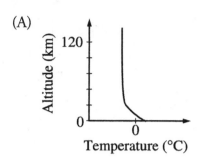

(B)
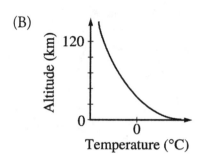

(C)
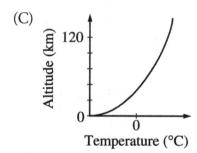

(D)
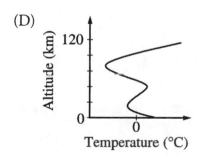

VARIATION OF SOLAR RADIATION RECEIVED ON HORIZONTAL SURFACES
AT DIFFERENT LATITUDES

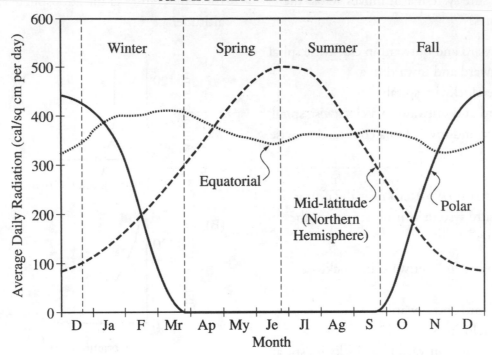

44. The diagram shown above depicts the variation in solar radiation received on horizontal surfaces at different latitudes. Which of the following locations receives about the same amount of average daily solar radiation throughout the year?

(A) Arctic
(B) Midlatitude (Northern Hemisphere)
(C) Equatorial
(D) Antarctic

45. Which of the following statements about island arcs is correct?

(A) They generally form far from plate boundaries.
(B) They rarely have earthquakes associated with them.
(C) The only lava produced at island arcs is basalt.
(D) The Aleutians are an example of an island arc.

46. How does the composition of the basaltic lava from Hawaiian volcanoes compare to the composition of the pyroclastic material emitted from Mount St. Helens?

(A) The basalt is more silicic.
(B) The basalt contains more light-colored minerals.
(C) The basalt has a higher concentration of ferromagnesian minerals.
(D) The basalt has a lower concentration of olivine.

SEQUENCE OF MINERALS FORMED IN METAMORPHOSED BASALT

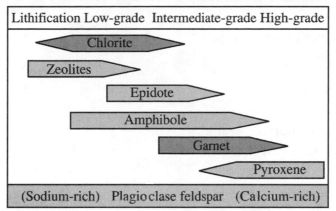

47. On the basis of the diagram above, which of the following groups of minerals is most likely to make up a large fraction of an intermediate-grade metamorphosed basalt?

(A) Chlorite, zeolite, and pyroxene
(B) Chlorite, pyroxene, and sodium-rich plagioclase
(C) Zeolite, garnet, and calcium-rich plagioclase
(D) Epidote, amphibole, garnet, and plagioclase

48. Which of the following processes most likely accounts for the features in the diagram above being out of alignment?

(A) Mudflow
(B) Slumping
(C) Rockslide
(D) Soil creep

49. A sequence of cirrus, cirrostratus, altostratus, and stratus clouds most likely indicates which of the following weather changes from the initial fair weather condition?

    (A) Extended precipitation followed by warmer weather
    (B) Hailstorms followed by warmer weather
    (C) Rain and sleet followed by clear and cooler weather
    (D) Thunderstorms followed by clear and cooler weather

50. Which of the following best helps account for the fact that many low-lying islands are suffering from increased flooding?

    (A) Volcanic eruptions
    (B) Movement of tectonic plates
    (C) Rising sea levels
    (D) Urban sprawl

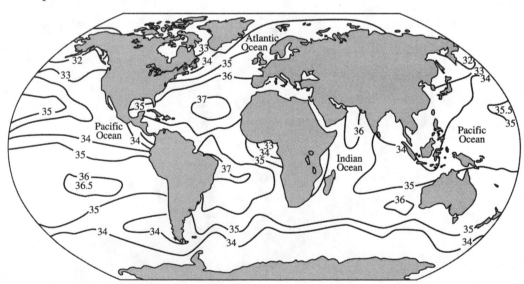

51. Which of the following properties of seawater is plotted on the world map above?

    (A) Density
    (B) Temperature
    (C) Dissolved oxygen concentration
    (D) Salinity

52. Which of the following types of seawater has the greatest density?

    (A) Warm, with low salinity
    (B) Warm, with high salinity
    (C) Cold, with low salinity
    (D) Cold, with high salinity

53. Which of the following is associated with the end of the Cretaceous period?

    (A) Mass extinctions
    (B) The evolution of the first mammals
    (C) The formation of Pangaea
    (D) The last ice age

54. Which of the following is generally NOT associated with midocean ridges?

    (A) Rift valleys
    (B) Guyots
    (C) Fracture zones
    (D) Hydrothermal vents

55. Which of the following best explains why the magnetic bands recorded on isochron maps of a midocean ridge of the eastern Pacific Ocean are farther apart than similar bands on either side of the Mid-Atlantic Ridge?

    (A) The magma formed at the eastern Pacific Ridge is less viscous than the magma formed at the Mid-Atlantic Ridge.
    (B) The rate of spreading at the eastern Pacific Ridge is less than that of the Mid-Atlantic Ridge.
    (C) The rate of spreading at the eastern Pacific Ridge is greater than that of the Mid-Atlantic Ridge.
    (D) There are more subduction zones in the Pacific Ocean than in the Atlantic Ocean.

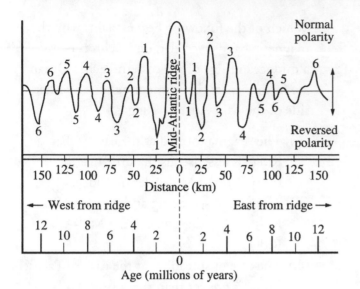

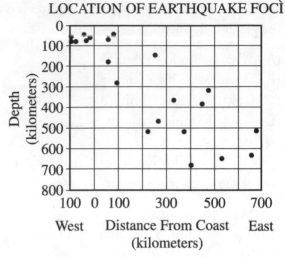

LOCATION OF EARTHQUAKE FOCÌ

56. Based on the diagram above, what is the average rate of movement of the plates on each side of the Mid-Atlantic Ridge?

(A) 0.8 cm/yr
(B) 1.3 cm/yr
(C) 1.6 cm/yr
(D) 2.6 cm/yr

57. Which of the following forces is responsible for the movement along a strike-slip fault such as the San Andreas Fault?

(A) Shearing
(B) Compression
(C) Tension
(D) Gravity

58. Which of the following features commonly form at continent-continent convergent plate boundaries?

(A) Oceanic trenches
(B) Island arcs
(C) Folded and/or faulted mountains
(D) Guyots

59. The information in the graph above was most likely obtained from which of the following tectonic settings?

(A) Subduction zone
(B) Midocean ridge
(C) Rift valley
(D) Transform fault

60. Regions that geologists refer to as "exotic terranes" would most likely be found in which of the following locations?

(A) Iceland
(B) Hawaii
(C) The Florida Everglades
(D) The west coast of Canada

61. Which of the following is mostly directly responsible for the textural foliation (schistosity) in metamorphic rocks?

(A) High temperature
(B) High pressure
(C) Low temperature
(D) Low pressure

ROCK COMPOSITION

	Rock A	Rock B	Rock C	Rock D
Quartz	5	35	0	0
Potassium feldspar	0	15	0	0
Plagioclase feldspar	55	25	0	55
Biotite	15	15	0	10
Amphibole	25	10	0	30
Pyroxene	0	0	40	5
Olivine	0	0	60	0

62. Which of the rocks in the diagram above could be a granite?

(A) A
(B) B
(C) C
(D) D

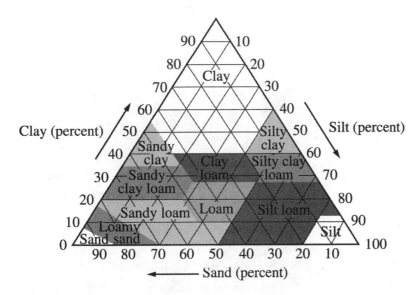

63. Based on the diagram above, a soil sample consisting of 50 percent sand, 20 percent silt, and 30 percent clay would be classified as

(A) loam
(B) sandy clay loam
(C) silt loam
(D) clay

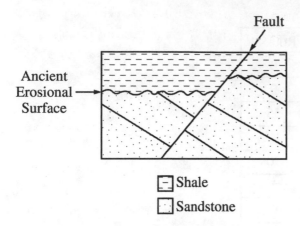

Shale

Sandstone

64. On the basis of the geologic cross section above, which of the following most likely occurred first?

(A) Movement along the fault
(B) Tilting of the sandstone
(C) Deposition of the shale material
(D) Deposition of the sandstone material

65. Which of the following diagrams best shows the cross section of a cold front?

(A)

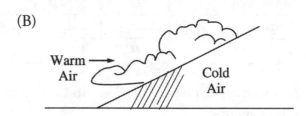

(B)

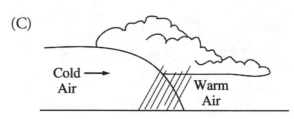

(C)

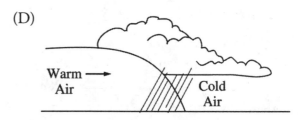

(D)

66. Which of the following is NOT a major cause of pollution in surface water and groundwater?

(A) Landfill leachate
(B) Industrial effluent
(C) Chlorofluorocarbons
(D) Agricultural chemicals

67. A student conducts an experiment on heat absorption using equal masses of soil and water in identical containers. The soil and water start out at the same temperature, which is lower than the air temperature. Which of the following would most likely be observed after the soil and water have been exposed to bright sunlight for 30 minutes?

    (A) The temperature of the soil and the water did not change.
    (B) The temperature of the soil did not change, but the temperature of the water increased.
    (C) The temperature of the water increased more than the temperature of the soil.
    (D) The temperature of the soil increased more than the temperature of the water.

68. Overuse of groundwater in coastal areas would most likely result in which of the following?

    (A) The intrusion of salt water into the aquifer
    (B) The contamination of the aquifer with bacteria
    (C) A decrease in the porosity of the aquifer
    (D) An increase in the rate of dissolution of calcium carbonate into the groundwater

69. Scientists have proposed that the burning of fossil fuels increases the concentration of CO_2 in the atmosphere. It has been predicted that which of the following will occur if the concentration of CO_2 continues to rise?

    (A) Earth's surface will have increased exposure to ultraviolet rays.
    (B) The average annual surface temperature will increase.
    (C) Animals will be harmed by breathing the higher levels of CO_2.
    (D) The ozone layer will disappear.

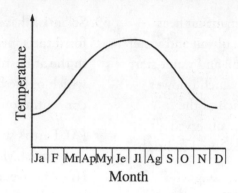

70. The average monthly temperature for a noncoastal city in the continental United States is shown in the graph above. Which of the following graphs most likely shows the average monthly temperature for a city on the West Coast at the same latitude?

(A)

(B)

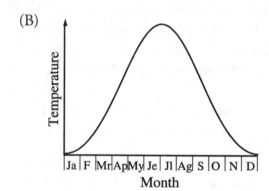

(C)

(D)

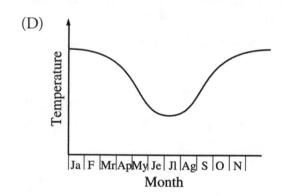

71. Which of the following best explains why a hypothesis is easier to disprove than to prove?

    (A) Formulating a hypothesis is the first step in the application of scientific thinking to a problem; disproving a second step is easier than disproving the first step.
    (B) The scientific method does not need to be followed in an experiment designed to disprove a hypothesis.
    (C) Measurements with precision can disprove a hypothesis; measurements must have both accuracy and precision to prove a hypothesis.
    (D) One experiment may disprove a hypothesis, but favorable results from many experiments do not necessarily prove a hypothesis.

72. Which of the following factors help(s) to account for the fact that, in the United States, lands to the east of a mountain range generally receive less precipitation than lands to the west of the mountain range?

    I. Air masses often move from west to east in the United States.
    II. An air mass cools as it rises on its way over a mountain range.
    III. The maximum amount of water vapor that a sample of cold air can contain is less than the amount that a sample of warm air can contain.

    (A) I only
    (B) II only
    (C) II and III only
    (D) I, II, and III

73. Some lakes in southeastern Canada and the northeastern United States are becoming depleted of living organisms. Which of the following is most often the primary cause?

    (A) Nuclear waste
    (B) Lowered water levels
    (C) Garbage dumping
    (D) Acid deposition

74. Which of the following properties of water most directly helps account for its ability to dissolve many salts?

    (A) Its molecules are polar.
    (B) It has a high heat capacity.
    (C) It has a high surface tension.
    (D) It expands when it freezes.

75. Which of the following best describes cosmic background radiation?

    (A) The most dangerous radiation given off during supernova explosions
    (B) Residual radiation from the big bang
    (C) The harmful radiation given off by the Sun, which the atmosphere usually blocks
    (D) The radiation emitted from matter that enters a black hole

Chapter 14

Right Answers and Explanations for the Practice Questions for the *Earth and Space Sciences: Content Knowledge* Test

▶ ▶ ▶ ▶ ▶ ▶ ▶ ▶ ▶ ▶ ▶ ▶

Right Answers and Explanations for the Practice Questions

Now that you have answered all of the practice questions, you can check your work.
Compare your answers with the correct answers in the table below.

Question Number	Correct Answer	Content Category
1	D	Astronomy
2	C	Astronomy
3	D	Basic Scientific Principles of Earth and Space Sciences
4	C	Astronomy
5	B	Astronomy
6	A	Astronomy
7	D	Astronomy
8	B	Astronomy
9	B	Earth Materials and Surface Processes
10	A	Earth Materials and Surface Processes
11	B	Earth Materials and Surface Processes
12	A	Earth Materials and Surface Processes
13	B	History of Earth and Its Life Forms
14	A	History of Earth and Its Life Forms
15	B	History of Earth and Its Life Forms
16	B	Earth's Atmosphere and Hydrosphere
17	A	Earth's Atmosphere and Hydrosphere
18	D	Tectonics and Internal Earth Processes
19	C	Tectonics and Internal Earth Processes
20	D	Tectonics and Internal Earth Processes
21	D	Earth Materials and Surface Processes
22	A	Earth Materials and Surface Processes
23	C	Earth Materials and Surface Processes
24	C	Earth Materials and Surface Processes
25	D	Astronomy
26	A	Earth's Atmosphere and Hydrosphere
27	D	Earth Materials and Surface Processes
28	B	Earth Materials and Surface Processes
29	A	Earth's Atmosphere and Hydrosphere
30	D	History of Earth and Its Life Forms
31	A	Earth Materials and Surface Processes
32	D	Earth Materials and Surface Processes
33	B	Earth Materials and Surface Processes
34	C	Earth Materials and Surface Processes
35	B	Basic Scientific Principles of Earth and Space Sciences
36	B	Earth Materials and Surface Processes
37	A	Earth's Atmosphere and Hydrosphere
38	C	Earth's Atmosphere and Hydrosphere

Question Number	Correct Answer	Content Category
39	D	Earth's Atmosphere and Hydrosphere
40	C	Astronomy
41	A	Earth's Atmosphere and Hydrosphere
42	D	Earth's Atmosphere and Hydrosphere
43	D	Earth's Atmosphere and Hydrosphere
44	C	Earth's Atmosphere and Hydrosphere
45	D	Tectonics and Internal Earth Processes
46	C	Tectonics and Internal Earth Processes
47	D	Earth Materials and Surface Processes
48	D	Earth Materials and Surface Processes
49	A	Earth's Atmosphere and Hydrosphere
50	C	Earth's Atmosphere and Hydrosphere
51	D	Earth's Atmosphere and Hydrosphere
52	D	Earth's Atmosphere and Hydrosphere
53	A	History of Earth and its Life Forms
54	B	Tectonics and Internal Earth Processes
55	C	Tectonics and Internal Earth Processes
56	B	Basic Scientific Principles of Earth and Space Sciences (Use of Measurement Systems)
57	A	Tectonics and Internal Earth Processes
58	C	Tectonics and Internal Earth Processes
59	A	Tectonics and Internal Earth Processes
60	D	Tectonics and Internal Earth Processes
61	B	Earth Materials and Surface Processes
62	B	Earth Materials and Surface Processes
63	B	Earth Materials and Surface Processes
64	D	History of Earth and Its Life Forms
65	C	Earth's Atmosphere and Hydrosphere
66	C	Earth's Atmosphere and Hydrosphere
67	D	Basic Scientific Principles of Earth and Space Sciences
68	A	Earth's Atmosphere and Hydrosphere
69	B	Basic Scientific Principles of Earth and Space Sciences
70	A	Earth's Atmosphere and Hydrosphere
71	D	Basic Scientific Principles of Earth and Space Sciences
72	D	Earth's Atmosphere and Hydrosphere
73	D	Basic Scientific Principles of Earth and Space Sciences
74	A	Basic Scientific Principles of Earth and Space Sciences
75	B	Astronomy

Explanations of Right Answers

1. The Moon does not emit its own light but reflects light received from the Sun. The half of the Moon facing the Sun is lit, and the phases of the Moon, as observed from Earth, depend on how much of the lit portion of the Moon is visible at the time of observation. The amount changes as the Moon revolves around Earth. The correct answer, therefore, is (D).

2. Since the time of Newton, the motion of astronomical bodies has been modeled successfully using gravitational force alone. The other forces, if they have any effect, are much less important. The correct answer, therefore, is (C).

3. Three of the four choices are consistent with the data given. Although statistical fluctuations are present in the data, the fact that the counts decrease by approximately one-half each hour indicates that the half-life is approximately one hour. An increasing count rate in the coming hours is not consistent with the data. The correct answer, therefore, is (D).

4. A light-year is one of the units astronomers use to measure distances in space. A light-year is defined as the distance light travels in one year and is equal to 9.5×10^{12} kilometers.

Since the number of years =
$$\frac{\text{distance in kilometers}}{\text{speed in kilometers per year}}$$
then the number of years =
$$\frac{8.3 \times 10^{13} \text{ kilometers}}{9.5 \times 10^{12} \text{ kilometers per year}}$$
which is 8.7 years. The correct answer, therefore, is (C).

5. The seasons are primarily due to Earth's tilt on its axis as it revolves around the Sun. On the first day of summer in the Northern Hemisphere, the Northern Hemisphere is tilted towards the Sun and the Sun is directly overhead at the tropic of Cancer at solar noon. When Sun angles are high (high solar path through the sky), the intensity of radiation is high. If Earth were tilted even more on its axis, on the first day of summer the Sun would be directly overhead at a latitude further north than the tropic of Cancer. Sun angles at midlatitudes of the Northern Hemisphere would be higher, and the intensity of the radiation would be greater. The number of hours of daylight at midlatitudes would also be greater, further increasing the amount of radiation received at a given location. The opposite would happen in the winter: Sun angles would be lower and the days would be shorter. The correct answer, therefore, is (B).

6. A hot, dense gas emits a continuous spectrum. The continuous spectrum of the Sun initially includes all wavelengths of visible light. When this radiation enters the relatively cool, less-dense gas cloud around the Sun, some of the radiation that matches energy-level differences in the atoms of the cooler gas is absorbed by the atoms. The resulting spectrum thus contains a series of dark absorption lines whose wavelengths are characteristic of elements in the relatively cool gas cloud. The correct answer, therefore, is (A).

7. The four inner planets, Mercury, Venus, Earth, and Mars, are called terrestrial planets. Jupiter, Saturn, Uranus, and Neptune are giant planets; they are much larger than the terrestrial planets and differ from them greatly in composition. Uranus is a gas- and ice-rich planet with a relatively low density. It is much farther away from the Sun than Mars, takes much longer to orbit the Sun, and has a much lower surface temperature. The correct answer, therefore, is (D).

8. Both Earth and the Moon were hit by many meteorites early in their history, but the frequency of the impacts has decreased significantly. Erosion and processes associated with plate tectonics have removed most of Earth's impact structures. In addition, small meteoroids burn up in Earth's atmosphere. The correct answer, therefore, is (B).

9. The horizontal layers of sedimentary rock seen in the walls of the Grand Canyon are composed of alternating layers of sandstone, shale, limestone, and so on. The limestone layers in the Grand Canyon are quite resistant to weathering in the dry climate, while the shale layers tend to be less resistant. This leads to differential weathering and erosion whereby the limestone layers yield steep slopes while the shale layers have gentler slopes. The correct answer, therefore, is (B).

10. A youthful stream, a stream beginning to develop a drainage system, generally has a relatively steep gradient. Its velocity is greatest, and it cuts straight, steep, and narrow valleys. Base level is the level where the stream enters a larger body of water. Streams cannot go lower than base level. As streams develop, they cut down toward base level, widen their valleys, and may start to meander. The stream with the steepest gradient, therefore, is (A).

11. Quartz is a major component of some common igneous and metamorphic rocks, such as granite and quartzite. When these rocks weather, quartz grains are likely to survive because quartz is a relatively hard and insoluble mineral, and therefore very resistant to physical and chemical weathering. Also, when the cement in a quartz sandstone dissolves, the resistant quartz grains may be transported and become part of another sedimentary rock. The correct answer, therefore, is (B).

12. The most common field test for whether or not a rock specimen contains calcium carbonate is the acid test. A few drops of cold, dilute hydrochloric acid (HCl) are placed on the surface of the rock and observed. If bubbles are produced, the sample contains a carbonate mineral, most likely $CaCO_3$. Calcite is the most common carbonate mineral. Some carbonates fizz only if the acid is hot or if the mineral is powered (e.g., dolomite). The correct answer, therefore, is (A).

13. In this area, the basement rock (labeled W) is schist, a metamorphic rock. A layer of sand was deposited on top of the schist, and then the other sedimentary layers that are now below the angular unconformity (labeled Z) were deposited. Sometime after the first sandstone, shale, and limestone layers were formed, faulting occurred at Y. The fault must be younger than the layers it offsets. The rock units in the region were tilted (it may have been before, during, or after the faulting), and then the surface was eroded, producing a new surface at Z. The sedimentary layers at X were then deposited. Molten igneous material cut through the existing tilted layers and the layers labeled X, producing the igneous rock at V. The correct answer, therefore, is (B).

14. The law of superposition states that in a sequence of sedimentary strata that has not been overturned, the oldest rock layer is on the bottom and the youngest layer is at the top. The rock layers in the two stratigraphic columns can be correlated. The Kaibab Formation is found in both canyons, being the youngest formation shown in the Grand Canyon stratigraphic column and the oldest formation shown in the Zion Canyon column. The Coconino sandstone is below the Kaibab Formation in the Grand Canyon stratigraphic column, and therefore the oldest of the four choices given. The correct answer, therefore, is (A).

15. The principle of uniformitarianism states that geological processes and natural laws now operating also operated in the past. Past geological events can be explained by phenomena and forces observable today. The correct answer is (B).

16. The water levels in streams generally increase as a result of precipitation or snowmelt. From the trend in the graph, winter is a time of relatively high precipitation, while fall is a time of low precipitation. The correct answer, therefore, is (B).

17. The load of a stream consists of all that a stream can move in solution (dissolved load), bounce along the bed (bed load), or carry in suspension (suspended load). The capacity of a stream to transport its load depends on its discharge, the volume of water that flows past a given point per unit time. Water levels were highest in this river in January, so the discharge was highest then. The correct answer, therefore, is (A).

18. The Hawaiian Islands are near the center of the Pacific Plate, not at a plate boundary. It is suggested that the chain of Hawaiian Islands was the result of the Pacific plate's moving over a hot spot. The correct answer, therefore, is (D).

19. Earthquakes occur most often at plate boundaries, but they also occur in other areas. The focus of an earthquake can be hundreds of

kilometers below Earth's surface. At a fault, two blocks are pushed in different directions, but the friction between them can prevent them from moving. The rock is strained, and elastic energy is stored in the rock until the frictional bond at the fault breaks and energy is released in the form of seismic vibrations. The Richter scale (which has largely been replaced with different scales, such as the moment magnitude scale) is related to the logarithm of the maximum amplitude of seismic waves. The difference in the amount of energy released by earthquakes of different magnitudes is much greater than the difference in magnitude. An earthquake with a magnitude of 4 releases, very roughly, about a thousand times as much energy as one with a magnitude of 2. The correct answer, therefore, is (C).

20. No vertical movement is indicated. The arrows show movement parallel to the strike of the fault. In a left-lateral strike-slip fault, the side opposite the observer appears to be displaced to the left. The correct answer, therefore, is (D).

21. Color is not always a reliable characteristic in helping to identify minerals. In this case, both specimens could be the same color. Streak is the color of the powder of the mineral obtained by rubbing the mineral on an unglazed tile. Both specimens have a colorless or white streak. Luster is the way the mineral's surface reflects light. Fluorite and quartz have the same luster. Hardness is the mineral's

resistance to scratching. Quartz has a hardness of 7 on the Mohs scale, and fluorite has a hardness of 4. The correct answer, therefore, is (D).

22. Chemical sedimentary rocks are the result of processes such as evaporation or precipitation. Clastic sedimentary rocks are made of particles compressed or cemented together. The correct answer, therefore, is (A).

23. Sedimentation is the process by which sediments accumulate in layers, perhaps to undergo lithification (the conversion of sediment to rock) at a later time. Metamorphic rocks are derived from preexisting igneous, sedimentary, or metamorphic rock in response to increases in temperature and pressure. The sequence identified is typical of metamorphism. The correct answer, therefore, is (C).

24. Aridisols are soils of dry regions. They are typical of desert areas, including cold polar deserts, cool temperate deserts, and warm deserts. The correct answer, therefore, is (C).

25. The lunar maria are relatively smooth and dark areas with few craters. As known from lunar rock samples and surface features, the maria are vast layers of thin basaltic lava that flowed into depressions and flooded large parts of the lunar surface. The correct answer, therefore, is (D).

26. Permeability is the capability of sediment or rock to permit the flow of fluids through its pore spaces. The rate at which water can flow is related to the size of the pores in the sediment or rock and to what degree the pore spaces are connected. The smaller and less connected the pore spaces, the lower the permeability. The larger and more connected the pore spaces, the greater the rate of flow. The correct answer, therefore, is (A).

27. Poorly sorted sediment consists of particles of many sizes mixed together. The correct answer, therefore, is (D).

28. Caliche is a calcareous material commonly found in layers on or near the surface of soils in arid and semiarid regions. The correct answer, therefore, is (B).

29. El Niño is a large-scale anomaly in the ocean and atmosphere often signaled by changes in atmospheric conditions in which the trade winds are weaker than average over the equatorial Pacific. Because of the weakened condition of the trade winds, warm surface water drifts to the east. The upwelling of cold, nutrient-rich ocean waters is cut off. The resulting impact is El Niño. The correct answer, therefore, is (A).

30. The present continents were derived from the supercontinent Pangaea through fragmentation and continental drift. The maps show several stages in this breakup. The correct answer is (D).

31. Ultramafic igneous rocks are composed chiefly of mafic minerals, which are ferromagnesian minerals such as olivine and certain types of pyroxene. Mafic and ultramafic rocks are dark colored. Basalt and gabbro are mafic rocks, and peridotite is classified as an ultramafic rock. The correct answer, therefore, is (A).

32. Quartz and feldspar are both in the silicate group of minerals. Gypsum is a sulfate ($CaSO_4 \cdot 2H_2O$), and dolomite is a carbonate, $CaMg(CO_3)_2$. The correct answer, therefore, is (D).

33. Earth's innermost layer, the core, is made mostly of iron, with some nickel, and with minor amounts of less dense elements, possibly silicon, sulfur, or oxygen. The correct answer, therefore, is (B).

34. Contour lines on a topographic map are used to show shape and elevation. The close spacing of contour lines in a short distance indicates a rapid change in elevation. The correct answer, therefore, is (C).

35. In mechanical weathering, rock is broken into fragments without involving chemical change. Water can go into tiny cracks in rocks. When the water freezes and expands, the force can enlarge the cracks and finally help split the rock. Options (A) and (C) are related to chemical weathering, not physical weathering. The correct answer, therefore, is (B).

36. A breccia is a coarse-grained rock composed of angular fragments in a finer-grained matrix. Sediment particles generally become more well rounded the further they are transported from their source. The correct answer, therefore, is (B).

37. Clouds form when a parcel of air cools to its dew point. The dew point is the temperature at which the air reaches 100 percent relative humidity and becomes saturated. Since both lines represent temperature and X is the actual temperature, then line Y must indicate the changing dew point with altitude. The correct answer, therefore, is (A).

38. The dew point is the temperature to which air must be cooled for it to be saturated (100% relative humidity). The dew point can be determined by using a psychrometer and a table like the one given. To find the dew point, subtract the wet-bulb reading from the dry-bulb reading. Locate that number (in this case 6°F) in the top row of numbers in the table. Interpolate where 73°F would be in the left-most column, and move to the right until you get to the column with the 6°F wet-bulb depression. The dew point is between 61°F and 66°F. The correct answer, therefore, is (C).

39. The temperature and dew point should be lower at point X, where the cold front has already passed, than at the point where the conditions are known. Point X is also closer to the center of low pressure, so the pressure should be lower than 1,009 mb. The difference in dew point shows that the air to the west of the front is drier than the air to the east of it. Since point X is close to the front, it is likely that it will be cloudy there. The passing of a cold front is also associated with a shift in the wind direction, as shown in (D). The correct answer, therefore, is (D).

40. The international date line keeps calendars on the correct date for world travelers. When it is midnight on the international date line, the entire world is on the same day for just that moment. The correct answer, therefore, is (C).

41. Air flows away from the center of a high-pressure system, and air from higher altitudes moves down to take its place. In the Northern Hemisphere, the surface air moves away from the high in a clockwise spiral. The correct answer, therefore, is (A).

42. Air flows toward the center of a low-pressure system, and its convergence causes air to rise. In the Northern Hemisphere, the surface air flowing toward the low moves in a counterclockwise spiral. The correct answer, therefore, is (D).

43. Temperature decreases with altitude in the troposphere, but the pattern of temperature in the atmosphere is not simple. For example, the ozone layer strongly absorbs radiation of certain wavelengths, which results in the high temperature at about 50 kilometers altitude. The correct answer, therefore, is (D).

44. The graph shows that the curve for equatorial regions has the least variation in average daily radiation over the course of a year. The average daily radiation at a given location depends on the number of hours of daylight and the intensity of the radiation. The correct answer, therefore, is (C).

45. Island arcs form at convergent boundaries where two oceanic plates meet. A system of volcanoes, intrusions, and metamorphic rocks forms on the edge of the overriding plate. The igneous rocks produced tend to be andesitic lava and granitic intrusives, though other types are possible. The correct answer, therefore, is (D).

46. Basalt is composed mostly of pyroxene, plagioclase feldspar, and olivine. Ferromagnesian minerals, such as olivine and pyroxene, are dark-colored minerals that contain a significant amount of iron and/or magnesium. The material emitted from Mount St. Helens was more silicic. The correct answer, therefore, is (C).

47. The diagram shows the sequence of minerals that forms from basalt as it passes through higher and higher grades of metamorphism. Epidote, amphibole, garnet, and a plagioclase feldspar of intermediate composition line up vertically and are likely to coexist in an intermediate-grade metamorphic rock. The correct answer, therefore, is (D).

48. Soil creep is the gradual downhill movement of soil and loose rock material on a slope. Material on the hillside shows evidence of moving downhill under the influence of gravity. Note the tilted fence, telephone pole, sign, guardrails, conifers, and the curved trunk of the deciduous tree. The correct answer, therefore, is (D).

49. A lowering sequence of stratiform clouds signifies an approaching warm front, which usually means some steady rain, followed by clearing and warmer weather. The correct answer, therefore, is (A).

50. The melting of glaciers and polar ice over the past several thousand years has resulted in an increase in sea level. Higher air temperatures also warm the ocean waters and cause an expansion of the water. The correct answer, therefore, is (C).

51. In subtropical regions of the ocean, evaporation generally exceeds precipitation, thereby resulting in relatively high salinity of surface ocean waters. Abundant rainfall in equatorial areas results in low salinity. It is possible to note where some large rivers drain into the oceans. The isolines summarize salinity, which is, on average, about 35 parts per thousand in surface ocean water. The correct answer, therefore, is (D).

52. The density of seawater depends on temperature, salinity, and pressure. Cold water is denser than warm water, and seawater is denser than freshwater. The correct answer, therefore, is (D).

53. Mammals first appeared in the Triassic, Pangaea existed between about 200 million and 300 million years ago, and the latest glacial epoch was the Pleistocene. There were mass extinctions at the end of the Cretaceous, possibly due to climate changes brought about by the impact of a large meteorite. The correct answer, therefore, is (A).

54. A guyot is a flat-topped seamount (undersea mountain). The flat top is caused by erosion during emergence. Seamounts are formed from molten material rising at hot spots and are thus not generally associated with midocean ridges. The correct answer, therefore, is (B).

55. The magnetic anomalies found on each side of midocean ridges are associated with reversals of Earth's magnetic field that are recorded in the basalts of the ocean floor. The bands are wider in the eastern Pacific Ocean because the rates of spreading are greater than those of the Mid-Atlantic Ridge. The correct answer, therefore, is (C).

56. The rock 150 kilometers on either side of the Mid-Atlantic Ridge is approximately 12 million years old. This means that each plate moved 1.5×10^7 centimeters in 1.2×10^7 years, or 1.25 centimeters/year. The correct answer, therefore, is (B).

57. A strike-slip fault is a fault for which the movement is parallel to the fault's strike. Shear forces cause bodies to move parallel to their plane of contact. The correct answer, therefore, is (A).

58. At convergent boundaries, lithospheric plates move toward each other. When low-density continental lithosphere is at the leading edge of both plates, neither plate is subducted. Instead, the lithosphere crumples and deforms, forming folded and faulted mountains. The correct answer, therefore, is (C).

59. Oceanic crust is forced downward under less-dense continental crust at subduction zones. The graph shows that the foci to the west are shallow whereas the foci to the east are deep. Earthquakes occur frequently in the zone where relatively brittle lithosphere sinks deep into the mantle. In this region, the oceanic crust is sinking into the mantle toward the east. The correct answer, therefore, is (A).

60. A terrane is a body of rock with a common geologic history, which is different from that of the surrounding area. An exotic terrane is a crustal fragment that was transported a large distance and then accreted onto a continent. This is true of much of the land on the Pacific coast of Canada and Alaska. The correct answer, therefore, is (D).

61. High pressure during metamorphism forces minerals whose crystals are flat or needlelike to crystallize or recrystallize with their long axes perpendicular to the force. A large number of crystals in a preferred orientation results in easily recognized layers or foliation. The correct answer, therefore, is (B).

62. The identification of igneous rocks is based on texture and mineral composition. There is a range of compositions for rocks classified as granites; they contain relatively high concentrations of quartz, potassium feldspar, and plagioclase feldspar, with smaller amounts of other minerals. The correct answer, therefore, is (B).

63. One method of soil classification is based on the percentages of silt, clay, and sand present in the soil sample. To identify the soil, follow the percent lines for the three categories and find where all three lines intersect. The correct answer, therefore, is (B).

64. According to the principle of superposition, if sedimentary rock layers have not been overturned, the bottommost layer is the oldest. The material that made up the sandstone was deposited, and then the layers were tilted. The material that made up the shale was deposited on top of this. Since the fault cuts across both layers, it is younger than both layers. The correct answer, therefore, is (D).

65. A cold, dry air mass is more dense than a warm, moist air mass. A cold front is a transition between relatively cold, dense air that is advancing on relatively warm, less-dense air. The dense air displaces the less-dense air by pushing under it. The lifting of air results in expansional cooling, and often cloud development and precipitation. Option (B) is a cross section of a warm front, and option (C) is a cross section of a cold front. The correct answer, therefore, is (C).

66. Leachate from landfills, industrial effluent, and agricultural chemicals all contribute significantly to water pollution. Chlorofluorocarbons are implicated in the destruction of the stratospheric ozone layer. The correct answer, therefore, is (C).

67. Water has a very high specific heat, so it takes more energy to increase the temperature of a given mass of water by one degree than to increase the temperature of the same mass of soil by one degree. The temperature of the soil, therefore, will increase faster than the temperature of the water. The correct answer, therefore, is (D).

68. When excessive water is pumped from a coastal aquifer, the salt water moves inland to replace the withdrawn freshwater. The correct answer, therefore, is (A).

69. When fossil fuels are burned, carbon dioxide, a greenhouse gas, is produced. The average concentration of CO_2 in the atmosphere increased about 20 percent between 1850 and 1986. When energy from the Sun reaches Earth, much of it is radiated back into space as infrared energy. As the concentration of CO_2 increases, more heat will be reradiated back to Earth and the average temperature will rise. The correct answer, therefore, is (B).

70. Since water has a high specific heat, large bodies of water tend to moderate climate. Areas near oceans exhibit smaller seasonal temperature variations than do inland areas. The correct answer, therefore, is (A).

71. A hypothesis is a temporary working explanation of a problem. A hypothesis can be supported by the results of many experiments; however, one experiment with reproducible results may be enough to disprove it. The correct answer, therefore, is (D).

72. Global wind belts determine the movement of weather over Earth's surface. In the United States, the westerlies are prevalent in the midlatitudes. Orographic lifting results in cooling of air forced over mountain ranges, chilling the air to its dew point and thus causing precipitation on the western slopes. Air moving downslope on the leeward side is compressed and warmed. Regions on the leeward slopes of mountain ranges are often arid. The saturation vapor pressure of water increases with increasing temperature. All three statements (I, II, and III) contain correct information relevant to the question. The correct answer, therefore, is (D).

73. Power plants that burn fossil fuels emit sulfur dioxide and nitrogen oxides into the atmosphere. These compounds and compounds formed from these (such as sulfuric acid) are carried into other areas by prevailing winds and eventually fall as acid deposition. This acid deposition often results in lakes with a low pH, which is intolerable for many forms of aquatic life. The correct answer, therefore, is (D).

74. Water is a good solvent for ionic compounds because water molecules are small and polar. There is a slight negative charge on the oxygen side of a water molecule and a slight positive charge on the side with the hydrogen atoms. The negative side of the water molecule is attracted to positive ions and helps pull them away from the crystal lattice, while the positive side is attracted to negative ions. In solution, the positive and negative ions are surrounded by water molecules (i.e., they are hydrated). The correct answer, therefore, is (A).

75. At the time of the big bang, the universe was filled with intense radiation. Cooling has shifted this radiation to longer wavelengths (microwaves). This radiation is known as cosmic background radiation and is believed to exist in all of space. The correct answer, therefore, is (B).

Chapter 15

Practice Questions for the
General Science: Content Knowledge Tests

▶   ▶   ▶   ▶   ▶   ▶   ▶   ▶   ▶   ▶   ▶   ▶

Practice Questions

Now that you have studied the content topics and have worked through strategies relating to multiple-choice questions, you should take the following practice test. You will probably find it helpful to simulate actual testing conditions, giving yourself about 75 minutes to work on the questions. You can cut out and use the answer sheet provided if you wish.

Keep in mind that the test you take at an actual administration will have different questions.

You should not expect the percentage of questions you answer correctly in these practice questions to be exactly the same as when you take the test at an actual administration, since numerous factors affect a person's performance in any given testing situation.

When you have finished the practice questions, you can score your answers and read the explanations of the best answer choices in chapter 16.

THE PRAXIS SERIES

Professional Assessments for Beginning Teachers®

TEST CODE:

TEST NAME:
General Science: Content Knowledge

Practice Questions

Calculators Prohibited

Time—75 Minutes
75 Questions

(Note, at the official administration of tests 0431 and 0432, there will be 60 questions, and you will be allowed 60 minutes to complete the test; for test 0435, there will be 120 questions, and you will be allowed 120 minutes to complete the test.)

THE PRAXIS SERIES
Professional Assessments for Beginning Teachers®

Answer Sheet C

PAGE 1

DO NOT USE INK

Use only a pencil with soft back lead (No. 2 or HB) to complete this answer sheet.
Be sure to fill in completely the oval that corresponds to the proper letter or number.
Completely erase any errors or stray marks.

1. NAME

Enter your last name and first initial.
Omit spaces, hyphens, apostrophes, etc.

Last Name (first 6 letters) F I

(ovals A–Z grid for Last Name and First Initial)

2.

YOUR NAME: _____ _____ ____
(Print)   Last Name (Family or Surname)   First Name (Given)   M. I.

MAILING ADDRESS: _____ _____
(Print)   P.O. Box or Street Address   Apt. # (If any)

_____ _____
City   State or Province

_____ _____
Country   Zip or Postal Code

TELEPHONE NUMBER: ( ) _____   ( ) _____
Home   Business

SIGNATURE: _____   TEST DATE: _____

3. DATE OF BIRTH

Month	Day
Jan.	
Feb.	
Mar.	
April	
May	
June	
July	
Aug.	
Sept.	
Oct.	
Nov.	
Dec.	

(Day ovals: 0–9)

4. SOCIAL SECURITY NUMBER

(ovals 0–9)

5. CANDIDATE ID NUMBER

(ovals 0–9)

6. TEST CENTER / REPORTING LOCATION

Center Number _____   Room Number _____

Center Name _____

City _____ State or Province _____

Country _____

7. TEST CODE / FORM CODE

0
1
(ovals 0–9)

8. TEST BOOK SERIAL NUMBER

9. TEST FORM

10. TEST NAME

Educational Testing Service, ETS, the ETS logo, and THE PRAXIS SERIES:PROFESSIONAL
ASSESSMENTS FOR BEGINNING TEACHERS and its logo are registered trademarks of
Educational Testing Service.

(ETS) Educational Testing Service

51055 • 08920 • TF71M500   Q2573-06
MH01159

I.N. 202974

1   2   3   4

CERTIFICATION STATEMENT: (Please write the following statement below. DO NOT PRINT.)

"I hereby agree to the conditions set forth in the *Registration Bulletin* and certify that I am the person whose name and address appear on this answer sheet."

_____

_____

_____

SIGNATURE: _____   DATE: _____ / _____ / _____

Month   Day   Year

BE SURE EACH MARK IS DARK AND COMPLETELY FILLS THE INTENDED SPACE AS ILLUSTRATED HERE: ● .

1 Ⓐ Ⓑ Ⓒ Ⓓ	41 Ⓐ Ⓑ Ⓒ Ⓓ	81 Ⓐ Ⓑ Ⓒ Ⓓ	121 Ⓐ Ⓑ Ⓒ Ⓓ
2 Ⓐ Ⓑ Ⓒ Ⓓ	42 Ⓐ Ⓑ Ⓒ Ⓓ	82 Ⓐ Ⓑ Ⓒ Ⓓ	122 Ⓐ Ⓑ Ⓒ Ⓓ
3 Ⓐ Ⓑ Ⓒ Ⓓ	43 Ⓐ Ⓑ Ⓒ Ⓓ	83 Ⓐ Ⓑ Ⓒ Ⓓ	123 Ⓐ Ⓑ Ⓒ Ⓓ
4 Ⓐ Ⓑ Ⓒ Ⓓ	44 Ⓐ Ⓑ Ⓒ Ⓓ	84 Ⓐ Ⓑ Ⓒ Ⓓ	124 Ⓐ Ⓑ Ⓒ Ⓓ
5 Ⓐ Ⓑ Ⓒ Ⓓ	45 Ⓐ Ⓑ Ⓒ Ⓓ	85 Ⓐ Ⓑ Ⓒ Ⓓ	125 Ⓐ Ⓑ Ⓒ Ⓓ
6 Ⓐ Ⓑ Ⓒ Ⓓ	46 Ⓐ Ⓑ Ⓒ Ⓓ	86 Ⓐ Ⓑ Ⓒ Ⓓ	126 Ⓐ Ⓑ Ⓒ Ⓓ
7 Ⓐ Ⓑ Ⓒ Ⓓ	47 Ⓐ Ⓑ Ⓒ Ⓓ	87 Ⓐ Ⓑ Ⓒ Ⓓ	127 Ⓐ Ⓑ Ⓒ Ⓓ
8 Ⓐ Ⓑ Ⓒ Ⓓ	48 Ⓐ Ⓑ Ⓒ Ⓓ	88 Ⓐ Ⓑ Ⓒ Ⓓ	128 Ⓐ Ⓑ Ⓒ Ⓓ
9 Ⓐ Ⓑ Ⓒ Ⓓ	49 Ⓐ Ⓑ Ⓒ Ⓓ	89 Ⓐ Ⓑ Ⓒ Ⓓ	129 Ⓐ Ⓑ Ⓒ Ⓓ
10 Ⓐ Ⓑ Ⓒ Ⓓ	50 Ⓐ Ⓑ Ⓒ Ⓓ	90 Ⓐ Ⓑ Ⓒ Ⓓ	130 Ⓐ Ⓑ Ⓒ Ⓓ
11 Ⓐ Ⓑ Ⓒ Ⓓ	51 Ⓐ Ⓑ Ⓒ Ⓓ	91 Ⓐ Ⓑ Ⓒ Ⓓ	131 Ⓐ Ⓑ Ⓒ Ⓓ
12 Ⓐ Ⓑ Ⓒ Ⓓ	52 Ⓐ Ⓑ Ⓒ Ⓓ	92 Ⓐ Ⓑ Ⓒ Ⓓ	132 Ⓐ Ⓑ Ⓒ Ⓓ
13 Ⓐ Ⓑ Ⓒ Ⓓ	53 Ⓐ Ⓑ Ⓒ Ⓓ	93 Ⓐ Ⓑ Ⓒ Ⓓ	133 Ⓐ Ⓑ Ⓒ Ⓓ
14 Ⓐ Ⓑ Ⓒ Ⓓ	54 Ⓐ Ⓑ Ⓒ Ⓓ	94 Ⓐ Ⓑ Ⓒ Ⓓ	134 Ⓐ Ⓑ Ⓒ Ⓓ
15 Ⓐ Ⓑ Ⓒ Ⓓ	55 Ⓐ Ⓑ Ⓒ Ⓓ	95 Ⓐ Ⓑ Ⓒ Ⓓ	135 Ⓐ Ⓑ Ⓒ Ⓓ
16 Ⓐ Ⓑ Ⓒ Ⓓ	56 Ⓐ Ⓑ Ⓒ Ⓓ	96 Ⓐ Ⓑ Ⓒ Ⓓ	136 Ⓐ Ⓑ Ⓒ Ⓓ
17 Ⓐ Ⓑ Ⓒ Ⓓ	57 Ⓐ Ⓑ Ⓒ Ⓓ	97 Ⓐ Ⓑ Ⓒ Ⓓ	137 Ⓐ Ⓑ Ⓒ Ⓓ
18 Ⓐ Ⓑ Ⓒ Ⓓ	58 Ⓐ Ⓑ Ⓒ Ⓓ	98 Ⓐ Ⓑ Ⓒ Ⓓ	138 Ⓐ Ⓑ Ⓒ Ⓓ
19 Ⓐ Ⓑ Ⓒ Ⓓ	59 Ⓐ Ⓑ Ⓒ Ⓓ	99 Ⓐ Ⓑ Ⓒ Ⓓ	139 Ⓐ Ⓑ Ⓒ Ⓓ
20 Ⓐ Ⓑ Ⓒ Ⓓ	60 Ⓐ Ⓑ Ⓒ Ⓓ	100 Ⓐ Ⓑ Ⓒ Ⓓ	140 Ⓐ Ⓑ Ⓒ Ⓓ
21 Ⓐ Ⓑ Ⓒ Ⓓ	61 Ⓐ Ⓑ Ⓒ Ⓓ	101 Ⓐ Ⓑ Ⓒ Ⓓ	141 Ⓐ Ⓑ Ⓒ Ⓓ
22 Ⓐ Ⓑ Ⓒ Ⓓ	62 Ⓐ Ⓑ Ⓒ Ⓓ	102 Ⓐ Ⓑ Ⓒ Ⓓ	142 Ⓐ Ⓑ Ⓒ Ⓓ
23 Ⓐ Ⓑ Ⓒ Ⓓ	63 Ⓐ Ⓑ Ⓒ Ⓓ	103 Ⓐ Ⓑ Ⓒ Ⓓ	143 Ⓐ Ⓑ Ⓒ Ⓓ
24 Ⓐ Ⓑ Ⓒ Ⓓ	64 Ⓐ Ⓑ Ⓒ Ⓓ	104 Ⓐ Ⓑ Ⓒ Ⓓ	144 Ⓐ Ⓑ Ⓒ Ⓓ
25 Ⓐ Ⓑ Ⓒ Ⓓ	65 Ⓐ Ⓑ Ⓒ Ⓓ	105 Ⓐ Ⓑ Ⓒ Ⓓ	145 Ⓐ Ⓑ Ⓒ Ⓓ
26 Ⓐ Ⓑ Ⓒ Ⓓ	66 Ⓐ Ⓑ Ⓒ Ⓓ	106 Ⓐ Ⓑ Ⓒ Ⓓ	146 Ⓐ Ⓑ Ⓒ Ⓓ
27 Ⓐ Ⓑ Ⓒ Ⓓ	67 Ⓐ Ⓑ Ⓒ Ⓓ	107 Ⓐ Ⓑ Ⓒ Ⓓ	147 Ⓐ Ⓑ Ⓒ Ⓓ
28 Ⓐ Ⓑ Ⓒ Ⓓ	68 Ⓐ Ⓑ Ⓒ Ⓓ	108 Ⓐ Ⓑ Ⓒ Ⓓ	148 Ⓐ Ⓑ Ⓒ Ⓓ
29 Ⓐ Ⓑ Ⓒ Ⓓ	69 Ⓐ Ⓑ Ⓒ Ⓓ	109 Ⓐ Ⓑ Ⓒ Ⓓ	149 Ⓐ Ⓑ Ⓒ Ⓓ
30 Ⓐ Ⓑ Ⓒ Ⓓ	70 Ⓐ Ⓑ Ⓒ Ⓓ	110 Ⓐ Ⓑ Ⓒ Ⓓ	150 Ⓐ Ⓑ Ⓒ Ⓓ
31 Ⓐ Ⓑ Ⓒ Ⓓ	71 Ⓐ Ⓑ Ⓒ Ⓓ	111 Ⓐ Ⓑ Ⓒ Ⓓ	151 Ⓐ Ⓑ Ⓒ Ⓓ
32 Ⓐ Ⓑ Ⓒ Ⓓ	72 Ⓐ Ⓑ Ⓒ Ⓓ	112 Ⓐ Ⓑ Ⓒ Ⓓ	152 Ⓐ Ⓑ Ⓒ Ⓓ
33 Ⓐ Ⓑ Ⓒ Ⓓ	73 Ⓐ Ⓑ Ⓒ Ⓓ	113 Ⓐ Ⓑ Ⓒ Ⓓ	153 Ⓐ Ⓑ Ⓒ Ⓓ
34 Ⓐ Ⓑ Ⓒ Ⓓ	74 Ⓐ Ⓑ Ⓒ Ⓓ	114 Ⓐ Ⓑ Ⓒ Ⓓ	154 Ⓐ Ⓑ Ⓒ Ⓓ
35 Ⓐ Ⓑ Ⓒ Ⓓ	75 Ⓐ Ⓑ Ⓒ Ⓓ	115 Ⓐ Ⓑ Ⓒ Ⓓ	155 Ⓐ Ⓑ Ⓒ Ⓓ
36 Ⓐ Ⓑ Ⓒ Ⓓ	76 Ⓐ Ⓑ Ⓒ Ⓓ	116 Ⓐ Ⓑ Ⓒ Ⓓ	156 Ⓐ Ⓑ Ⓒ Ⓓ
37 Ⓐ Ⓑ Ⓒ Ⓓ	77 Ⓐ Ⓑ Ⓒ Ⓓ	117 Ⓐ Ⓑ Ⓒ Ⓓ	157 Ⓐ Ⓑ Ⓒ Ⓓ
38 Ⓐ Ⓑ Ⓒ Ⓓ	78 Ⓐ Ⓑ Ⓒ Ⓓ	118 Ⓐ Ⓑ Ⓒ Ⓓ	158 Ⓐ Ⓑ Ⓒ Ⓓ
39 Ⓐ Ⓑ Ⓒ Ⓓ	79 Ⓐ Ⓑ Ⓒ Ⓓ	119 Ⓐ Ⓑ Ⓒ Ⓓ	159 Ⓐ Ⓑ Ⓒ Ⓓ
40 Ⓐ Ⓑ Ⓒ Ⓓ	80 Ⓐ Ⓑ Ⓒ Ⓓ	120 Ⓐ Ⓑ Ⓒ Ⓓ	160 Ⓐ Ⓑ Ⓒ Ⓓ

FOR ETS USE ONLY	R1	R2	R3	R4	R5	R6	R7	R8	TR	CS

PERIODIC TABLE OF THE ELEMENTS

1																	2
H 1.0079																	**He** 4.0026
3 **Li** 6.941	4 **Be** 9.012											5 **B** 10.811	6 **C** 12.011	7 **N** 14.007	8 **O** 16.00	9 **F** 19.00	10 **Ne** 20.179
11 **Na** 22.99	12 **Mg** 24.30											13 **Al** 26.98	14 **Si** 28.09	15 **P** 30.974	16 **S** 32.06	17 **Cl** 35.453	18 **Ar** 39.948
19 **K** 39.10	20 **Ca** 40.08	21 **Sc** 44.96	22 **Ti** 47.90	23 **V** 50.94	24 **Cr** 52.00	25 **Mn** 54.938	26 **Fe** 55.85	27 **Co** 58.93	28 **Ni** 58.69	29 **Cu** 63.55	30 **Zn** 65.39	31 **Ga** 69.72	32 **Ge** 72.59	33 **As** 74.92	34 **Se** 78.96	35 **Br** 79.90	36 **Kr** 83.80
37 **Rb** 85.47	38 **Sr** 87.62	39 **Y** 88.91	40 **Zr** 91.22	41 **Nb** 92.91	42 **Mo** 95.94	43 **Tc** (98)	44 **Ru** 101.1	45 **Rh** 102.91	46 **Pd** 106.42	47 **Ag** 107.87	48 **Cd** 112.41	49 **In** 114.82	50 **Sn** 118.71	51 **Sb** 121.75	52 **Te** 127.60	53 **I** 126.91	54 **Xe** 131.29
55 **Cs** 132.91	56 **Ba** 137.33	57 ***La** 138.91	72 **Hf** 178.49	73 **Ta** 180.95	74 **W** 183.85	75 **Re** 186.21	76 **Os** 190.2	77 **Ir** 192.2	78 **Pt** 195.08	79 **Au** 196.97	80 **Hg** 200.59	81 **Tl** 204.38	82 **Pb** 207.2	83 **Bi** 208.98	84 **Po** (209)	85 **At** (210)	86 **Rn** (222)
87 **Fr** (223)	88 **Ra** 226.02	89 **†Ac** 227.03	104 **Rf** (261)	105 **Db** (262)	106 **Sg** (263)	107 **Bh** (262)	108 **Hs** (265)	109 **Mt** (266)	110 § (269)	111 § (272)	112 § (277)						

§Not yet named

*Lanthanide Series	58 **Ce** 140.12	59 **Pr** 140.91	60 **Nd** 144.24	61 **Pm** (145)	62 **Sm** 150.4	63 **Eu** 151.97	64 **Gd** 157.25	65 **Tb** 158.93	66 **Dy** 162.50	67 **Ho** 164.93	68 **Er** 167.26	69 **Tm** 168.93	70 **Yb** 173.04	71 **Lu** 174.97
†Actinide Series	90 **Th** 232.04	91 **Pa** 231.04	92 **U** 238.03	93 **Np** 237.05	94 **Pu** (244)	95 **Am** (243)	96 **Cm** (247)	97 **Bk** (247)	98 **Cf** (251)	99 **Es** (252)	100 **Fm** (257)	101 **Md** (258)	102 **No** (259)	103 **Lr** (260)

TABLE OF INFORMATION

Electron rest mass	m_e	=	9.11×10^{-31} kilogram
Proton rest mass	m_p	=	1.672×10^{-27} kilogram
Neutron rest mass	m_n	=	1.675×10^{-27} kilogram
Magnitude of the electron charge	e	=	1.60×10^{-19} coulomb
Bohr radius	a_0	=	5.29×10^{-11} meter
Avogadro's number	N_A	=	6.02×10^{23} per mole
Universal gas constant	R	=	8.314 joules/(mole • K)
		=	0.0821 L • atm/(mole • K)
Boltzmann constant	k	=	1.38×10^{-23} joule/K
Planck constant	h	=	6.63×10^{-34} joule • second
		=	4.14×10^{-15} eV • second
Speed of light	c	=	3.00×10^8 meters/second
Vacuum permittivity	ϵ_0	=	8.85×10^{-12} coulomb^2/(newton • meter^2)
Vacuum permeability	μ_0	=	4×10^{-7} newton/ampere^2
Coulomb constant	$1/4\,\epsilon_0$	=	8.99×10^9 newtons • meter^2/coulomb^2
Universal gravitational constant	G	=	6.67×10^{-11} newton • meter^2/kilogram^2
Acceleration due to gravity	g	=	9.80 meters/second^2
1 atmosphere pressure	1 atm	=	1.0×10^5 newtons/meter^2
		=	1.0×10^5 pascals (Pa)
Faraday constant	$\mathscr{F}$	=	9.65×10^4 coulombs/mole
1 atomic mass unit	1 amu	=	1.66×10^{-27} kilogram
1 electron volt	1 eV	=	1.602×10^{-19} joule

For H_2O:

heat of fusion	3.33×10^2 joules/gram
heat of vaporization	2.26×10^3 joules/gram
mean specific heat (liquid)	4.19 joules/(gram • K)

Volume of 1 mole of ideal gas at 0°C, 1 atmosphere	22.4 liters

GENERAL SCIENCE: CONTENT KNOWLEDGE

Questions 1-2 refer to the following information.

The onset of stomach ulcers and gastroesophageal reflux disease (GERD) has been directly linked to stomach hyperacidity in some cases. Data collected from an experiment measuring the effect of three new drugs, X, Y and Z, on stomach pH are shown below.

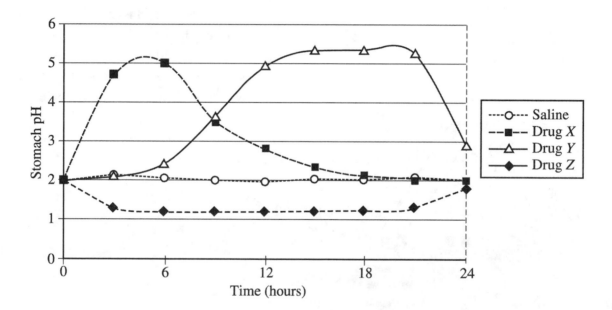

1. Treatment with which of the following was the most effective in reducing stomach acid during the course of the experiment?

   (A) Saline
   (B) Drug X
   (C) Drug Y
   (D) Drug Z

2. The dependent variable in this experiment is

   (A) time
   (B) drug concentration
   (C) stomach pH
   (D) the various drugs tested

3. Which of the following best describes a scientific hypothesis?

   (A) It must first be formulated by a famous scientist.
   (B) It is based on observations and can be evaluated experimentally.
   (C) Once proposed, it must be accepted by the scientific community.
   (D) It can be tested only by using laboratory equipment.

5. In preparing diluted sulfuric acid, H_2SO_4, the concentrated acid should be added to the water during the dilution, not the other way around. Which of the following reasons accounts for this procedure?

   (A) The density of water is greater than that of the acid, so it is easier to add the acid to the water.
   (B) The diluting process is quite exothermic, so that the solution may splatter if diluted by the addition of water.
   (C) Fewer fumes are given off when the concentrated acid is added to the water than when water is added to the acid.
   (D) Carbon dioxide from the air will dissolve into the acid while it is being poured, which tends to neutralize the acid.

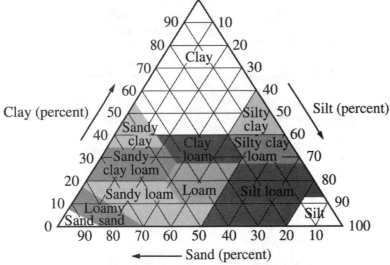

4. Based on the diagram above, a soil sample consisting of 50 percent sand, 20 percent silt, and 30 percent clay would be classified as

   (A) loam
   (B) sandy clay loam
   (C) silt loam
   (D) clay

6. A portion of a buret containing a liquid is shown above. The correct volume reading for this buret is

   (A) 20.68 mL
   (B) 20.7 mL
   (C) 21.3 mL
   (D) 21.32 mL

7. How many significant figures are in the measurement 0.0120 meter?

   (A) Two
   (B) Three
   (C) Four
   (D) Five

8. Which of the following scientists is NOT correctly linked with one of his major contributions to scientific knowledge?

   (A) Mendel and the periodic table
   (B) Newton and the laws of motion
   (C) Hutton and uniformitarianism
   (D) Boyle and law of gas behavior

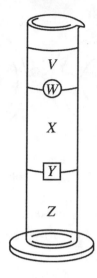

9. The diagram above represents a graduated cylinder containing two solid objects (*Y* and *W*) and three immiscible liquids (*V*, *X*, and *Z*). All of the substances have different densities. Which of the following correctly lists the substances in the cylinder in order of increasing density?

   Smallest Density ⟶ Greatest Density

   (A) $Z < Y < X < W < V$
   (B) $Z < X < V < Y < W$
   (C) $W < Y < V < X < Z$
   (D) $V < W < X < Y < Z$

10. Which of the following is closest to the average mass of an adult human?

    (A)   0.6 kg
    (B)   6.0 kg
    (C)   60.0 kg
    (D) 500.0 kg

11. When a sponge is compressed, which of the following physical properties changes?

    (A) Volume
    (B) Mass
    (C) Inertia
    (D) Weight

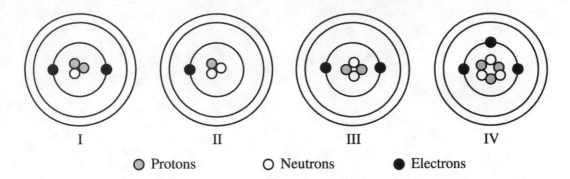

I   II   III   IV

◉ Protons   ○ Neutrons   ● Electrons

12. The diagrams above represent atoms. The numbers of protons, neutrons, and electrons in each are indicated by the differently shaded circles in each diagram. Which of the following are isotopes of the same element?

(A) I and II only
(B) I and III only
(C) I and IV only
(D) I, II, III, and IV

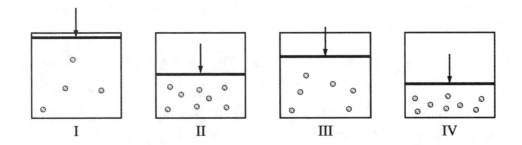

I   II   III   IV

13. The four diagrams above represent a cylinder with a movable, frictionless piston as seen during four different experiments. The external pressure, shown by the arrows, is the same in all four experiments. Contained in each cylinder is a sample of a gas behaving ideally, i.e., the molecules are moving with random, chaotic motion. The small spheres represent the relative number of molecules present in the cylinder during the different experiments. Rank the cylinders in order from lowest absolute temperature to highest absolute temperature for each of the four experiments.

Lowest Temperature ⟶ Highest Temperature

(A) I   <   II   <   III   <   IV
(B) II   <   IV   <   III   <   I
(C) III   <   IV   <   II   <   I
(D) IV   <   II   <   III   <   I

14. How much heat is absorbed by 10.0 grams of water as the temperature is increased from 30°C to 50°C?

(A) 66,600 J
(B) 3,330 J
(C) 838 J
(D) 200 J

$$^{220}_{86}Rn$$

15. Which of the following results when the nucleus of the radon atom shown above emits an alpha particle?

(A) $^{216}_{84}Po$

(B) $^{220}_{85}At$

(C) $^{220}_{86}Rn$

(D) $^{224}_{88}Fr$

16. Which of the following can produce a real image of an object?

(A) A plane mirror
(B) A converging lens
(C) A diverging lens
(D) A convex mirror

17. A frequency of 2,000 hertz is measured as an ambulance siren recedes from a detector. What frequency will be detected when the ambulance is at rest relative to the detector?

(A) Less than 2,000 Hz
(B) 2,000 Hz
(C) Greater than 2,000 Hz
(D) No sound will be detected.

18. The nodal separation in a one-dimensional standing wave is 0.5 meter. If the frequency of the wave is 100.0 Hertz, then the speed of the wave is

(A) 25.0 m/s
(B) 50.0 m/s
(C) 100.0 m/s
(D) 200.0 m/s

19. When light travels from water to air, which of the following occurs?

(A) The frequency stays the same and the velocity increases.
(B) Both the frequency and the velocity increase.
(C) Both the wavelength and the velocity decrease.
(D) The frequency increases and the wavelength stays the same.

20. A rubber rod is rubbed with fur, and the rod becomes negatively charged. Which of the following statements explains this phenomenon?

(A) Neutrons are exchanged between the rod and the fur.
(B) Protons are transferred from the fur to the rod.
(C) Electrons are transferred from the fur to the rod.
(D) Electrons are transferred from the rod to the fur.

21. Tiny bits of paper are attracted to a charged rubber rod as a result of which of the following?

    (A) Paper naturally has a positive charge.
    (B) Paper naturally has a negative charge.
    (C) The paper becomes polarized by induction.
    (D) The paper acquires a net positive charge by induction.

22. A charged particle with constant velocity enters a uniform magnetic field whose direction is parallel to the particle's velocity. Neglecting the gravitational field, the particle will

    (A) speed up
    (B) slow down
    (C) experience no change in velocity
    (D) follow a circular path

23. Three different resistors R_1, R_2, and R_3 are connected in parallel to a battery. R_1 has an electrical potential of 4.0 volts, R_2 has a resistance of 4.0 ohms, and R_3 dissipates 6.0 watts. What is the current in R_3?

    (A)   0.66 amp
    (B)   1.5 amp
    (C)   3.0 amp
    (D) 12.0 amp

24. An object is thrown vertically upward. What is the acceleration of the object at the top of its path?

    (A) Zero
    (B) 9.8 m/s^2 up
    (C) 9.8 m/s^2 down
    (D) Between zero and 9.8 m/s^2, depending on air resistance

25. How much work is done in holding an object of mass 10.0 kilograms at a height of 2.0 meters above the floor for 10.0 seconds? (Assume the acceleration due to gravity is 10.0 m/s^2.)

    (A) zero
    (B)   20.0 J
    (C)   200.0 J
    (D) 2,000.0 J

26. A simple pendulum has a period, T, on Earth. Which of the following would decrease the period of the pendulum if the pendulum were kept at the same location?

    (A) Increasing the length of the pendulum
    (B) Increasing the mass of the pendulum bob
    (C) Decreasing the length of the pendulum
    (D) Decreasing the mass of the pendulum bob

27. A tractor is pulling a wagon full of hay. The mass of the hay and wagon is two times the mass of the tractor. When the tractor accelerates forward, the force that the wagon exerts on the tractor is

    (A) two times greater than the force of the tractor on the wagon
    (B) equal to the force of the tractor on the wagon
    (C) one-half the force of the tractor on the wagon
    (D) zero, since the tractor is pulling the wagon forward

28. Which of the following elements is correctly paired with its most likely oxidation state or charge?

   (A) Oxygen, -2
   (B) Magnesium, $+1$
   (C) Sulfur, $+4$
   (D) Silicon, $+2$

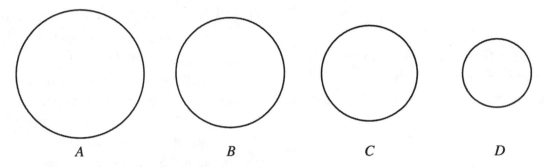

29. The diagram above represents atoms from the halogen group. On the basis of relative size, which of the following correctly lists the atoms from the top of the group to the bottom?

   (A) A, B, C, D
   (B) C, A, B, D
   (C) D, B, A, C
   (D) D, C, B, A

30. The formula for tin(II) phosphate (stannous phosphate) is

   (A) $SnPO_4$
   (B) Sn_3PO_4
   (C) $Sn_3(PO_4)_2$
   (D) $Sn_3(PO_4)_4$

31. Metals conduct electricity well. Which of the following properties of metals accurately accounts for this observation?

(A) Valence electrons are transferred from one atom to another to form ions.

(B) Valence electrons are shared between two discrete atoms simultaneously.

(C) Valence electrons are held loosely in a network of atoms.

(D) Covalent bonds form between the atoms.

$$Li_3N(s) + ...H_2O(l) \rightarrow ...Li^+(aq) + ...OH^-(aq) + ...NH_3(g)$$

32. When the equation above is balanced and all coefficients are reduced to the lowest whole-number terms, the coefficient for $OH^-(aq)$ is

(A) 2

(B) 3

(C) 4

(D) 6

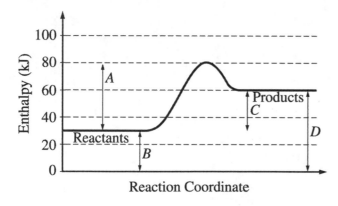

33. The heat of reaction, ΔH, for the reaction above is represented by arrow

(A) A

(B) B

(C) C

(D) D

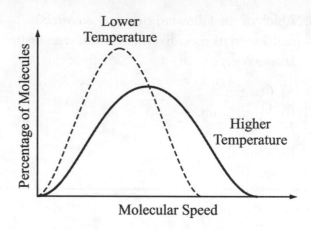

34. The diagram above shows the distribution of molecular speeds of a one-mole sample of nitrogen molecules at two different temperatures. The nitrogen is in the gas phase at both temperatures and is kept at a constant volume. Which of the following correctly describes the molecules of nitrogen in the sample at the lower temperature?

(A) The average distance between molecules is greater at the lower than at the higher temperature.

(B) The intermolecular attraction between molecules is greater at the lower than at the higher temperature.

(C) The mass of individual molecules is less at the lower than at the higher temperature.

(D) The average speed of the molecules is smaller at the lower than at the higher temperature.

35. A sample of water starts off as ice at $-10°C$ and is heated until it is transformed into steam at a temperature of $110°C$. Which of the following graphs best represents the change in temperature of the sample of water as heat is added to it at a constant rate?

(A)
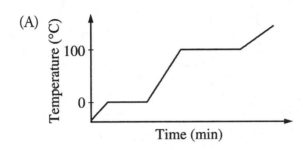

(B)
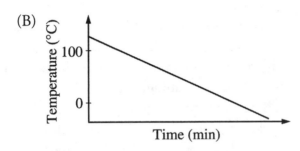

(C)
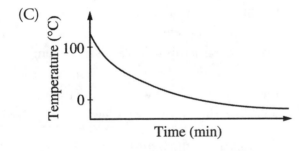

(D)
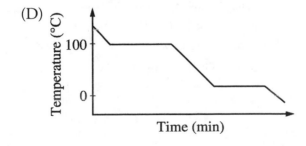

36. Which of the following solutions would be most resistant to a change in pH when a small amount of an acid or a base is added?

(A) 0.1 M HNO_3 and 0.1 M $NaNO_3$
(B) 0.1 M HNO_3 and 0.1 M NaOH
(C) 0.1 M $HC_2H_3O_3$ and 0.1 M $NaC_2H_3O_2$
(D) 0.1 M Na_2CO_3

37. Which of the following 0.5 M aqueous solutions would have the lowest freezing point?

(A) $C_6H_{12}O_6$
(B) $Al(NO_3)_3$
(C) $AgCl_2$
(D) KBr

38. If a mixture of 7 grams of iron filings and 4 grams of sulfur is heated in a test tube, a red glow spreads throughout the tube. Heat energy is obviously released. After cooling, the test tube and contents are weighed. If the empty tube weighed 17 grams and if it is assumed that no atmospheric gases were involved in the reaction, then the total mass of the test tube and its contents should be approximately

(A)   6 grams
(B) 17 grams
(C) 27 grams
(D) 28 grams

39. Which of the following cellular structures would you expect to find in high numbers within a phagocytic white blood cell as compared to a muscle cell?

(A) Ribosomes
(B) Lysosomes
(C) Golgi apparatus
(D) Endoplasmic reticulum

40. All of the following are characteristics of the human immunodeficiency virus (HIV) EXCEPT:

    (A) HIV causes acquired immunodeficiency syndrome (AIDS).
    (B) HIV may be spread by body fluid contact, including blood and semen.
    (C) HIV binds to CD4 receptors on the surface of target cells within its host.
    (D) HIV is a retrovirus, having DNA as its genetic material.

41. When caribou migrate, the weaker ones often become the prey of wolves and other carnivores. If the vegetation eaten by caribou is sparse for several consecutive years, which of the following statements is most likely correct concerning the wolf population during that same time period?

    (A) The wolf population initially increases due to an increase in the availability of food.
    (B) The wolf population initially decreases because the wolves compete with the caribou for the same food.
    (C) The wolf population initially decreases because the stronger caribou will begin to use wolves as a food source.
    (D) The wolf population does not change significantly, only the caribou population declines.

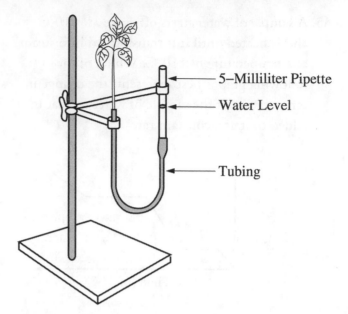

42. Experiments were conducted to test the rate of transpiration in plants under different environmental conditions. The stem of a plant shoot was cut. Tubing, attached at one end to a water-filled pipette, was placed over the cut end of the shoot. The tubing and pipette were clamped as shown in the diagram above. Measurements of the water level in the pipette were recorded every 15 minutes. The experimental setup was placed in a room with partial sunlight at 25°C. Which of the following conditions would cause the most rapid lowering of the water level in the pipette?

    (A) Increasing the light intensity
    (B) Misting the leaves with water
    (C) Removing half of the leaves
    (D) Placing the experimental set-up inside a sealed, clear glass container

43. All of the following are believed to be factors that are involved in causing essential hypertension (persistent high blood pressure) EXCEPT

    (A) hardening of the arteries
    (B) high cholesterol levels
    (C) high dietary salt intake
    (D) anemia

44. Which of the following diagrams best represents a cell (diploid number, $2N = 4$) that, when finished division, would result in the production of diploid, genetically identical daughter cells?

    (A)
    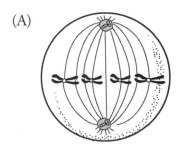

    (B)
    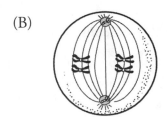

    (C)
    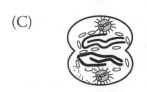

    (D)
    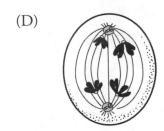

45. Cystic fibrosis (CF) is a genetic, autosomal recessive disease. If a woman with CF has children with a man who does not have CF and is not a carrier, what fraction of their offspring will have CF?

    (A) 0
    (B) $\frac{1}{4}$
    (C) $\frac{1}{2}$
    (D) 1

46. Which of the following statements is accurate regarding global population growth?

    (A) The infant mortality rate exceeds the death rate.
    (B) Earth has reached its ultimate carrying capacity.
    (C) The human population is exhibiting exponential growth.
    (D) The human population exhibits characteristics of an r-selected population.

47. Which of the following physiological responses would be appropriate to help reduce body temperature?

    (A) Contraction of skeletal muscle
    (B) Release of thyroid hormone
    (C) Activation of the sweat glands
    (D) Release of prostaglandins from the hypothalamus

48. Human beings, reptiles, birds, and fish all belong to the same

    (A) class
    (B) family
    (C) order
    (D) phylum

49. In which of the following cell types would a random DNA mutation have the greatest possibility of having an impact on the gene pool of a population?

(A) Liver
(B) Neuron
(C) Skin
(D) Sperm

50. Male stickleback fish have a characteristic red belly coloration. A male stickleback fish will attack other male sticklebacks or any non-fishlike model with a red belly sign stimulus to defend its territory. Attacking the non-fishlike model is an example of which of the following?

(A) Fixed action pattern
(B) Habituation
(C) Imprinting
(D) Operant conditioning

51. Which of the following is NOT an example of Darwin's concept of the mechanism of natural selection?

(A) Selective breeding produces a variety of corn that will survive drought conditions.
(B) Average beak size in a population of birds changes over time following their migration to an environment with larger seeds for food.
(C) Bacteria develop resistance to antibiotics.
(D) Infants tend to have birth weights between 3 and 4 kilograms, neither higher nor lower.

52. An insect species lays its eggs on a specific type of plant leaf. The leaves hide the insect eggs from predators and protect them from the environment. As the eggs hatch, the insect larvae feed on the leaves. Which of the following best describes the relationship between the insect and plant?

(A) Commensalism
(B) Mimicry
(C) Mutualism
(D) Parasitism

53. In a cancer patient, which of the following would LEAST likely be damaged by chemotherapy treatment?

(A) Bone marrow
(B) Skeletal muscle
(C) Epidermis
(D) Lining of the gastrointestinal tract

54. Which of the following would best describe the Earth/Sun relationship on the first day of summer in the Northern Hemisphere?

(A) Earth is at its closest approach to the Sun.
(B) Earth is at its farthest point from the Sun.
(C) The Sun is directly overhead at local noon at 23.5 degrees north.
(D) The Sun's perpendicular rays are over the equator at local noon.

55. Approximately how many years does it take for the light from Sirius, the Dog Star, to reach Earth if Sirius is about 8.3×10^{13} kilometers from Earth? (1 light-year = 9.5×10^{12} kilometers.)

    (A) 0.87 yr
    (B) 1.1 yr
    (C) 8.7 yr
    (D) 11 yr

56. All of the following statements relating to fossil record are true EXCEPT:

    (A) The oldest layers of sedimentary rock contain the most ancient fossils.
    (B) Many species have become extinct over time.
    (C) All fossils are actual remains of past organisms.
    (D) Life-forms have changed over time.

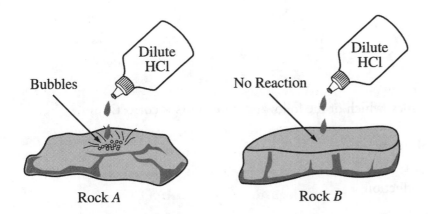

Rock A   Rock B

57. What can be inferred about the rock samples shown in the diagram above?

    (A) Rock A probably contains $CaCO_3$.
    (B) Rock B probably contains $CaCO_3$.
    (C) Rock A and B are the same kind of rock.
    (D) Rock A and B were found together.

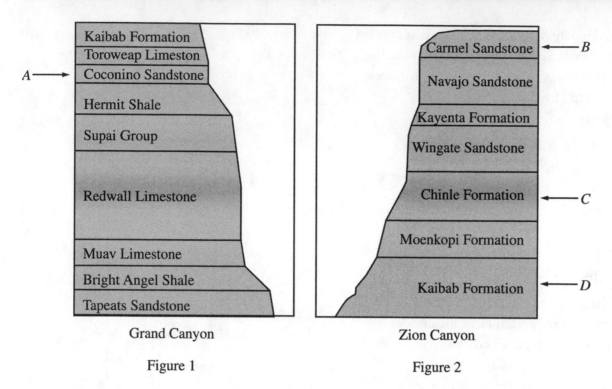

Grand Canyon

Figure 1

Zion Canyon

Figure 2

58. The figures shown above are rock columns from two different canyons on the Colorado Plateau. Of the following, which layer is the oldest?

(A) *A*
(B) *B*
(C) *C*
(D) *D*

59. According to the theory of plate tectonics, which of the following statements is correct?

(A) Midocean ridges and continental rifts form at convergent plate boundaries.
(B) Crustal plates are destroyed at subduction zones.
(C) Earth's crust is one solid plate.
(D) Earthquakes occur most frequently in the center of crustal plates.

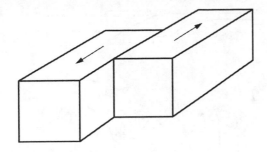

60. In the diagram above, which of the following types of faulting is shown?

(A) Normal
(B) Reverse
(C) Right-lateral strike slip
(D) Left-lateral strike slip

Time (hours)	Observed Counts per Minute
0	204
1	106
2	51
3	22
4	13

61. A radioactive source is monitored for one minute at hourly intervals by use of a Geiger counter, yielding the data above. Which of the following statements is INCONSISTENT with these data?

(A) Statistical fluctuations are present in the data.
(B) Doubling the observation times to two minutes will approximately double the number of counts recorded.
(C) The half-life of the source is approximately one hour.
(D) The count rate will increase in the coming hours.

62. Which of the following mineral properties would be most useful in distinguishing fluorite from quartz?

(A) Color
(B) Streak
(C) Luster
(D) Hardness

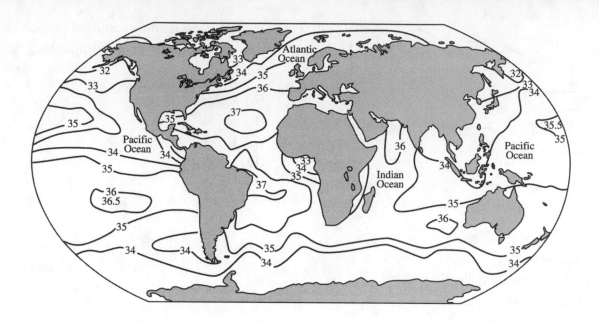

63. Which of the following properties of seawater is plotted on the world map above?

(A) Density
(B) Temperature
(C) Salinity
(D) Dissolved oxygen concentration

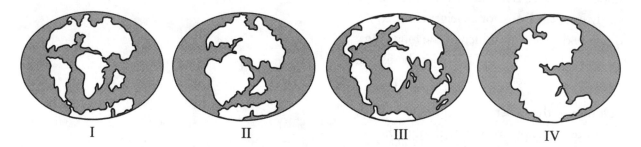

64. The maps above show the orientation of Earth's landmasses during four different periods of time. Which of the following gives the correct sequence, first to last?

(A) I, II, III, IV
(B) II, III, IV, I
(C) III, I, II, IV
(D) IV, II, I, III

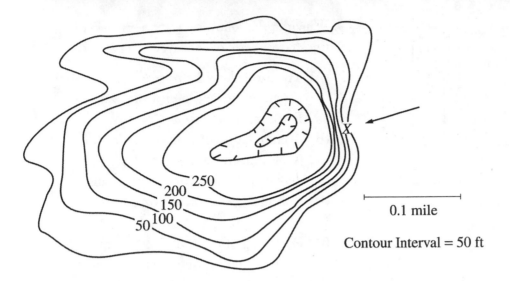

0.1 mile

Contour Interval = 50 ft

65. Which of the following land features is represented at location *X*?

(A) Valley
(B) Depression
(C) Cliff
(D) Hilltop

66. What is the airflow pattern in the center of a low-pressure system as it moves across the United States?

(A) Downward and outward in clockwise spiral
(B) Downward and inward in a counterclockwise spiral
(C) Upward and outward in a clockwise spiral
(D) Upward and inward in a counterclockwise spiral

Table of Dew Points

Dry-Bulb Temperature	Dry-Bulb Temperature Minus Wet-Bulb Temperature					
	3	4	5	6	7	8
65	60	59	57	55	53	51
70	65	64	62	61	59	57
75	71	69	68	66	64	63

67. Based on the table above, if the dry-bulb temperature is 73°F and the wet-bulb temperature is 67°F, the dew point is closest to

(A) 68°F
(B) 66°F
(C) 64°F
(D) 61°F

68. The phases of the Moon are due to

(A) the varying distance of the Moon from Earth
(B) the varying distance of Earth from the Sun
(C) the rotation of Earth on its axis
(D) changes in the relative positions of the Sun, Earth, and the Moon

69. Which of the following statements regarding the stratospheric ozone layer is accurate?

(A) The ozone layer helps to absorb infrared radiation, preventing it from reaching Earth's surface.
(B) Accumulation of chlorofluorocarbons (CFCs) in the atmosphere has led to depletion of the ozone layer because chlorine atoms convert ozone into molecular oxygen.
(C) Depletion of the ozone layer is most apparent in atmospheric regions above the equator, because warm temperatures accelerate the depletion reaction.
(D) Scientists believe that if the use of ozone-depleting agents is stopped, the damage to the ozone layer will repair itself within five years.

70. Which of the following procedures would provide the best evidence for the presence of a suspect at the scene of a crime?

(A) Blood-typing of the suspect and of a blood sample found at the crime scene
(B) Microscopic analysis of hair strands from the suspect and of those found at the crime scene
(C) Karyotyping of cells isolated from the suspect and of cells found at the crime scene
(D) Comparison of DNA sequences from the tissues of the suspect and from a tissue sample collected from the crime scene

71. The addition of fertilizers to a lake, e.g., by runoff from lawns or agricultural fields, will initially affect the oxygen cycle in the lake by

    (A) promoting growth of algae
    (B) increasing populations of decomposers
    (C) causing more oxygen from the air to dissolve in the water at the lake's surface
    (D) killing the fish and invertebrates within the lake

72. Lakes in southeastern Canada and the northeastern United States are becoming depleted of living organisms. Which of the following is most often the primary cause?

    (A) Nuclear waste
    (B) Lowered water levels
    (C) Garbage dumping
    (D) Acid deposition

73. The symbol shown above is used in context with which of the following?

    (A) Recycling of plastics
    (B) Disposal of biomedical waste
    (C) Radioactive materials warnings
    (D) Disposal of hazardous materials

74. Which of the following is NOT a major cause of pollution in surface water and groundwater?

    (A) Landfill leachate
    (B) Industrial effluent
    (C) Chlorofluorocarbons
    (D) Agricultural chemicals

75. Radon is an odorless, radioactive gas and poses a health hazard. Which of the following can be used to reduce radon in the home?

    (A) Increasing the insulation in the walls and ceilings
    (B) Keeping the basement door closed
    (C) Using masonry walls on the outside of the home
    (D) Increasing the ventilation throughout the home

Chapter 16

Right Answers and Explanations for the Practice
Questions for the *General Science:
Content Knowledge* Tests

▶   ▶   ▶   ▶   ▶   ▶   ▶   ▶   ▶   ▶   ▶   ▶

Right Answers and Explanations for the Practice Questions

Now that you have answered all of the practice questions, you can check your work.
Compare your answers with the correct answers in the table below.

Question Number	Correct Answer	Content Category
1	C	History and Nature of Science
2	C	History and Nature of Science
3	B	History and Nature of Science
4	B	History and Nature of Science
5	B	History and Nature of Science
6	A	History and Nature of Science
7	B	History and Nature of Science
8	A	History and Nature of Science
9	D	Physical Sciences - Basic Principles, Matter and Energy
10	C	Physical Sciences - Basic Principles, Matter and Energy
11	A	Physical Sciences - Basic Principles, Matter and Energy
12	B	Physical Sciences - Basic Principles, Atomic and Nuclear Structure
13	D	Physical Sciences - Basic Principles, Heat and Thermodynamics
14	C	Physical Sciences - Basic Principles, Heat and Thermodynamics
15	A	Physical Sciences - Basic Principles, Atomic and Nuclear Structure
16	B	Physical Sciences - Physics, Waves
17	C	Physical Sciences - Physics, Waves
18	C	Physical Sciences - Physics, Waves
19	A	Physical Sciences - Physics, Waves
20	C	Physical Sciences - Physics, Electricity and Magnetism
21	C	Physical Sciences - Physics, Electricity and Magnetism
22	C	Physical Sciences - Physics, Electricity and Magnetism
23	B	Physical Sciences - Physics, Electricity and Magnetism
24	C	Physical Sciences - Physics, Mechanics
25	A	Physical Sciences - Physics, Mechanics
26	A	Physical Sciences - Physics, Mechanics
27	B	Physical Sciences - Physics, Mechanics
28	A	Physical Sciences - Chemistry, Chemical Reactions
29	D	Physical Sciences - Chemistry, Periodicity
30	C	Physical Sciences - Chemistry, Moles and Bonding, Nomenclature
31	C	Physical Sciences - Chemistry, Moles and Bonding
32	B	Physical Sciences - Chemistry, Chemical Reactions
33	C	Physical Sciences - Chemistry, Chemical Reactions, Endothermic and Exothermic
34	D	Physical Sciences - Chemistry, Kinetics Molecular Theory and States of Matter
35	A	Physical Sciences - Chemistry, Kinetics Molecular Theory and States of Matter
36	C	Physical Sciences - Chemistry, Solutions and Solubility
37	B	Physical Sciences - Chemistry, Solutions and Solubility
38	D	Physical Sciences - Chemistry, Chemical Reactions

Question Number	Correct Answer	Content Category
39	B	Life Sciences - The Cell
40	D	Life Sciences - Diversity of Life
41	A	Life Sciences - Ecology
42	A	Life Sciences - Plants
43	D	Life Sciences - Animals
44	A	Life Sciences - The Cell
45	A	Life Sciences - Classical Genetics
46	C	Life Sciences - Ecology
47	C	Life Sciences - Animals
48	D	Life Sciences - Diversity of Life
49	D	Life Sciences - Molecular Basis of Heredity / Evolution
50	A	Life Sciences - Animals
51	A	Life Sciences - Evolution
52	D	Life Sciences - Ecology
53	B	Life Sciences - The Cell
54	C	Earth/Space Sciences - Astronomy, Seasons
55	C	Earth/Space Sciences - Astronomy, units of distance
56	C	Earth/Space Sciences - Historical Geology, fossil record
57	A	Earth/Space Sciences - Physical Geology, identify minerals
58	A	Earth/Space Sciences - Physical Geology, stratigraphy
59	B	Earth/Space Sciences - Physical Geology, plate tectonics
60	D	Earth/Space Sciences - Physical Geology, faulting
61	D	Earth/Space Sciences - Historical Geology, relative vs. absolute time
62	D	Earth/Space Sciences - Physical Geology, identify minerals
63	C	Earth/Space Sciences - Oceanography, property of sea water
64	D	Earth /Space Sciences - Physical Geology, plate tectonics
65	C	Earth/Space Sciences - Physical Geology, topography
66	D	Earth/Space Sciences - Meteorology, low-pressure system
67	C	Earth/Space Sciences - Meteorology, dew point
68	D	Earth /Space Sciences - Astronomy, moon phases
69	B	Science, Technology and Social Perspectives
70	D	Science, Technology and Social Perspectives
71	A	Science, Technology and Social Perspectives
72	D	Science, Technology and Social Perspectives
73	A	Science, Technology and Social Perspectives
74	C	Science, Technology and Social Perspectives
75	D	Science, Technology and Social Perspectives

Explanations of Right Answers

1. This question requires fundamental understanding of how to interpret graphic data. You must also understand the relationship between the numerical values on the pH scale and the classification of these values as acidic or basic. The data show that only drugs X and Y reduce acid (increase the pH value) as compared to the saline control. Drug Y's maximal effects last 9 to 10 hours, while drug X's effects last only 3 to 4 hours. The correct answer, therefore, is (C).

2. This question requires an understanding of dependent versus independent variables in experimental design. In this experiment, changes in the stomach pH depend on the presence of different drugs over a 24-hour time period. The correct answer, therefore, is (C).

3. Hypotheses are testable statements that lead to predictions that can be confirmed or rejected experimentally. They do not need to be proposed by a famous scientist (A), nor are they accepted until supported by data and observations gathered under controlled conditions (C). These data may be obtained in the field as well as the laboratory, i.e., under the appropriate condition for testing the validity of the hypothesis. The correct answer, therefore, is (B).

4. One method of soil classification is based on the percentages of silt, clay, and sand present in the soil sample. To identify the soil, follow the percent lines for the three categories and find where all three lines intersect. The correct answer, therefore, is (B).

5. Water has a very high specific heat capacity. The excess water can absorb much of the heat released by the dissolving process when it is in greater amount. If water is added to acid, the water is in a lesser amount and will boil. A boiling solution of concentrated sulfuric acid is quite dangerous. The correct answer, therefore, is (B).

6. Burets are read to the nearest 0.01 mL. Estimate one decimal beyond the calibration. The correct answer, therefore, is (A).

7. A significant digit in a measurement is used to express the precision of the measure. All nonzero digits in a measurement are considered significant digits. In our example, the digits 1 and 2 from 0.0120 meter are significant. Zeros are significant if their purpose is to express precision. Zeros that hold decimal location do not express precision. In our example, the two 0's to the left of the 1 in 0.0120 meter are placeholders and therefore are not significant. The 0 to the right of the 2 expresses the precision of the measure to the nearest 0.0001 meter and is therefore significant. The total number of significant figures in the measurement is three. The correct answer, therefore, is (B).

8. Mendel was a biologist directly associated with the development of concepts involving inheritance that he developed while studying pea plants and their offspring. Mendeleev, on the other hand, was a Russian chemist who was one of the major contributors to the development of the periodic table. The correct answer, therefore, is (A).

9. Substances with greater densities will sink when placed in liquids of lesser densities. Physical states have no bearing on the situation. The correct answer, therefore, is (D).

10. One kilogram is approximately 2.2 pounds [60.0 kg ≈ 132.0 pounds]. The correct answer, therefore, is (C).

11. Inertia is the natural tendency of an object to remain at rest or in motion at a constant speed along a straight line. The mass of the object is a quantitative measure of inertia. The deformation of the sponge will not affect the mass or inertia of the object. The weight is dependent on the mass and acceleration due to gravity, which remain constant. The volume of the sponge is equal to the length, L, times the width, W, times the height, H [$V = L \times W \times H$]. Compressing the sponge decreases one or all of these measurements. The correct answer, therefore, is (A).

12. Isotopes have the same number of protons but different numbers of neutrons. The number of electrons is irrelevant. The correct answer, therefore, is (B).

13. As the temperature of a gas increases, the kinetic energy of the molecules also increases. Under conditions of constant pressure, a fixed amount of gas will occupy a greater volume as temperature increases. This means that the gas should have its smallest volume at the lowest temperature. The fact that there are fewer molecules present in piston I than in piston III means that the temperature would be even greater in piston I. This is true because the volume of a gas at a fixed pressure is also proportional to the number of molecules. The only reason that the gas occupies a greater volume must be that there is an even greater increase in temperature. The correct answer, therefore, is (D).

14. The amount of heat needed to raise the temperature of a substance over a specific temperature range is determined by multiplying the specific heat × the mass × the change in temperature.

$$Q = C \times m \times \Delta t, Q = 4.19 \text{ J/g·°C} \times 10.0 \text{ g} \times (50.0°C - 30°C) = 838 \text{ joules}$$

The correct answer, therefore, is (C).

15. Alpha decay occurs when an unstable parent nucleus emits an alpha (α) particle and is converted into a different nucleus in the process. The alpha particle has two protons and a nucleon number of 4.

$$^{220}_{86}\text{Rn} \rightarrow ^{4}_{2}\text{He} + ^{216}_{84}\text{Po}$$

The mass number and electric charge are conserved. The correct answer, therefore, is (A).

16. A plane mirror, a diverging lens, and a convex mirror always produce a virtual image. A converging lens produces a real image when the object is placed beyond the focal point. The correct answer, therefore, is (B).

17. The Doppler effect is a change in the frequency of a sound as detected by an observer that results because the sound source and the observer have different velocities with respect to the medium of sound propagation. The frequency f is detected when the source is stationary relative to the observer. A greater frequency f' is detected when the source is moving towards the detector. A smaller frequency f is detected when the source is moving away from the detector. The correct answer, therefore, is (C).

18. A wavelength is the horizontal length of one cycle of the wave or the horizontal distance between two successive points in phase. A wavelength for a standing wave is the distance between every other node or every other antinode. The distance between two nodes is half a wavelength. The speed of the wave is equal to the frequency times the wavelength $[v = f\lambda = (100.0 \text{ Hz})(1.0 \text{ m}) = 100.0 \text{ m/s}]$. The correct answer, therefore, is (C).

19. When light strikes the interface between two media, part of the light is reflected, and the remainder is transmitted. The part that is transmitted changes speeds and might change direction depending on the angle of entry. The change in direction or speed is due to the different refractive indexes of the media. The refractive index n of a material is the ratio of the speed of light in a vacuum, c, to the speed of light in the material, v, $[n = c/v]$. Water (1.33) has a larger refractive index than air (1.0). The smaller the refractive index the faster light will travel in that medium. When light travels from water to air, the speed and wavelength will increase, but the frequency in both media will remain the same $[f = v/\lambda]$. The correct answer, therefore, is (A).

20. When a rubber rod is rubbed against fur, electrons from the fur are transferred to the rod. This transfer gives the rod a negative charge and leaves a positive charge on the fur. The correct answer, therefore, is (C).

21. When the charged rubber rod is brought near the neutral paper, a separation of charge occurs on the paper. On the paper, unlike charges will be attracted to the charged rubber rod and like charges will be repelled. The unlike charges will be closer to the charged rod. The electrostatic force between two objects is dependent on the distance. The electrostatic force of attraction between rod and paper will be larger for the unlike charges than for the like charges since the distance between unlike charges is less than that between like charges. The correct answer, therefore, is (C).

22. A charged particle moving in a magnetic field will experience a force **F** that is perpendicular to both the velocity **v** and the magnetic field **B**. $[\mathbf{F} = q\mathbf{v} \times \mathbf{B}$ or $F = qvB(\sin\theta)$, where θ is the angle between the velocity **v** and the magnetic field **B**]. The particle will not accelerate since there is no force when the particle's motion is parallel to the magnetic field. The correct answer, therefore, is (C).

23. When resistors are connected in parallel, they have the same difference in potential [$V_1 = V_2 = V_3 = 4$ volts]. The power dissipated in a resistor is equal to the current times the potential difference [$P = IV$]. Solving for the current in resistor R_3, [$I_3 = P_3/V_3 = 1.5$ amps]. The correct answer, therefore, is (B).

24. There is no air resistance at the top of the path because the object is not moving. The only force acting on the object is gravity, the force of Earth on the object. The force is directed toward Earth or downward. The acceleration due to gravity is 9.8 m/s² down near Earth's surface. The correct answer, therefore, is (C).

25. The work, W, done on an object is dependent on the force **F** and the displacement **d** [$W = F \times d(\cos\theta)$]. **F** is the magnitude of the force, **d** is the magnitude of the displacement, and θ is the angle between the force and displacement. No work was done on the object since there was no displacement. The correct answer, therefore, is (A).

26. The period of a simple pendulum is dependent on the length and the acceleration due to gravity. The period of the pendulum does not depend on the mass of the pendulum bob. Acceleration due to gravity does not change because the location did not change. A long pendulum has a greater period than a short pendulum. The correct answer, therefore, is (A).

27. Newton's third law states that for every action there is an equal and opposite reaction. There are two objects and two forces that interact. The reaction of the "tractor on wagon" equals "wagon on tractor." These forces are equal and opposite. The correct answer, therefore, is (B).

28. Oxygen has space for two electrons in its valence shell. As such, the most common oxidation number for oxygen is -2. The correct answer, therefore, is (A).

29. As you proceed down a group (column) on the periodic table, atomic radius typically increases. This is the case in option (D). The correct answer, therefore, is (D).

30. The charge of tin, Sn, is $+2$, as indicated by the (II) part of the name. The formula and charge of the phosphate polyatomic ion is PO_4^{3-}. In order to maintain charge neutrality, three tin(II) ions and two phosphate ions are required. The subscripts in option (C) represent such a combination. The correct answer, therefore, is (C).

31. The atoms of metal elements have atoms in the valence shell with only weak attractions to the nuclei of the atoms. These weak attractions result in a "sea of electrons." This means that the electrons flow between atoms with little resistance. The correct answer, therefore, is (C).

32. This equation is tricky. An initial thought might be to balance the hydrogen atoms by using a coefficient of 2 before the H_2O. This process causes a conflict with respect to the number of oxygen atoms. Keeping in mind that the ratio of hydrogen atoms to oxygen atoms is 2 to 1, using a 3 for OH^- will give 3 oxygen atoms and 6 hydrogen atoms on the product side. Using a coefficient of 3 for the water will balance these elements. The remaining elements can be balanced by using the concept that the subscripts on one side often suggest the coefficients on the other side. When the coefficients used are $Li_3N(s) + 3 H_2O(l) \rightarrow 3 Li^+(aq) + 3 OH^-(aq) + NH_3(g)$, the number of atoms of each element is the same on both sides of the equation. The correct answer, therefore, is (B).

33. The heat of reaction equals the difference between the heat stored in the products and the heat stored in the reactants. The concept is often illustrated by an enthalpy profile. The stored energy of the products and reactants are indicated by the vertical displacement on the profile. The difference between the two in this case is represented by letter C. The actual value would be $+30$ kJ, since the stored energy in the products is greater than that of the reactants. This reaction would be endothermic in the forward direction. During these types of reactions, the temperature of the surroundings decreases as the reaction absorbs the heat. The correct answer, therefore, is (C).

34. In the sample, the individual molecules of gas travel at different speeds. Because there are so many collisions, the speeds of the molecules vary from almost zero to some very high value, well above the average. At a given temperature, the number of molecules that move at very high or very low speeds is small, while the number of molecules at intermediate speeds is much greater and centered around some average speed. At a higher temperature, the whole curve shifts to higher speeds. The correct answer, therefore, is (D).

35. As the ice is heated, it first increases in temperature, as indicated by the sloped line to the lower left on the scale in graph (A). Once the melting point (0°C) is reached, the temperature stops increasing until all of the solid is melted. Once only liquid is present, the temperature again rises with time, as indicated by a second sloped line segment. The boiling point (100°C) is reached. Again, the temperature stops increasing while the liquid goes through a phase change to gas. The final sloped segment represents the increasing temperature of the gas form once only gas is present. The correct answer, therefore, is (A).

36. A solution that resists changes in pH upon the addition of small amounts of an acid or a base is called a buffer. Buffers are solutions or mixtures of a weak acid and one of its soluble salts or of a weak base and one of its soluble salts. In option (C), $HC_2H_3O_2$ is a weak acid and $NaC_2H_3O_2$ is a soluble salt containing the $C_2H_3O_2^-$ ion. The correct answer, therefore, is (C).

37. The freezing point of a solution depends on the concentration of the ions in solution as well as other factors. In this specific case, (A) forms no ions, (B) forms approximately four ions, (C) forms approximately three ions, and (D) forms approximately two ions. The correct answer, therefore, is (B).

38. According to the law of conservation of mass, the total mass during any physical or chemical change remains constant. If no atmospheric gases are involved in the reaction, then the total mass of the test tube and its contents after the reaction should be the sum of 17, 4, and 7, or 28 grams. Adding the masses of the test tube, the iron, and the sulfur will give the total mass. The correct answer, therefore, is (D).

39. This question requires knowledge of cell structure and function. Phagocytic cells engulf large particulate substances and degrade them (e.g., destruction of bacteria by leukocytes). Lysosomes are organelles that contain hydrolytic enzymes and function in intracellular digestion. The correct answer, therefore, is (B).

40. This question requires knowledge of the general characteristics of viruses, viral replication, and HIV specifically. HIV is a retrovirus, but retroviruses carry RNA as their genetic material and then synthesize DNA, using reverse transcriptase, to incorporate their genetic material into the host's genome. The correct answer, therefore, is (D).

41. This question requires you to understand interspecies relationships and predator-prey relationships within a community. In this scenario, the caribou population will weaken due to lack of food (caribou are herbivores), making the caribou easier prey for the wolves. With the increase in food, more wolves will survive, and they will produce more offspring. The correct answer, therefore, is (A).

42. This question requires an understanding of factors that regulate transpiration in plants. Transpiration is the evaporation of water through stomata in plant leaves, which creates a negative pressure and causes water to be absorbed into the plant through the roots. In this setup, an increase in transpiration rate will be indicated by a decrease in water level in the pipet. Of the choices, only increasing the light intensity will increase the transpiration rate. Additional light will allow photosynthesis to occur more rapidly, causing the stomata to open more fully and possibly also increasing the temperature on the leaf surface. The correct answer, therefore, is (A).

43. This question requires an understanding of the causes of a common health problem, high blood pressure. Blockage of the arteries, high cholesterol, and high salt intake (by causing an increase in blood volume) are all causes of hypertension. Anemia, or low blood cell / low hemoglobin count, can result in hypotension (low blood pressure). The correct answer, therefore, is (D).

44. This question requires you to distinguish between the phases and resulting genetic makeup of cells in mitosis and meiosis. Mitosis results in the production of genetically identical, diploid cells, whereas meiosis results in genetically unique, haploid daughter cells. The first diagram is the only one to depict a cell during a mitotic event. The correct answer, therefore, is (A).

45. This question requires you to predict the outcome of a genetic cross and understand Mendelian genetics. (Assume standard nomenclature for a dominant/recessive trait: *D* for a "normal" allele, *d* for a diseased allele.) Since CF is an autosomal recessive trait, the woman must have a *dd* genotype. If the man is homozygous dominant, he must have a *DD* genotype. When *dd* is crossed with *DD*, all the F1 generation offspring will have a *Dd* genotype. Heterozygotes will not express the recessive disease trait. The correct answer, therefore, is (A).

46. This question requires knowledge of population ecology and the trend of human population growth. The human population has continued to grow exponentially since the mid-1600's. Earth's ultimate carrying capacity is debatable. Defining the carrying capacity for humans is difficult because it has been observed to change with the evolution of human culture, e.g., the advent of agriculture and the influence of industrial technology. The correct answer, therefore, is (C).

47. This question requires an understanding of thermoregulation in warm-blooded animals. Sweat gland activation will release sweat onto the surface of the skin and allow for evaporative cooling. All of the other responses would lead to an increase in metabolic heat production and therefore raise the body temperature. The correct answer, therefore, is (C).

48. This question requires knowledge of taxonomic classification and animal characteristics. Human beings, reptiles, birds, and fish are all members of the Phylum *Chordata* but have unique Classes, Orders, and Families. The correct answer, therefore, is (D).

49. This question tests knowledge of the mechanisms of evolution. Mutations in DNA may result in changes in protein structure and expression. These changes may impact the fitness of the individual in its environment. If these changes occur in gametes (i.e., sperm, ova), not in somatic cells, then the changes can be inherited and influence the population's gene pool. Inherited changes may lead to evolution of a population. Changes in somatic cells will affect only the individual. The correct answer, therefore, is (D).

50. This question requires understanding of animal behavior. Fixed action patterns are a sequence of behaviors, triggered by an external sensory stimulus that remain unchanged. Male sticklebacks will act aggressively toward anything that bears a red marking on its underside. The correct answer, therefore, is (A).

51. This question tests understanding of Darwin's concept of the process of natural selection versus that of artificial selection. Artificial selection is employed when a farmer selectively breeds corn to produce a drought-resistant variety. In this case, the farmer, not nature, i.e., the environment, selects for particular traits. The correct answer, therefore, is (A).

52. This question requires understanding of interspecific relationships in a community. In the relationship between the insect and plant, the insect is protected and gains nutrients from the plant but the plant is damaged by the insect. The correct answer, therefore, is (D).

53. This question tests your knowledge of cell division and cancer. Chemotherapy generally targets rapidly dividing cells, whether they are cancerous or not. Muscle cells do not actively divide after their initial development. The correct answer, therefore, is (B).

54. The seasons are due to the tilt of Earth's axis at 23.5 degrees. On the first day of summer, the Northern Hemisphere is tilted toward the Sun and the perpendicular rays of the Sun are directly overhead at local noon on the Tropic of Cancer (23.5 degrees north). The correct answer, therefore, is (C).

55. A light-year is one of the ways astronomers measure distances in space. A light-year is defined as the distance light travels in one year and is equal to 9.5×10^{12} kilometers.

Since the number of years $= \dfrac{\text{distance in kilometers}}{\text{speed in kilometers per year}}$,

then the number of years $= \dfrac{8.3 \times 10^{13} \text{ kilometers}}{9.5 \times 10^{12} \text{ kilometers per year}}$,

which is 8.7 years. The correct answer, therefore, is (C).

56. A fossil is any evidence of past life. It is not necessarily the actual organism preserved in some way (such as petrification, permineralization, lucky burial, tar pits, etc.). A footprint or impression (mold or cast) may be all that a paleontologist has found. The correct answer, therefore, is (C).

57. The most common field test for whether or not a rock specimen contains calcium carbonate is the acid test. A few drops of cold dilute hydrochloric acid (HCl) are placed on the surface of the rock and observed. If bubbles are produced, the sample contains a carbonate mineral, most likely $CaCO_3$. Calcite is the most common carbonate mineral. The correct answer, therefore, is (A).

58. The law of superposition states that in a sequence of sedimentary strata that has not been overturned, the oldest rock layer is on the bottom and the youngest layer is at the top.

The rock layers in the two stratigraphic columns can be correlated. The Kaibab Formation is found in both canyons, being the youngest formation shown in the Grand Canyon stratigraphic column and the oldest formation shown in the Zion Canyon column. The Coconino sandstone is below the Kaibab Formation, and therefore is the oldest of the four choices given. The correct answer, therefore, is (A).

59. Subduction zones mark a convergent plate boundary at which one plate slides beneath the other. The subducting plate is destroyed in the mantle, frequently becoming the ingredients of eruptions on the surface above. New material is added to the edges of plates at the midocean ridges, where paleomagnetism has revealed the history of seafloor spreading. The correct answer, therefore, is (B).

60. No vertical faults are indicated. The arrows show a movement in the strike direction of the fault. In a left-lateral strike-slip fault, the side opposite the observer appears to be displaced to the left. The correct answer, therefore, is (D).

61. Three of the four choices are consistent with the data given. Although statistical fluctuations are present in the data, the fact that the counts decrease by approximately one half each hour indicates that the half-life is approximately one hour. In option (D), an increasing count rate in the coming hours is not consistent with the data. The correct answer, therefore, is (D).

62. Color is not always a reliable characteristic in helping to identify minerals. In this case, both specimens could be the same color. Streak, the color of the powder of the mineral obtained by rubbing the mineral on an unglazed tile, is also an aid. Both specimens have a colorless or white streak. Luster is the way the mineral's surface reflects light. Fluorite and quartz have the same luster. Hardness is the mineral's resistance to scratching. Quartz has a hardness of 7 on Mohs' scale, and fluorite has a hardness of 4. The correct answer, therefore, is (D).

63. In subtropical regions, rates of evaporation exceed precipitation, thereby resulting in relatively high salinity. Abundant rainfall in equatorial areas results in low salinity. It is possible to note where large rivers drain into the oceans. Lower salinity at the Arctic and Antarctic regions is related to melting ice. The isolines summarize salinity that is, on average, about 35 parts per thousand. The correct answer, therefore, is (C).

64. The present continents were derived from the supercontinent Pangaea through fragmentation and continental drift. The maps show several stages in this breakup. The correct answer, therefore, is (D).

65. Contour lines on a topographic map are used to show shape and elevation. In this case, the close spacing of contour lines in a short distance must mean rapid change in elevation. The correct answer, therefore, is (C).

66. Air in the center of a low typically flows inward, rises, and cools, with the surface winds generating a counterclockwise spiral. The correct answer, therefore, is (D).

67. The dew point is the temperature at which air would be saturated (100% relative humidity). The dew point is related to the rate of evaporation and can be determined by using a psychrometer and a table like the one in the question. To find the dew point, subtract the wet-bulb reading from the dry-bulb reading. Locate that number (in this case 6°F) in the top row of numbers in the table. Interpolate where 73°F would be in the leftmost column, and move to the right until you get to the column with the 6°F wet-bulb depression. The dew point is between 61°F and 66°F. The correct answer, therefore, is (C).

68. The Moon does not emit its own light but reflects light received from the Sun. The half of the Moon facing the Sun is lit, and the phases of the Moon, as observed from Earth, are based on how much of the lit portion of the Moon is visible at the time of observation. The amount changes as the Moon revolves around Earth. The correct answer, therefore, is (D).

69. This question requires understanding the importance of the ozone layer and how its integrity has been influenced by humankind. Liberation of chlorine atoms from CFCs has been a major factor in formation of the "ozone hole" above Antarctica and thinning of the layer around the globe. Once in the atmosphere, chlorine atoms can remain there for decades, destroying ozone molecules and thus allowing increased penetration of ultraviolet light through the atmosphere. The correct answer, therefore, is (B).

70. This question tests understanding of how scientific evidence can be used in criminal investigations. Identification of individuals based on their genetic makeup is one of the most accurate techniques used in crime solving. DNA sequence analysis can distinguish between billions of different individuals, giving an accuracy rating of greater than 99.9 percent. The only major error that can occur with this type of technology is that it cannot distinguish between genetically identical individuals (i.e., identical twins). The correct answer, therefore, is (D).

71. Fertilizers contain nitrates, phosphates, and potassium that can cause excessive growth of algae when allowed to pollute lakes, leading to cultural eutrophication. These algal blooms may result in increased oxygen production during the day, but they may also cause oxygen depletion at night due to respiration. Oxygen depletion will cause the death of other organisms within the lake. As the algae die, decomposers break down the organic matter, and this leads to further oxygen depletion. The correct answer, therefore, is (A).

72. Many lakes in southeastern Canada and the northeastern United States are becoming depleted of living organisms because the lakes have a low pH. This low pH renders the lakes uninhabitable by many forms of aquatic life. Power plants that burn fossil fuels emit sulfur oxides and nitrogen oxides into the atmosphere. Prevailing winds carry these compounds, which react with water to form acid deposition. The correct answer, therefore, is (D).

73. The triangle made of circling arrows surrounding a number is used to symbolize the type of plastic of which the object is made. Generally speaking, the lower the value of the number the easier the recycling of the plastic. The correct answer, therefore, is (A).

74. Leachate from landfills, industrial effluent, and agricultural chemicals all contribute significantly to water pollution. Chlorofluorocarbons are implicated in the destruction of the stratospheric ozone layer. The correct answer, therefore, is (C).

75. Radon is a major contributor to natural background radiation. There is a growing concern about radon as a health hazard because it can be trapped in houses, entering primarily through cracks in walls and floors in the foundation and in the drinking water. The entry of radon can be reduced significantly by sealing the foundation against the entry of the gas and providing good ventilation so that it does not accumulate. The correct answer, therefore, is (D).

Chapter 17

Practice Questions for the
Physics: Content Knowledge Tests

▶   ▶   ▶   ▶   ▶   ▶   ▶   ▶   ▶   ▶   ▶   ▶

Practice Questions

Now that you have studied the content topics and have worked through strategies relating to multiple-choice questions, you should take the following practice test. You will probably find it helpful to simulate actual testing conditions, giving yourself about 90 minutes to work on the questions. You can cut out and use the answer sheet provided if you wish.

Keep in mind that the test you take at an actual administration will have different questions.

You should not expect the percentage of questions you answer correctly in these practice questions to be exactly the same as when you take the test at an actual administration, since numerous factors affect a person's performance in any given testing situation.

When you have finished the practice questions, you can score your answers and read the explanations of the best answer choices in chapter 18.

THE PRAXIS SERIES
Professional Assessments for Beginning Teachers®

TEST CODE:

TEST NAME:
Physics:
Content Knowledge

Practice Questions

Calculators Prohibited

Time—90 Minutes
75 Questions

(Note, at the official administration of test 0261, there will be 50 questions, and you will be allowed 60 minutes to complete the test; for test 0265, there will be 100 questions, and you will be allowed 120 minutes to complete the test.)

Answer Sheet C

PAGE 1

THE PRAXIS SERIES®
Professional Assessments for Beginning Teachers®

DO NOT USE INK

Use only a pencil with soft black lead (No. 2 or HB) to complete this answer sheet.
Be sure to fill in completely the oval that corresponds to the proper letter or number.
Completely erase any errors or stray marks.

1. NAME
Enter your last name and first initial.
Omit spaces, hyphens, apostrophes, etc.

Last Name (first 6 letters) — F I

A B C D E F G H I J K L M N O P Q R S T U V W X Y Z

2.

YOUR NAME: (Print)
Last Name (Family or Surname) — First Name (Given) — M. I.

MAILING ADDRESS: (Print)
P.O. Box or Street Address — Apt. # (If any)

City — State or Province

Country — Zip or Postal Code

TELEPHONE NUMBER: ( ) Home — ( ) Business

SIGNATURE:

TEST DATE:

3. DATE OF BIRTH

Month	Day
Jan.	
Feb.	
Mar.	
April	
May	
June	
July	
Aug.	
Sept.	
Oct.	
Nov.	
Dec.	

4. SOCIAL SECURITY NUMBER

0 1 2 3 4 5 6 7 8 9

5. CANDIDATE ID NUMBER

0 1 2 3 4 5 6 7 8 9

6. TEST CENTER / REPORTING LOCATION

Center Number — Room Number

Center Name

City — State or Province

Country

7. TEST CODE / FORM CODE

0 1 2 3 4 5 6 7 8 9

8. TEST BOOK SERIAL NUMBER

9. TEST FORM

10. TEST NAME

Educational Testing Service, ETS, the ETS logo, and THE PRAXIS SERIES:PROFESSIONAL
ASSESSMENTS FOR BEGINNING TEACHERS and its logo are registered trademarks of
Educational Testing Service.

ETS Educational Testing Service

I.N. 202974

51055 • 08920 • TF71M500   Q2573-06
MH01159

1 2 3 4

CERTIFICATION STATEMENT: (Please write the following statement below. DO NOT PRINT.)

"I hereby agree to the conditions set forth in the *Registration Bulletin* and certify that I am the person whose name and address appear on this answer sheet."

_____

_____

_____

SIGNATURE: _____   DATE: _____ / _____ / _____

Month   Day   Year

BE SURE EACH MARK IS DARK AND COMPLETELY FILLS THE INTENDED SPACE AS ILLUSTRATED HERE: ⬤ .

1 Ⓐ Ⓑ Ⓒ Ⓓ	41 Ⓐ Ⓑ Ⓒ Ⓓ	81 Ⓐ Ⓑ Ⓒ Ⓓ	121 Ⓐ Ⓑ Ⓒ Ⓓ
2 Ⓐ Ⓑ Ⓒ Ⓓ	42 Ⓐ Ⓑ Ⓒ Ⓓ	82 Ⓐ Ⓑ Ⓒ Ⓓ	122 Ⓐ Ⓑ Ⓒ Ⓓ
3 Ⓐ Ⓑ Ⓒ Ⓓ	43 Ⓐ Ⓑ Ⓒ Ⓓ	83 Ⓐ Ⓑ Ⓒ Ⓓ	123 Ⓐ Ⓑ Ⓒ Ⓓ
4 Ⓐ Ⓑ Ⓒ Ⓓ	44 Ⓐ Ⓑ Ⓒ Ⓓ	84 Ⓐ Ⓑ Ⓒ Ⓓ	124 Ⓐ Ⓑ Ⓒ Ⓓ
5 Ⓐ Ⓑ Ⓒ Ⓓ	45 Ⓐ Ⓑ Ⓒ Ⓓ	85 Ⓐ Ⓑ Ⓒ Ⓓ	125 Ⓐ Ⓑ Ⓒ Ⓓ
6 Ⓐ Ⓑ Ⓒ Ⓓ	46 Ⓐ Ⓑ Ⓒ Ⓓ	86 Ⓐ Ⓑ Ⓒ Ⓓ	126 Ⓐ Ⓑ Ⓒ Ⓓ
7 Ⓐ Ⓑ Ⓒ Ⓓ	47 Ⓐ Ⓑ Ⓒ Ⓓ	87 Ⓐ Ⓑ Ⓒ Ⓓ	127 Ⓐ Ⓑ Ⓒ Ⓓ
8 Ⓐ Ⓑ Ⓒ Ⓓ	48 Ⓐ Ⓑ Ⓒ Ⓓ	88 Ⓐ Ⓑ Ⓒ Ⓓ	128 Ⓐ Ⓑ Ⓒ Ⓓ
9 Ⓐ Ⓑ Ⓒ Ⓓ	49 Ⓐ Ⓑ Ⓒ Ⓓ	89 Ⓐ Ⓑ Ⓒ Ⓓ	129 Ⓐ Ⓑ Ⓒ Ⓓ
10 Ⓐ Ⓑ Ⓒ Ⓓ	50 Ⓐ Ⓑ Ⓒ Ⓓ	90 Ⓐ Ⓑ Ⓒ Ⓓ	130 Ⓐ Ⓑ Ⓒ Ⓓ
11 Ⓐ Ⓑ Ⓒ Ⓓ	51 Ⓐ Ⓑ Ⓒ Ⓓ	91 Ⓐ Ⓑ Ⓒ Ⓓ	131 Ⓐ Ⓑ Ⓒ Ⓓ
12 Ⓐ Ⓑ Ⓒ Ⓓ	52 Ⓐ Ⓑ Ⓒ Ⓓ	92 Ⓐ Ⓑ Ⓒ Ⓓ	132 Ⓐ Ⓑ Ⓒ Ⓓ
13 Ⓐ Ⓑ Ⓒ Ⓓ	53 Ⓐ Ⓑ Ⓒ Ⓓ	93 Ⓐ Ⓑ Ⓒ Ⓓ	133 Ⓐ Ⓑ Ⓒ Ⓓ
14 Ⓐ Ⓑ Ⓒ Ⓓ	54 Ⓐ Ⓑ Ⓒ Ⓓ	94 Ⓐ Ⓑ Ⓒ Ⓓ	134 Ⓐ Ⓑ Ⓒ Ⓓ
15 Ⓐ Ⓑ Ⓒ Ⓓ	55 Ⓐ Ⓑ Ⓒ Ⓓ	95 Ⓐ Ⓑ Ⓒ Ⓓ	135 Ⓐ Ⓑ Ⓒ Ⓓ
16 Ⓐ Ⓑ Ⓒ Ⓓ	56 Ⓐ Ⓑ Ⓒ Ⓓ	96 Ⓐ Ⓑ Ⓒ Ⓓ	136 Ⓐ Ⓑ Ⓒ Ⓓ
17 Ⓐ Ⓑ Ⓒ Ⓓ	57 Ⓐ Ⓑ Ⓒ Ⓓ	97 Ⓐ Ⓑ Ⓒ Ⓓ	137 Ⓐ Ⓑ Ⓒ Ⓓ
18 Ⓐ Ⓑ Ⓒ Ⓓ	58 Ⓐ Ⓑ Ⓒ Ⓓ	98 Ⓐ Ⓑ Ⓒ Ⓓ	138 Ⓐ Ⓑ Ⓒ Ⓓ
19 Ⓐ Ⓑ Ⓒ Ⓓ	59 Ⓐ Ⓑ Ⓒ Ⓓ	99 Ⓐ Ⓑ Ⓒ Ⓓ	139 Ⓐ Ⓑ Ⓒ Ⓓ
20 Ⓐ Ⓑ Ⓒ Ⓓ	60 Ⓐ Ⓑ Ⓒ Ⓓ	100 Ⓐ Ⓑ Ⓒ Ⓓ	140 Ⓐ Ⓑ Ⓒ Ⓓ
21 Ⓐ Ⓑ Ⓒ Ⓓ	61 Ⓐ Ⓑ Ⓒ Ⓓ	101 Ⓐ Ⓑ Ⓒ Ⓓ	141 Ⓐ Ⓑ Ⓒ Ⓓ
22 Ⓐ Ⓑ Ⓒ Ⓓ	62 Ⓐ Ⓑ Ⓒ Ⓓ	102 Ⓐ Ⓑ Ⓒ Ⓓ	142 Ⓐ Ⓑ Ⓒ Ⓓ
23 Ⓐ Ⓑ Ⓒ Ⓓ	63 Ⓐ Ⓑ Ⓒ Ⓓ	103 Ⓐ Ⓑ Ⓒ Ⓓ	143 Ⓐ Ⓑ Ⓒ Ⓓ
24 Ⓐ Ⓑ Ⓒ Ⓓ	64 Ⓐ Ⓑ Ⓒ Ⓓ	104 Ⓐ Ⓑ Ⓒ Ⓓ	144 Ⓐ Ⓑ Ⓒ Ⓓ
25 Ⓐ Ⓑ Ⓒ Ⓓ	65 Ⓐ Ⓑ Ⓒ Ⓓ	105 Ⓐ Ⓑ Ⓒ Ⓓ	145 Ⓐ Ⓑ Ⓒ Ⓓ
26 Ⓐ Ⓑ Ⓒ Ⓓ	66 Ⓐ Ⓑ Ⓒ Ⓓ	106 Ⓐ Ⓑ Ⓒ Ⓓ	146 Ⓐ Ⓑ Ⓒ Ⓓ
27 Ⓐ Ⓑ Ⓒ Ⓓ	67 Ⓐ Ⓑ Ⓒ Ⓓ	107 Ⓐ Ⓑ Ⓒ Ⓓ	147 Ⓐ Ⓑ Ⓒ Ⓓ
28 Ⓐ Ⓑ Ⓒ Ⓓ	68 Ⓐ Ⓑ Ⓒ Ⓓ	108 Ⓐ Ⓑ Ⓒ Ⓓ	148 Ⓐ Ⓑ Ⓒ Ⓓ
29 Ⓐ Ⓑ Ⓒ Ⓓ	69 Ⓐ Ⓑ Ⓒ Ⓓ	109 Ⓐ Ⓑ Ⓒ Ⓓ	149 Ⓐ Ⓑ Ⓒ Ⓓ
30 Ⓐ Ⓑ Ⓒ Ⓓ	70 Ⓐ Ⓑ Ⓒ Ⓓ	110 Ⓐ Ⓑ Ⓒ Ⓓ	150 Ⓐ Ⓑ Ⓒ Ⓓ
31 Ⓐ Ⓑ Ⓒ Ⓓ	71 Ⓐ Ⓑ Ⓒ Ⓓ	111 Ⓐ Ⓑ Ⓒ Ⓓ	151 Ⓐ Ⓑ Ⓒ Ⓓ
32 Ⓐ Ⓑ Ⓒ Ⓓ	72 Ⓐ Ⓑ Ⓒ Ⓓ	112 Ⓐ Ⓑ Ⓒ Ⓓ	152 Ⓐ Ⓑ Ⓒ Ⓓ
33 Ⓐ Ⓑ Ⓒ Ⓓ	73 Ⓐ Ⓑ Ⓒ Ⓓ	113 Ⓐ Ⓑ Ⓒ Ⓓ	153 Ⓐ Ⓑ Ⓒ Ⓓ
34 Ⓐ Ⓑ Ⓒ Ⓓ	74 Ⓐ Ⓑ Ⓒ Ⓓ	114 Ⓐ Ⓑ Ⓒ Ⓓ	154 Ⓐ Ⓑ Ⓒ Ⓓ
35 Ⓐ Ⓑ Ⓒ Ⓓ	75 Ⓐ Ⓑ Ⓒ Ⓓ	115 Ⓐ Ⓑ Ⓒ Ⓓ	155 Ⓐ Ⓑ Ⓒ Ⓓ
36 Ⓐ Ⓑ Ⓒ Ⓓ	76 Ⓐ Ⓑ Ⓒ Ⓓ	116 Ⓐ Ⓑ Ⓒ Ⓓ	156 Ⓐ Ⓑ Ⓒ Ⓓ
37 Ⓐ Ⓑ Ⓒ Ⓓ	77 Ⓐ Ⓑ Ⓒ Ⓓ	117 Ⓐ Ⓑ Ⓒ Ⓓ	157 Ⓐ Ⓑ Ⓒ Ⓓ
38 Ⓐ Ⓑ Ⓒ Ⓓ	78 Ⓐ Ⓑ Ⓒ Ⓓ	118 Ⓐ Ⓑ Ⓒ Ⓓ	158 Ⓐ Ⓑ Ⓒ Ⓓ
39 Ⓐ Ⓑ Ⓒ Ⓓ	79 Ⓐ Ⓑ Ⓒ Ⓓ	119 Ⓐ Ⓑ Ⓒ Ⓓ	159 Ⓐ Ⓑ Ⓒ Ⓓ
40 Ⓐ Ⓑ Ⓒ Ⓓ	80 Ⓐ Ⓑ Ⓒ Ⓓ	120 Ⓐ Ⓑ Ⓒ Ⓓ	160 Ⓐ Ⓑ Ⓒ Ⓓ

FOR ETS USE ONLY	R1	R2	R3	R4	R5	R6	R7	R8	TR	CS

PERIODIC TABLE OF THE ELEMENTS

1 H 1.0079																	2 He 4.0026
3 Li 6.941	4 Be 9.012											5 B 10.811	6 C 12.011	7 N 14.007	8 O 16.00	9 F 19.00	10 Ne 20.179
11 Na 22.99	12 Mg 24.30											13 Al 26.98	14 Si 28.09	15 P 30.974	16 S 32.06	17 Cl 35.453	18 Ar 39.948
19 K 39.10	20 Ca 40.08	21 Sc 44.96	22 Ti 47.90	23 V 50.94	24 Cr 52.00	25 Mn 54.938	26 Fe 55.85	27 Co 58.93	28 Ni 58.69	29 Cu 63.55	30 Zn 65.39	31 Ga 69.72	32 Ge 72.59	33 As 74.92	34 Se 78.96	35 Br 79.90	36 Kr 83.80
37 Rb 85.47	38 Sr 87.62	39 Y 88.91	40 Zr 91.22	41 Nb 92.91	42 Mo 95.94	43 Tc (98)	44 Ru 101.1	45 Rh 102.91	46 Pd 106.42	47 Ag 107.87	48 Cd 112.41	49 In 114.82	50 Sn 118.71	51 Sb 121.75	52 Te 127.60	53 I 126.91	54 Xe 131.29
55 Cs 132.91	56 Ba 137.33	57 *La 138.91	72 Hf 178.49	73 Ta 180.95	74 W 183.85	75 Re 186.21	76 Os 190.2	77 Ir 192.2	78 Pt 195.08	79 Au 196.97	80 Hg 200.59	81 Tl 204.38	82 Pb 207.2	83 Bi 208.98	84 Po (209)	85 At (210)	86 Rn (222)
87 Fr (223)	88 Ra 226.02	89 †Ac 227.03	104 Rf (261)	105 Db (262)	106 Sg (263)	107 Bh (262)	108 Hs (265)	109 Mt (266)	110 § (269)	111 § (272)	112 § (277)						

§Not yet named

*Lanthanide Series

58 Ce 140.12	59 Pr 140.91	60 Nd 144.24	61 Pm (145)	62 Sm 150.4	63 Eu 151.97	64 Gd 157.25	65 Tb 158.93	66 Dy 162.50	67 Ho 164.93	68 Er 167.26	69 Tm 168.93	70 Yb 173.04	71 Lu 174.97

† Actinide Series

90 Th 232.04	91 Pa 231.04	92 U 238.03	93 Np 237.05	94 Pu (244)	95 Am (243)	96 Cm (247)	97 Bk (247)	98 Cf (251)	99 Es (252)	100 Fm (257)	101 Md (258)	102 No (259)	103 Lr (260)

TABLE OF INFORMATION

Electron rest mass	m_e	= 9.11×10^{-31} kilogram
Proton rest mass	m_p	= 1.672×10^{-27} kilogram
Neutron rest mass	m_n	= 1.675×10^{-27} kilogram
Magnitude of the electron charge	e	= 1.60×10^{-19} coulomb
Bohr radius	a_0	= 5.29×10^{-11} meter
Avogadro's number	N_A	= 6.02×10^{23} per mole
Universal gas constant	R	= 8.314 joules/(mole • K)
		= 0.0821 L • atm/(mole • K)
Boltzmann constant	k	= 1.38×10^{-23} joule/K
Planck constant	h	= 6.63×10^{-34} joule • second
		= 4.14×10^{-15} eV • second
Speed of light	c	= 3.00×10^8 meters/second
Vacuum permittivity	ϵ_0	= 8.85×10^{-12} coulomb^2/(newton • meter^2)
Vacuum permeability	μ_0	= 4×10^{-7} newton/ampere^2
Coulomb constant	$1/4\,\epsilon_0$	= 8.99×10^9 newtons • meter^2/coulomb^2
Universal gravitational constant	G	= 6.67×10^{-11} newton • meter^2/kilogram^2
Acceleration due to gravity	g	= 9.80 meters/second^2
1 atmosphere pressure	1 atm	= 1.0×10^5 newtons/meter^2
		= 1.0×10^5 pascals (Pa)
Faraday constant	$\mathscr{F}$	= 9.65×10^4 coulombs/mole
1 atomic mass unit	1 amu	= 1.66×10^{-27} kilogram
1 electron volt	1 eV	= 1.602×10^{-19} joule

For H_2O:

heat of fusion	3.33×10^2 joules/gram
heat of vaporization	2.26×10^3 joules/gram
mean specific heat (liquid)	4.19 joules/(gram • K)

Volume of 1 mole of ideal gas at 0°C, 1 atmosphere   22.4 liters

PHYSICS: CONTENT KNOWLEDGE

1. A ball rolls up an inclined plane and then rolls back down to its initial position. Which of the following graphs best represents the velocity of the ball as a function of time?

(A)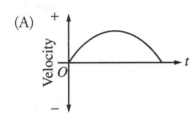

(B)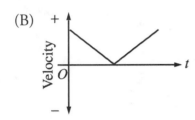

(C)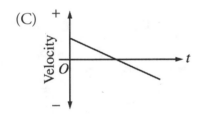

(D)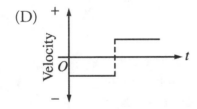

2. A student throws a ball upward at an acute angle. Which two of the following graphs best represent the vertical component of the motion of the ball? (Note that the y-axis differs on the graphs.)

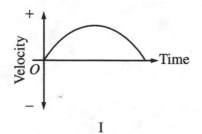

I

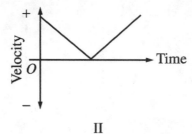

II

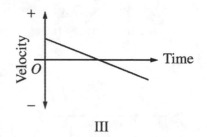

III

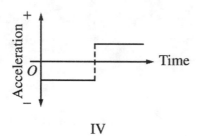

IV

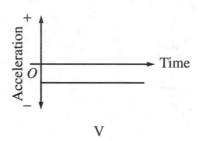

V

(A) I and IV
(B) II and IV
(C) III and IV
(D) III and V

3. A student walks 15 meters east and then turns and walks 20 meters north in a total time of 10 seconds. Which of the following gives the magnitude of the student's average velocity?

(A) 1.5 m/s
(B) 2.0 m/s
(C) 2.5 m/s
(D) 3.5 m/s

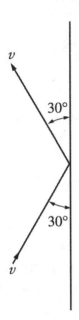

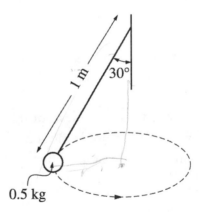

4. A 1.0-kilogram ball is moving at 4 meters per second on a horizontal surface and strikes a wall at an angle of 30 degrees relative to the wall, as shown in the figure above. The ball bounces off the wall at the same angle and speed. The magnitude of the change in momentum of the ball is

(A) zero
(B) 1.0 kg · m/s
(C) 2.0 kg · m/s
(D) 4.0 kg · m/s

5. A projectile is launched with a speed of 40 meters per second at an angle of 60 degrees with the horizontal. At the maximum height of its flight, the values for the speed and acceleration of the projectile are given by which of the following? (Assume air resistance is negligible.)

	Speed	Acceleration
(A)	40 m/s	0
(B)	40 m/s	9.8 m/s^2
(C)	20 m/s	0
(D)	20 m/s	9.8 m/s^2

6. The speed versus time graph shown above represents the motion of a car. Approximately how far did the car travel during the first 5 seconds?

(A) 100 m
(B) 150 m
(C) 200 m
(D) 250 m

7. A 0.5-kilogram mass is attached to a 1.0-meter-long string and whirled around in a horizontal circle, as shown in the figure above. If the frequency of the motion is 0.5 cycle per second and the string makes a constant angle of 30° with the vertical, the linear speed of the mass is

(A) 1.57 m/s
(B) 3.14 m/s
(C) 6.28 m/s
(D) 12.56 m/s

8. A simple pendulum on Earth has a period of 2.0 seconds. The same pendulum is taken to Planet X, which has an acceleration due to gravity that is one-fourth that of Earth's. What is the period of the pendulum on Planet X?

    (A) 0.25 seconds
    (B) 2.0 seconds
    (C) 4.0 seconds
    (D) 8.0 seconds

9. A mass is tied to a string and whirled in a horizontal circle at constant speed. The mass has a centripetal acceleration of magnitude a_c. If the speed of the mass is tripled without any change to the length of the string, then the magnitude of the centripetal acceleration of the mass is

    (A) $\frac{1}{9}a_c$
    (B) $\frac{1}{3}a_c$
    (C) $3a_c$
    (D) $9a_c$

10. A mass suspended from an ideal spring oscillates in simple harmonic motion. The restoring force must be proportional to the

    (A) frequency
    (B) displacement
    (C) velocity
    (D) amplitude

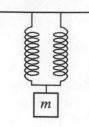

Figure 1   Figure 2

11. A mass m is attached to a spring of force constant k, as shown in Figure 1 above. The mass oscillates with period T_1. If a second spring of the same length and force constant is connected in parallel to the first spring, as shown in Figure 2, then the same mass m will oscillate with period

    (A) $2T_1$
    (B) $\sqrt{2}T_1$
    (C) T_1
    (D) $\dfrac{T_1}{\sqrt{2}}$

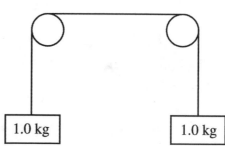

12 A string of negligible mass has a 1-kilogram block attached to each end. When the string is hung over two frictionless pulleys, as shown in the figure above, it remains at rest. Which of the following represents the tension in the string? (Assume that $g = 10$ m/s^2.)

    (A) Zero
    (B) 2 N
    (C) 10 N
    (D) 20 N

13. An object is accelerated when a net force is applied. Which of the following graphs gives the relationship between the acceleration of the object and its mass if the net force is kept constant but the mass of the object is continuously increased?

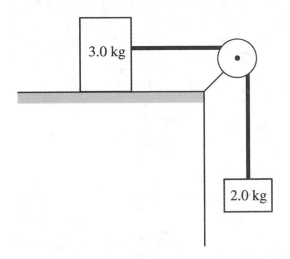

(A)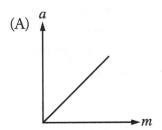

(B)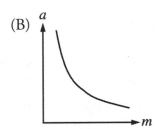

(C)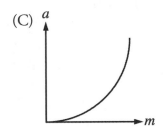

(D)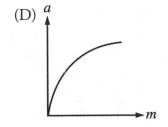

14. Blocks of 3.0 kilograms and 2.0 kilograms are connected to the ends of a string. As shown in the figure above, the 3.0-kilogram block sits on a level frictionless table, and the 2.0-kilogram block is hung over a frictionless, massless pulley. Which of the following represents the tension in the string that connects the blocks? (Assume that $g = 10$ m/s^2.)

(A) 10 N
(B) 12 N
(C) 20 N
(D) 28 N

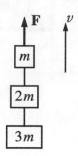

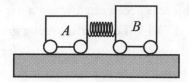

15. Three blocks with masses of m, $2m$, and $3m$ are connected by strings, as shown in the figure above. After an upward force **F** is applied on block m, the masses move upward at constant speed v. What is the net force on the block of mass $2m$?

(A) Zero
(B) $2mg$
(C) $3mg$
(D) $6mg$

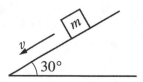

16. A block of mass m slides with constant speed v down an inclined plane of 30°, as shown in the figure above. Which of the following represents the coefficient of kinetic friction between the block and the plane?

(A) sin 30°
(B) cos 30°
(C) tan 30°
(D) $mg \cdot$ sin 30°

17. In the figure above, carts A and B are held together by a compressed spring. The mass of cart B is greater than the mass of cart A. Which of the following will be the same for both carts just after the spring is released?

(A) Speed
(B) Kinetic energy
(C) Magnitude of the acceleration
(D) Magnitude of the momentum

18. Planet X has twice the radius and six times the mass of Earth. Which of the following gives the acceleration of gravity at the surface of Planet X? (Assume that the acceleration due to gravity on Earth is 10.0 m/s².)

(A) 1.67 m/s²
(B) 6.67 m/s²
(C) 15.0 m/s²
(D) 60.0 m/s²

19. A single roller coaster car has a speed of 20 meters per second at the lowest point on the track. Which of the following represents the maximum height that the cart can reach on the track? (Neglect rolling friction and air resistance, and assume that g = 10 m/s².)

(A) 1 m
(B) 10 m
(C) 20 m
(D) 40 m

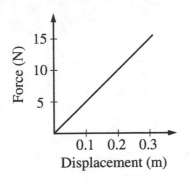

20. A graph of force versus the displacement of a bowstring is shown in the figure above. Which of the following represents the potential energy stored in the bowstring when the displacement is 0.2 meter?

(A) 1.0 J
(B) 2.0 J
(C) 5.0 J
(D) 10.0 J

21. Two artificial satellites, A and B, are traveling in circular orbits situated at the same altitude above Earth's surface. The mass of satellite A is twice the mass of satellite B. If the period of satellite A is T, what is the period of satellite B?

(A) $\frac{T}{4}$

(B) $\frac{T}{2}$

(C) T

(D) $2T$

22. In a head-on collision, a 3.0-kilogram puck moves at 8.0 meters per second toward a 4.0-kilogram puck that is initially at rest. The pucks move with negligible friction on a horizontal surface. After collision, the 3.0-kilogram puck is at rest. The speed of the 4.0-kilogram puck after collision is

(A) zero
(B) 3.4 m/s
(C) 6.0 m/s
(D) 8.0 m/s

23. Two objects of equal mass are attached to a circular platform that is rotating with increasing angular velocity about a fixed axis. If the two objects are located at different distances from the axis, which of the following is a true statement about the objects?

(A) Both objects have the same centripetal acceleration.
(B) Both objects have the same tangential acceleration.
(C) Both objects have the same moment of inertia about the fixed axis.
(D) Both objects have the same instantaneous angular velocity.

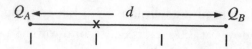

24. The figure above shows two point charges Q_A and Q_B separated by a distance d. Which of the following values of the charges will yield an electric field of zero at point X ?

	Q_A	Q_B
(A)	$-1q$	$-3q$
(B)	$+1q$	$+3q$
(C)	$+1q$	$-4q$
(D)	$+1q$	$+4q$

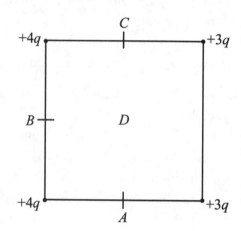

25. The figure above shows point charges $+4q$, $+4q$, $+3q$, and $+3q$ located at the corners of a square. At which of the labeled points shown does the electric field vector **E** point directly to the left? (A, B, and C are at the midpoints of the sides, and D is at the center of the square.)

(A) A
(B) B
(C) C
(D) D

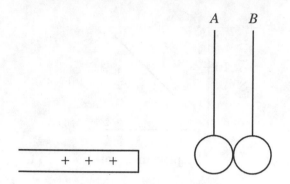

26. Two uncharged conducting spheres, A and B, are suspended from insulating threads so that they touch each other. A positively charged rod is brought near sphere A, but not touching it, as shown in the figure above. While the rod is in place, sphere B is separated from sphere A. Which of the following represents the charges on the two spheres?

	Sphere A	Sphere B
(A)	Uncharged	Negative
(B)	Positive	Uncharged
(C)	Positive	Negative
(D)	Negative	Positive

27. Two identical conducting spheres initially carry charges of $+4.0$ microcoulombs and -1.0 microcoulomb, respectively, and the centers of the spheres are separated by a distance of 2.0 centimeters. The charge on the -1.0 microcoulomb conducting sphere is then increased to -2.0 microcoulombs, and the distance between the centers of the spheres is increased to 4.0 centimeters. In terms of the original electrostatic force between the spheres, what is the magnitude of the new electrostatic force between them?

(A) It is equal to one-fourth the original force.
(B) It is equal to one-half the original force.
(C) It is equal to the original force.
(D) It is equal to twice the original force.

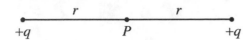

+q   P   +q

28. Two positive point charges are equidistant from a point P, as shown in the figure above. Which of the following is a true statement about this configuration of charges?

(A) The electrostatic force between the two charges is equal to zero.
(B) The electric field at point P is equal to zero.
(C) The electric field at point P is perpendicular to the line joining the two charges.
(D) The electric potential at point P is equal to zero.

29. Which of the following combinations of charges has the greatest electric potential energy?

(A) +2 q   +2 q
      d

(B) +2 q   −4 q
      d

(C) +2 q   +2 q
        2d

(D) +2 q   −4 q
        2d

30. A 5-ohm resistor and a 10-ohm resistor are connected in parallel to a battery. If heat is dissipated in the 5-ohm resistor at a rate of P, then the rate at which heat is dissipated in the 10-ohm resistor is

(A) $\dfrac{P}{2}$

(B) P
(C) $2P$
(D) $4P$

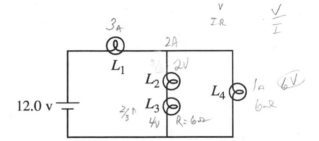

31. A 12.0-volt battery is connected to four lamps as shown in the circuit above. All the lamps are not identical. The current in lamp L_1 is 3 amperes, and the current in lamp L_4 is 1.0 ampere. The potential difference across lamp L_3 is 4.0 volts. The resistance of lamp L_4 is 6 ohms. Which of the following represents the resistance of lamp L_2?

(A) 1.0Ω
(B) 2.0Ω
(C) 3.0Ω
(D) 6.0Ω

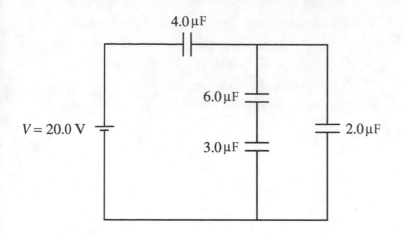

32. The equivalent capacitance of the circuit shown above is

    (A)   1.0 μF
    (B)   2.0 μF
    (C)   5.6 μF
    (D) 15.0 μF

33. A point charge q is located inside a spherical Gaussian surface of radius r. Which of the following is true of the net electric flux through the surface?

    (A) It is equal to zero.
    (B) It is proportional to q.
    (C) It is proportional to $1/r^2$.
    (D) It is independent of q and r.

34. A conductor moves through a uniform magnetic field **B** that is directed into the page of the paper, as shown in the figure above. If the induced charge separation in the conductor is as shown above, then the conductor is moving in which direction?

    (A) To the right
    (B) To the left
    (C) Toward the top of the page
    (D) Toward the bottom of the page

35. A charged particle with velocity **v** enters a region of magnetic field **B** whose magnetic field lines are perpendicular in direction to the particle's velocity. The particle moves in a circular path of radius r in this region. Suppose for this same charged particle that the particle's velocity and the magnetic field are both doubled in magnitude. The particle would then move in a circular path of radius

    (A) $\frac{r}{4}$

    (B) $\frac{r}{2}$

    (C) r
    (D) $2r$

36. Two large, oppositely charged plates are initially separated by air, with a uniform electric field between them. A slab of teflon is put between the plates. If the charge on the plates does not change, which of the following statements is true?

   I. The electric field strength decreases.
  II. The electric field strength increases.
 III. The potential difference between the plates increases.

(A) I only
(B) II only
(C) III only
(D) I and III

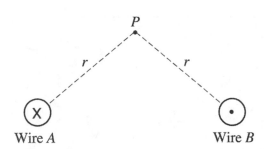

Wire *A*   Wire *B*

37. Two very long parallel conducting wires *A* and *B* carry equal conventional (positive) currents in opposite directions. Wire *A* carries a current into the page and wire *B* carries a current out of the page, as shown in the figure above. At point *P*, which is an equal distance *r* from each wire, the magnetic field is

(A) zero
(B) directed toward the top of the page
(C) directed toward the bottom of the page
(D) directed to the right of the page

38. An ion of charge $+e$ moving horizontally with a velocity v passes into a region in which there is a uniform vertical magnetic field **B**. Which of the following gives the magnitude of the smallest electric field that will allow the ion to pass through undeflected? (Ignore the gravitational force, which is rather small.)

(A) B/v
(B) qB/v
(C) Bv
(D) qBv

39. Which of the following gives the magnetic force $\mathbf{F_B}$ on a particle of charge q moving with velocity **v** in a uniform magnetic field **B**?

(A) $\mathbf{F_B} = q\mathbf{B}$
(B) $\mathbf{F_B} = q\,\mathbf{v} \cdot \mathbf{B}$
(C) $\mathbf{F_B} = q\,\mathbf{v} \times \mathbf{B}$
(D) $\mathbf{F_B} = \dfrac{q\mathbf{B}}{v}$

40. An ideal step-down transformer is characterized by which of the following?

  I. The current in the primary is larger than the current in the secondary.

  II. The number of turns in the secondary is less than the number of turns in the primary.

  III. The voltage in the secondary is less than the voltage in the primary.

(A) I only

(B) II only

(C) III only

(D) II and III

41. Which of the following waves would bend most readily around an obstacle such as a building?

(A) X-rays

(B) AM radio waves

(C) FM radio waves

(D) Ultraviolet radiation

42. Observer A is twice as far away as observer B is from an aerial fireworks display. If the fireworks emit sound uniformly in all directions, then the ratio of the sound intensity heard by observer A to the intensity heard by observer B is

(A) $\frac{1}{4}$

(B) $\frac{1}{2}$

(C) $\frac{2}{1}$

(D) $\frac{4}{1}$

43. When a fire truck is at rest relative to an observer, the observer finds that the sound emitted by the fire truck's siren has frequency f and wavelength λ. Which of the following would characterize the frequency and wavelength of the emitted sound if the fire truck were moving toward the observer?

(A) The frequency would be greater than f and the wavelength less than λ.

(B) The frequency would be greater than f and the wavelength greater than λ.

(C) The frequency would be less than f and the wavelength less than λ.

(D) The frequency would be less than f and the wavelength greater than λ.

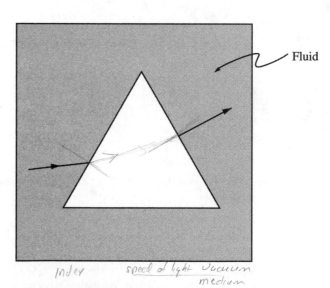

44. A glass prism bends a ray of light upward, as shown in the figure above. The index of refraction of the fluid surrounding the prism is

(A) zero

(B) less than the index of refraction of the glass prism

(C) equal to the index of refraction of the glass prism

(D) greater than the index of refraction of the glass prism

45. By which of the following means would sunlight become polarized?

   I. Reflection from a horizontal surface
   II. Scattering by molecules in the atmosphere
   III. Interference by passage through a diffraction grating

(A) I only
(B) II only
(C) III only
(D) I and II

46. A girl of height h stands in front of a plane mirror. Which of the following gives the minimum length of the plane mirror that is needed for the girl to see a full-sized image?

(A) $\frac{1}{4}h$
(B) $\frac{1}{2}h$
(C) h
(D) $2h$

47. If the image of an object in front of a mirror is virtual, enlarged, and upright, then the object is located between

(A) a concave mirror and its focal point
(B) a convex mirror and its focal point
(C) the focal point and center of curvature of a concave mirror
(D) the focal point and center of curvature of a convex mirror

48. If an object placed 10.0 centimeters in front of a convex mirror produces a virtual image 5.0 centimeters behind the mirror, the focal length of the convex mirror is

(A)   3.33 cm
(B)   5.0 cm
(C)   −5.0 cm
(D) −10.0 cm

49. A ball is at rest at the bottom of a pool of water that has a depth of 1.0 meter. If the index of refraction of the water is 4/3, how deep does the ball appear to be?

(A) 0.50 m
(B) 0.75 m
(C) 1.00 m
(D) 1.33 m

50. Which of the following is the phenomenon underlying fiber optics?

(A) Diffraction
(B) Interference
(C) Polarization
(D) Total internal reflection

51. A soap bubble is multicolored when viewed in the sunlight because of which of the following phenomena?

(A) Diffraction
(B) Polarization
(C) Interference
(D) Total internal reflection

52. If an object placed 0.25 meter from a converging lens forms a real image 1.0 meter from the lens, the focal length of the lens is

(A) less than 0.25 m
(B) between 0.25 m and 1.0 m
(C) equal to 1.0 m
(D) greater than 1.0 m

53. Which of the following electromagnetic waves has the longest wavelength?

(A) Infrared waves
(B) Ultraviolet waves
(C) Radio waves
(D) Gamma rays

54. A simple pendulum is made using a long, thin wire. When the temperature decreases, what happens to the period of the pendulum?

(A) The period of the pendulum increases.
(B) The period of the pendulum decreases.
(C) The period of the pendulum stays the same.
(D) The effect on the period cannot be determined without knowing the mass of the pendulum bob.

55. The Hubble space telescope is covered with a highly reflecting metal foil for which of the following reasons?

(A) To absorb radiant energy when the telescope is outside Earth's shadow
(B) To increase radiant energy loss when the telescope is inside Earth's shadow
(C) To minimize temperature changes as the telescope orbits
(D) To reduce glare

56. When someone steps out of a hot shower, why does a tile floor feel much colder to the touch than a cloth mat that is at the same temperature as the tile?

(A) The thermal conductivity of the tile is greater than that of the cloth mat.
(B) The thermal conductivity of the cloth mat is greater than that of the tile.
(C) The tile floor is a better convector of heat than is the cloth mat.
(D) The tile floor is a better radiator of heat than is the cloth mat.

57. When 1,000 joules of heat is added to a gas, the internal energy of the gas increases by 600 joules. The work done by the gas is most nearly

(A) zero
(B) 400 J
(C) 600 J
(D) 1,600 J

58. 100 grams of water at 20.0°C is added to a 100-gram aluminum cup initially at 50.0°C. The final temperature of the water and cup is

(A) 20.0°C
(B) greater than 20.0°C but less than 35.0°C
(C) 35.0°C
(D) greater than 35.0°C but less than 50.0°C

59. A piston compresses an ideal gas at 300 Kelvin to a volume one-tenth of its original volume and a pressure 50 times its original pressure. What is the temperature of the gas after compression?

(A)   60 K
(B)   300 K
(C) 1,500 K
(D) 150,000 K

60. The half-life of radium-226 is 1,500 years. How many years would have to elapse before the radioactivity of a sample of radium-226 is reduced to 1/8 of its original value?

    (A) 750
    (B) 1,500
    (C) 3,000
    (D) 4,500

    [handwritten: $1500 - \frac{1}{2}$; $1500 - \frac{1}{4}$; $1500 - \frac{1}{8}$; 45]

61. In the photoelectric effect, increasing the intensity of the incident light would do which of the following?

    (A) Increase the kinetic energy of the photoelectrons that are emitted.
    (B) Decrease the kinetic energy of the photoelectrons that are emitted.
    (C) Increase the number of photoelectrons that are emitted.
    (D) Decrease the number of photoelectrons that are emitted.

62. In the Bohr model of the hydrogen atom, the radius a_o of the first ($n = 1$) orbit is known as the Bohr radius. In terms of the Bohr radius, the radius of the third ($n = 3$) Bohr orbit of hydrogen is

    (A) $a_o/3$
    (B) $3a_o$
    (C) $6a_o$
    (D) $9a_o$

63. The process by which heavy nuclei are split into intermediate nuclei with an accompanying release of energy is known as

    (A) nuclear fusion
    (B) nuclear fission
    (C) chain reaction
    (D) beta decay

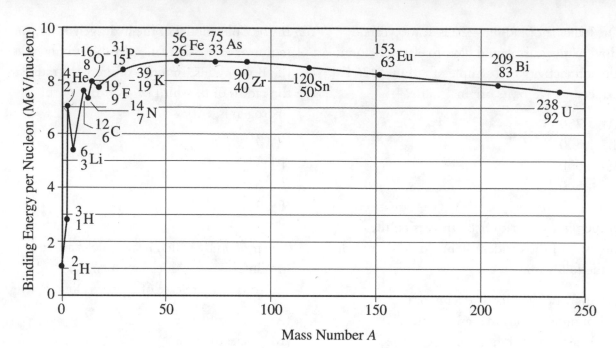

Mass Number A

64. A graph of the binding energy per nucleon
versus mass number is shown above. The region
of greatest nuclear stability would be for mass
numbers close to

(A) $A = 4$
(B) $A = 16$
(C) $A = 56$
(D) $A = 238$

65. A nucleus of $_{92}U^{238}$ decays by emitting an
alpha particle. The daughter nucleus that
results is given by which of the following?

(A) $_{90}Th^{234}$
(B) $_{91}Pa^{238}$
(C) $_{93}Np^{238}$
(D) $_{94}Pu^{242}$

$$U^{238}_{92} \longrightarrow Th^{234}_{90} + He^{4}_{2}$$

66. Which of the following materials would be used to shield and store a gamma ray source in the laboratory?

   (A) Plastic
   (B) Glass
   (C) Wood
   (D) Lead

67. Which of the following gives the equation of a parabola? (*m*, *a*, and *b* are constants.)

   (A) $xy = a$ hyperbola
   (B) $y = mx + b$ straight
   (C) $y = ax^2 + b$ parabola
   (D) $x^2 + y^2 = a^2$ circle

68. Suppose that a variable *y* is directly proportional to the square root of a variable *x*. Which of the following graphs best represents this relationship?

(A)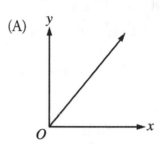

(B)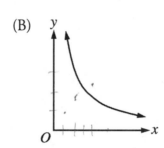

$y \sim \sqrt{x}$

4	2
16	4
36	6

(C)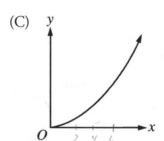

(D)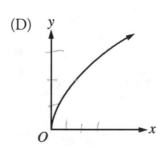

69. In an experiment to determine how the period of a simple pendulum is affected by its length, which of the following variables would most likely be the dependent variable?

    (A) The length of the pendulum
    (B) The period of the pendulum
    (C) The mass of the pendulum bob
    (D) The displacement of the pendulum bob

70. Which of the following circuits would be used to measure the resistance of a resistor, using a voltmeter and an ammeter?

    (A)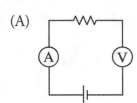

    (B)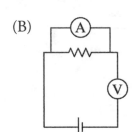

    (C)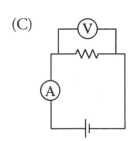

    (D)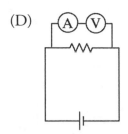

71. What temperature change in the Kelvin scale is equivalent to a 45-degree change in the Celsius scale?

    (A) 25 K
    (B) 45 K
    (C) 81 K
    (D) 273 K

72. Manufacturers are developing which of the following refrigerants in response to concerns over the destruction of ozone in the stratosphere?

    (A) Chlorinated methanes
    (B) Chlorine-free methanes
    (C) Freon
    (D) Benzene

73. All of the following techniques involve the use of ionizing radiation EXCEPT

    (A) x-ray imaging
    (B) magnetic resonance imaging (MRI)
    (C) computer tomography (CT) imaging
    (D) radiographic fluoroscopy

74. An underground site is being evaluated as a repository for the disposal of highly radioactive waste. Which of the following would be the LEAST important factor to consider?

    (A) Climate
    (B) Vulnerability to earthquakes
    (C) Volcanic activity
    (D) Groundwater flow

75. Radon is an odorless, radioactive gas and poses a health hazard when inhaled. Which of the following will reduce radon in the home?

    (A) Using masonry outside walls
    (B) Keeping the basement door closed
    (C) Increasing insulation in the walls and ceiling
    (D) Increasing ventilation

Chapter 18

Right Answers and Explanations for the Practice
Questions for the *Physics: Content Knowledge* Tests

▶   ▶   ▶   ▶   ▶   ▶   ▶   ▶   ▶   ▶   ▶   ▶

Right Answers and Explanations for the Practice Questions

Now that you have answered all of the practice questions, you can check your work.
Compare your answers with the correct answers in the table below.

Question Number	Correct Answer	Content Category	Question Number	Correct Answer	Content Category
1	C	Mechanics	39	C	Electricity and Magnetism
2	D	Mechanics	40	D	Electricity and Magnetism
3	C	Mechanics	41	B	Optics and Waves
4	D	Mechanics	42	A	Optics and Waves
5	D	Mechanics	43	A	Optics and Waves
6	B	Mechanics	44	D	Optics and Waves
7	A	Mechanics	45	D	Optics and Waves
8	C	Mechanics	46	B	Optics and Waves
9	D	Mechanics	47	A	Optics and Waves
10	B	Mechanics	48	D	Optics and Waves
11	D	Mechanics	49	B	Optics and Waves
12	C	Mechanics	50	D	Optics and Waves
13	B	Mechanics	51	C	Optics and Waves
14	B	Mechanics	52	A	Optics and Waves
15	A	Mechanics	53	C	Optics and Waves
16	C	Mechanics	54	B	Heat and Thermodynamics
17	D	Mechanics	55	C	Heat and Thermodynamics
18	C	Mechanics	56	A	Heat and Thermodynamics
19	C	Mechanics	57	B	Heat and Thermodynamics
20	A	Mechanics	58	B	Heat and Thermodynamics
21	C	Mechanics	59	C	Heat and Thermodynamics
22	C	Mechanics	60	D	Modern Physics, Atomic and Nuclear Structure
23	D	Mechanics	61	C	Modern Physics, Atomic and Nuclear Structure
24	D	Electricity and Magnetism	62	D	Modern Physics, Atomic and Nuclear Structure
25	B	Electricity and Magnetism	63	B	Modern Physics, Atomic and Nuclear Structure
26	D	Electricity and Magnetism	64	C	Modern Physics, Atomic and Nuclear Structure
27	B	Electricity and Magnetism	65	A	Modern Physics, Atomic and Nuclear Structure
28	B	Electricity and Magnetism	66	D	History and Nature of Science
29	B	Electricity and Magnetism	67	C	History and Nature of Science
30	A	Electricity and Magnetism	68	D	History and Nature of Science
31	A	Electricity and Magnetism	69	B	History and Nature of Science
32	B	Electricity and Magnetism	70	C	History and Nature of Science
33	B	Electricity and Magnetism	71	B	History and Nature of Science
34	A	Electricity and Magnetism	72	B	Science, Technology, and Social Perspectives
35	C	Electricity and Magnetism	73	B	Science, Technology, and Social Perspectives
36	A	Electricity and Magnetism	74	A	Science, Technology, and Social Perspectives
37	C	Electricity and Magnetism	75	D	Science, Technology, and Social Perspectives
38	C	Electricity and Magnetism			

Explanations of Right Answers

1. The net force on the ball is the component of the gravitational force (of Earth on the ball) parallel to the inclined plane. The ball slows down to a stop and then speeds up in the opposite direction. The rate of change of velocity stays the same. A constant rate of change of velocity is equal to the slope of a straight line on a velocity-time graph. The correct answer, therefore, is (C).

2. There is a net downward force on the ball due to Earth's gravitational field. The net downward force is a constant and produces a constant rate of change of velocity (i.e., constant acceleration) throughout the motion of the ball, which is represented by the straight line on the velocity-time graph in III. The horizontal line on the acceleration-time graph in V represents constant acceleration throughout the motion. The correct answer, therefore, is (D).

3. Velocity is the rate of change of position [$v = \Delta x/\Delta t$]. Adding the displacement vectors geometrically, you find that the student changed position by 25 meters in a time of 10 seconds. The correct answer, therefore, is (C).

4. The change in momentum [$\Delta p = p_f - p_i$] occurs only with the component of the momentum vector perpendicular to the wall, which is 2.0 kg · m/s [4.0 kg · m/s(sin 30°)]. Add the two vector components perpendicular to the wall: [2.0 kg · m/s $-(-2.0$ kg · m/s$) = 4.0$ kg · m/s]. The correct answer, therefore, is (D).

5. The horizontal component of the speed remains constant at 20 m/s [40 m/s(cos 60°)]. The vertical component of the speed changes and is zero at the maximum height because Earth's gravitational field slows the projectile down to a stop. Thus, the projectile's speed is 20 m/s at the maximum height. There is a net downward force due to Earth's gravitational field. The acceleration has only a vertical component, which is due to gravity, and has a constant value of 9.8 m/s^2 near Earth's surface. The correct answer, therefore, is (D).

6. The area under the curve is equal to the distance [$x = \frac{1}{2}$(20 m/s + 40 m/s) 5 s = 150 m].

   Alternatively, the acceleration is equal to the slope of the line [-4m/s^2]. Solve for the distance, using a constant-acceleration equation:

   [$x = v_0 t + \frac{1}{2}at^2 = $(40 m/s)(5 s)$ + \frac{1}{2}(-4$ m/s$^2)$ (25 s^2) = 200 m $-$ 50 m = 150 m].

   The correct answer, therefore, is (B).

7. The radius of the circle, r, is 0.5 m [$r = 1.0$ m (sin 30°)]. The linear speed of the mass is equal to the circumference [$2\pi r = 3.14$ m] multiplied by the frequency [0.5 Hz], which is equal to 1.57 m/s [$v = 2\pi rf$]. The correct answer, therefore, is (A).

8. The period (T) of a simple pendulum is dependent on its length (L) and the acceleration due to gravity (g).

$$T = 2\pi\sqrt{\frac{L}{g}}$$

The length of the pendulum was kept the same; therefore, $T^2 g$ is equal to a constant $[T_1^2 g_1 = T_2^2 g_2]$. Solve the equation for the period on Planet X: $[T_2^2 = (2s)^2 (g) / \frac{1}{4} g]$. The correct answer, therefore, is (C).

9. An object in uniform circular motion has a centripetal acceleration. The magnitude of the acceleration (a_c) is equal to the speed (v) squared divided by the radius (R) $[a_c = v^2/R]$. Since the radius was kept the same, the speed squared divided by the centripetal acceleration equals a constant $[v_1^2/a_{c1} = v_2^2/a_{c2}]$. Solve the equation for a_{c2}: $[a_{c2} = a_{c1}(9v_1^2/v_1^2)]$. The correct answer, therefore, is (D).

10. The restoring force on an object in simple harmonic motion is proportional to the displacement $[F = -kx]$. The correct answer, therefore, is (B).

11. The period of a harmonic oscillator is dependent on the mass and the force constant.

$$T = 2\pi\sqrt{\frac{m}{k}}$$

Since the mass was kept constant, the product of the period squared and force constant is constant $[T_1^2 k_1 = T_2^2 k_2]$. Adding a spring in parallel doubles the spring constant $[k_2 = 2k_1]$. Solve for T_2: $T_2^2 = T_1^2 k_1 / k_2$. The correct answer, therefore, is (D).

12. For a system to be at rest, the sum of the forces must add up to zero. The weight $[W = mg]$ of each mass is approximately 10 newtons, using 10 m/s^2 as the acceleration due to gravity (g). The net force on each mass must be zero. The downward force of Earth on the mass, its weight, is 10 newtons; therefore, the upward force of the string on the mass must be 10 newtons. The correct answer, therefore, is (C).

13. The quantitative representation of Newton's second law is net $F = ma$. The net force is kept constant; therefore, there is an inverse relationship between the mass and acceleration $[k = ma]$. A hyperbola represents an inverse relationship on a graph. The correct answer, therefore, is (B).

14. The net force acting on the system is 20 newtons due to the force of Earth on the 2.0-kilogram mass. The normal force of the table on the 3.0-kilogram mass cancels the force of Earth on the 3.0-kilogram mass. Use the whole system to solve for the acceleration of the system: $[a = \text{net } F/m = 20 \text{ N}/5 \text{ kg} = 4 \text{ m/s}^2]$.

Isolate either block to solve for the tension in the string. Isolating the 2-kilogram block and using net $F = ma$: $[20 \text{ N} - T = (2 \text{ kg})(4 \text{ m/s}^2); T = 12 \text{ N}]$ Isolating the 3-kilogram block and using net $F = ma$: $[T = (3 \text{ kg})(4 \text{ m/s}^2) = 12 \text{ N}]$ The correct answer, therefore, is (B).

15. When an object is at rest or moving at constant velocity, the sum of the forces acting on the object equals zero. The net force on each of the masses must be equal to zero. The correct answer, therefore, is (A).

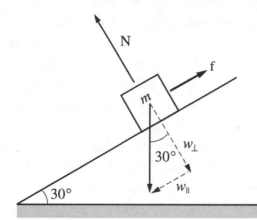

18. Newton's universal law of gravitation states that the force of attraction between two masses is directly proportional to the product of the masses (*m*) and inversely proportional to the square of the distance between the centers of their masses [$F = Gm_1m_2/r^2$]. The measure of the force of gravity (*F*) is the weight [$W = mg$].

$$mg = GMm/r^2$$

$$G = gr^2/M = k$$

$$g_1r_1{}^2/M_1 = g_2r_2{}^2/M_2$$

$$g_2 = g_1r_1{}^2M_2/M_1r_2{}^2 = 10 \text{ m/s}^2(R_e{}^2)(6M_e)/$$
$$(M_e)(2R_e)^2 = 10 \text{ m/s}^2(6/4) = 15 \text{ m/s}^2$$

The correct answer, therefore, is (C).

16. The sum of the forces acting on an object equals zero when the object is moving at constant velocity. The weight (*W*) is the measure of the force of gravity [$W = mg$]. The diagram shows that the frictional force (*f*) equals the component of the weight parallel to the inclined plane [$f = mg(\sin 30°)$]. The normal force equals the component of the weight perpendicular to the inclined plane [$N = mg(\cos 30°)$]. The coefficient of friction equals the frictional force divided by the normal force [$\mu = f/N$]. sin 30° divided by cos 30° is equal to tan 30°. The correct answer, therefore, is (C).

19. Mechanical energy is conserved. The kinetic energy ($\frac{1}{2}\,mv^2$) at the lowest position would be transformed into gravitational potential energy (*mgh*) at the highest position on the track.

$$\frac{1}{2}mv^2 = mgh \qquad \frac{1}{2}v^2 = gh \qquad h = \frac{1}{2}v^2/g$$
$$= \frac{1}{2}(20\text{m/s})^2/10 \text{ m/s}^2 = 20 \text{ m}$$

The correct answer, therefore, is (C).

17. Momentum is conserved. The momentum before the release of the compressed spring is zero; therefore, the momentum after release must be zero. The momentum of each cart before it is released is zero. The magnitudes of the momentum of carts *A* and *B* are equal after the carts are released. The vector sum is zero because the momentum of cart *A* is in the opposite direction of the momentum of cart *B*. Both carts have the same change in momentum. Since the carts have different masses, their speeds, accelerations, and kinetic energies will be different. The correct answer, therefore, is (D).

20. The area under the curve gives the work done in pulling back the bowstring. The area of the triangle is one-half the base times the height [$W = \frac{1}{2}(0.2 \text{ m})(10 \text{ N}) = 1.0 \text{ J}$]. The correct answer, therefore, is (A).

21. The gravitational force of Earth on a satellite in circular orbit is the centripetal force [$F = GM_Em_s/R^2 = m_sa_c = m_sv^2/R$]. The mass of the satellite cancels out, which means that the period of a satellite is independent of the mass of the satellite in a circular orbit. The correct answer, therefore, is (C).

22. Momentum is conserved during the collision.

    $(m_1v_1 + m_2v_2)_{before} = (m_1v_1 + m_2v_2)_{after}$

    (3.0 kg)(8.0 m/s) + (4.0 kg)(0) = (3.0 kg)(0) + (4.0 kg)($v_{2\ after}$)

    The correct answer, therefore, is (C).

23. The centripetal acceleration of an object is dependent on the radius of the circle in which it moves [$a_c = v^2/r$]. The tangential acceleration is equal to the radius times the angular acceleration [$a_t = r\alpha$]. The moment of inertia of a body about a fixed axis depends on the distribution of the mass [$I = \Sigma mr^2$]. The angular velocity is the rate of change of the angular displacement of the rotating body [$\omega = d\theta/dt$]. The definition of angular velocity holds not only for the rotating rigid body as a whole but also for every particle of the body. The correct answer, therefore, is (D).

24. The electric field is a measure of the force per unit test charge [$E = F/q_o$]. The magnitude of the electric field **E** of a point charge q is [$E = kq/r^2$]. The direction of **E** is away from the point charge if the charge is positive and toward the point charge if the charge is negative. To have a net force of zero on the test charge, charges A and B must be like charges. Equating the electric field strengths [$kQ_A/x^2 = kQ_B/(L-x)^2$] will give X a value of $L/3$ when the point charges $Q_A = +1q$ and $Q_B = +4q$ are substituted. The correct answer, therefore, is (D).

25. The direction of **E** is away from the point charge if the charge is positive and toward the point charge if the charge is negative. The electric field **E** is the electrostatic force **F** exerted on a positive test charge q_o [$\mathbf{E} = \mathbf{F}/q_o$]. A positive test charge at B will give a resultant electric field vector pointing directly to the left. None of the other locations for the test charge will give such a resultant electric field vector. The correct answer, therefore, is (B).

26. Like charges repel and unlike charges attract. Conductors are materials in which a significant number of charged particles (electrons) are free to move. The electrons in conducting spheres A and B move toward the positive rod. There is an excess of electrons on sphere A and a deficiency of electrons on sphere B when they are separated. The correct answer, therefore, is (D).

$$i^2 R = \left(\frac{V}{R}\right)^2$$

27. Coulomb's law states that the electrostatic force between point charges is directly proportional to the product of the charges and inversely proportional to the square of the distance between the charges $[F = kq_1q_2/r^2]$. One of the charges is doubled, and the distance between the centers of the spheres is doubled $[F_2 = kq_1 2q_2/(2r)^2 = F]$. The correct answer, therefore, is (B).

28. The direction of **E** is away from the point charge if the charge is positive. The magnitudes of **E** are equal at point P. Thus, the electric field is zero because the vectors have opposite directions. The electrostatic force between the two charges is nonzero and repulsive. The potential due to a single point charge is dependent on the charge and the distance from the charge $[V = kq/r]$. Potential is a scalar quantity and it will be positive or negative but not zero. The correct answer, therefore, is (B).

29. The electric potential energy of a system of point charges is equal to the work needed to assemble the system with the charges initially at rest and infinitely distant from each other $[W = qV]$. When two charges are separated, the potential energy is directly proportional to the product of the charges and inversely proportional to the distance between the charges $[U = W = kq_1q_2/r]$. The charges can be negative or positive. (B) and (D) have the largest product of the charges, but (B) has a smaller distance than (D). The correct answer, therefore, is (B).

30. Power is the rate of energy transfer in an electric device across which a potential difference is maintained $[P = W/t = iV]$. For a resistor we can substitute Ohm's law ($V = iR$): $[P = iV = i^2R = V^2/R]$. Resistors in parallel have the same potential difference across their terminals. Since the potential difference is constant, a proportion can be developed: $[V^2 = PR = k, P_1R_1 = P_2R_2]$. Solve the equation for P_2 $[P_2 = P_1(R_1/R_2)]$. The correct answer, therefore, is (A).

31. Ohm's law will give the potential difference across lamp L_4 $[V_4 = iR = 6.0 \text{ volts}]$. The potential across resistors that are in parallel is the same. The series combination of lamps L_2 and L_3 is in parallel with lamp L_4. Potential is additive in series; therefore, V_2 is 2.0 volts since V_3 is given $[V_4 = V_2 + V_3]$. The current through lamp L_1 splits when it gets to the junction leading to lamps L_2 and L_4 $[i_1 = i_2 + i_4]$. The current in lamp L_2 is 2.0 amperes $[i_2 = 3.0 \text{ amps} - 1.0 \text{ amp}]$. Ohm's law gives the resistance of lamp L_2 to be 1.0 ohm. The correct answer, therefore, is (A).

32. To find the equivalent capacitance of a series combination, add the reciprocals [$1/C_t = 1/C_1 + 1/C_2$]. The 6.0 μF and 3.0 μF capacitors are in series. The equivalent capacitance is 2.0 μF [$1/C = 1/6 + 1/3$]. To find the equivalent capacitance of a parallel combination, add [$C_t = C_1 + C_2$]. The series combination of 6.0 μF and 3.0 μF is in parallel with the 2.0 μF capacitor. The equivalent capacitance of this parallel combination is 4.0 μF. The combination of 6.0 μF, 3.0 μF, and 2.0 μF is in series with the 4.0 μF. The equivalent capacitance of the circuit is 2.0 μF [$1/C_t = \frac{1}{4} + \frac{1}{4}$]. The correct answer, therefore, is (B).

33. By Gauss's law, the net electric flux through any closed Gaussian surface is equal to the net charge within the surface divided by the electric permittivity, ϵ_o. The correct answer, therefore, is (B).

34. When a conductor moves through a uniform magnetic field, an emf is induced in the conductor. Electromagnetic induction arises as a result of the magnetic force that acts on a moving charge [$\mathbf{F_B} = q\mathbf{v} \times \mathbf{B}$]. The velocity $\mathbf{v}$ of the wire is perpendicular to the uniform magnetic field $\mathbf{B}$. Each charge q within the conductor also moves with a velocity $\mathbf{v}$ perpendicular to the magnetic field $\mathbf{B}$ and experiences a magnetic force of magnitude $F = qvB$. The right-hand rule can be used to determine the direction of velocity $\mathbf{v}$ of the moving charge q (or conductor). The correct answer, therefore, is (A).

35. The force $\mathbf{F}$ exerted by the magnetic field $\mathbf{B}$ is given by $\mathbf{F_B} = q\mathbf{v} \times \mathbf{B}$. Since the velocity $\mathbf{v}$ is perpendicular to the magnetic field $\mathbf{B}$, the magnitude of the magnetic force is $F_B = qvB$. The particle is moving in a circular path; therefore, the magnetic force accelerates the particle toward the center of the circular path [$F_c = mv^2/r$]. Equating qvB to mv^2/r gives the equation for the radius $r = mv/qB$. If the speed and the magnetic field $\mathbf{B}$ are both doubled, the radius stays the same. The answer, therefore, is (C).

36. If the charge on the capacitor plates is maintained, as in this case, the effect of a dielectric is to reduce the potential difference between the plates. The electric field in the dielectric is in the opposite direction of the original electric field [$E = E_o - E_d$]. The effect of the dielectric is to weaken the original field E_o by a factor κ, the dielectric constant [$\kappa = E_o/E$]. The correct answer, therefore, is (A).

37. For a long, straight wire carrying a current i, the Biot-Savart law gives, for a magnetic field a distance r from the wire, $B = \mu i/2\pi r$. The magnetic field lines for a current i in a long straight wire are concentric circles. Their direction is given by the right-hand rule. The correct answer, therefore, is (C).

38. For the ion to go through undeflected, the total force must be zero [$\mathbf{F} = e(\mathbf{E} + \mathbf{v} \times \mathbf{B}) = 0$]. The magnetic field $\mathbf{B}$ must be perpendicular to the electric field $\mathbf{E}$ to determine the magnitude of the smallest electric field E [$eE = evB$]. The correct answer, therefore, is (C).

39. The force on a moving charge in a magnetic field is given by the Lorentz force, $\mathbf{F_B} = q\mathbf{v} \times \mathbf{B}$. The correct answer, therefore, is (C).

40. For an ideal transformer, the primary and secondary voltages are related by $V_S/V_p = N_S/N_p$. An ideal step-down transformer steps down voltage, which means $V_S < V_p$. Thus, $N_S < N_p$. For an ideal transformer, the average power delivered to the primary is equal to the average power delivered to the secondary; namely, $I_pV_p = I_SV_S$. Thus, $I_p < I_S$ for a step-down transformer. The correct answer, therefore, is (D).

41. The bending of a wave around an obstacle is called diffraction. The extent of the diffraction depends on the ratio of the wavelength of the wave to the size of the opening [$\sin\theta = \lambda/D$]. If the ratio of the wavelength λ to the size of the opening D is small, then the bending is small. Longer-wavelength electromagnetic waves bend more readily than do shorter-wavelength waves. AM radio waves have the longest wavelengths of the electromagnetic waves listed. The correct answer, therefore, is (B).

42. The intensity of sound uniformly distributed in all directions at any distance is inversely proportional to the square of the distance from the sound [$I = P/4\pi r^2$]. Observing the same aerial display [$I_1/I_2 = r_2^2/r_1^2$], the ratio of the sound intensity is 1 to 4 for observer A to observer B. The correct answer, therefore, is (A).

43. The Doppler effect is a change in the frequency of a sound that is detected by an observer because the sound source and the observer have different velocities with respect to the medium of sound propagation. The frequency f is detected when the source is stationary relative to the observer. A greater frequency f' is detected when the source is moving toward the detector. The speed of sound is v and the speed of the source is v_s.

$$f' = f\,\frac{v}{v-v_s}$$

The speed of the sound is constant in the same medium [$v = f\lambda = k$]. The wavelength λ is inversely proportional to the frequency f. The correct answer, therefore, is (A).

44. The ray bends upward, or away from the normal, as it enters the prism. A ray bends away from the normal when it travels from a medium with a larger refractive index into a medium with a smaller refractive index. When the ray leaves the prism, it again bends upward, which is toward the normal at the point of exit. A ray bends toward the normal when traveling from a medium with a smaller refractive index toward a medium with a larger refractive index. The situation could arise if the prism were immersed in a fluid that has a larger refractive index than does the glass prism. The correct answer, therefore, is (D).

45. Light from the sun is unpolarized, but a considerable amount of horizontally polarized sunlight originates by reflection from horizontal surfaces such as the hood of a car or the surface of a lake. Polarized sunlight also originates from the scattering of light by molecules in the atmosphere. The correct answer, therefore, is (D).

46. According to the law of reflection, the angle of incidence equals the angle of reflection. Any light from the girl's feet must strike the mirror at a point halfway up her body length to be reflected into her eyes. Any light from the top of her forehead must strike the mirror at a point halfway down her forehead to be reflected into her eyes. Refer to the diagram below. Only a half-sized mirror is needed to see a full-sized image. The correct answer, therefore, is (B).

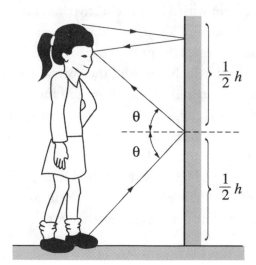

47. A concave mirror is the only mirror that will produce an image that is virtual, enlarged, and upright. When the object is placed between the focal point F and the concave mirror, three rays can be drawn to find the image. Refer to the diagram below. A ray #1, parallel to the principal axis, is reflected through the focal point. A ray #2, passing through the focal point, is reflected parallel to the principal axis. A ray #3, passing through the center of curvature C, is reflected back in itself. In this case, the rays diverge from each other and do not converge to a common point. When the three rays are projected behind the mirror, the rays appear to come from a common point behind the mirror. A virtual image is formed that is upright and larger than the object. The correct answer, therefore, is (A).

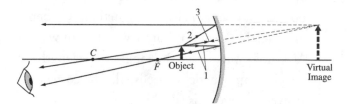

48. For a plane mirror, the image and the object are the same distance on either side of the mirror. The virtual image would be 10.0 cm behind the plane mirror. A convex mirror always forms a virtual image. If the image is 5.0 cm closer, it must be 5.0 cm behind the convex mirror. When the object distance $d_o = 10.0$ cm, the image distance for the convex mirror is $d_i = -5.0$ cm (negative because the image is virtual). The mirror equation can be used to find the focal length [$1/f = 1/d_o + 1/d_i = -1/10.0$ cm]. The focal length is 10.0 cm. The correct answer, therefore, is (D).

49. Because of refraction, an object lying underwater appears to be closer to the surface than it actually is. When the observer is directly above a submerged object, the apparent depth d' is related to the actual depth d and the index of refraction of air ($n_1 = 1.0$) and water ($n_2 = 4/3$) by the formula $[\frac{d'}{d} = \frac{n_{air}}{n_{water}}]$. Solving the relationship for d' $[d' = 1.0 \text{ m} (\frac{3}{4})]$ gives an apparent depth of 0.75 meter. The correct answer, therefore, is (B).

50. Total internal reflection is the phenomenon underlying fiber optics. Light enters one end of the fiber and follows a zigzag path through the fiber because its angle of incidence is greater than the critical angle of reflection. The correct answer, therefore, is (D).

51. When light travels through a material with a smaller refractive index toward a material with a larger refractive index (air to soapy water), reflection at the boundary occurs along with a phase change that is equivalent to one-half a wavelength. Destructive interference removes certain colors from the reflected sunlight. The thickness of the film is the key. Constructive interference can also cause certain colors to appear brighter and give the film a colored appearance. Which colors are enhanced by constructive interference and which are removed by destructive interference depends on the thickness of the film. The thickness of the film changes; therefore, we see different colors. The correct answer, therefore, is (C).

52. To find the focal length f, use the thin-lens equation, with $d_o = 0.25$ m and $d_i = 1.0$ m $[1/f = 1/d_o + 1/d_i]$.

$1/f = 1/0.25 \text{ m} + 1/1.0 \text{ m} = 5.0/1.0 \text{ m}$

The reciprocal of $1/f$ is 0.20 m. The correct answer, therefore, is (A).

53. Infrared waves have wavelengths ranging from about 1 millimeter to 700 nanometers. Ultraviolet waves have wavelengths ranging from about 380 nanometers to 60 nanometers. Gamma rays have wavelengths less than 0.1 nanometer. Radio waves have wavelengths greater than 1 meter. The correct answer, therefore, is (C).

54. As the temperature drops, the length of the thin wire will decrease due to linear thermal expansion. The greater the change in temperature, the greater the change in length. The period of a simple pendulum is directly proportional to the square root of the length $[T^2 \propto L]$, and it is independent of the mass of the pendulum bob. The correct answer, therefore, is (B).

55. During the orbital period of a satellite, it travels in and out of Earth's shadow. The temperature within a satellite would decrease or increase sharply during an orbital period. The satellites are covered with highly reflecting metal foil. The metal foil reflects the sunlight and does not absorb the radiant energy. The foil is also a poor emitter and reduces energy losses when in Earth's shadow. The metal foil reduces temperature changes that would occur during each orbit. The correct answer, therefore, is (C).

56. Conduction is the process in which heat is transferred directly through a material independent of the bulk motion of the material. The thermal conductivity of the tile is greater than the thermal conductivity of the cloth mat. Heat flows from the warmer body (feet) to the cooler body (tile). The correct answer, therefore, is (A).

57. The change in the internal energy of a system ΔU is dependent on the heat Q and the work W [$\Delta U = Q - W$]. The value of heat is positive when the system gains heat and negative when it loses heat. The value of work is positive when work is done by the system and negative when work is done on the system. The correct answer, therefore, is (B).

58. According to the principle of energy conservation, the heat gained by the water ($cm\Delta T$) equals the heat lost by the aluminum cup ($cm\Delta T$). The specific heat capacity c is greater for water than aluminum. Since the masses are equal, the change in temperature (ΔT) is greater for the aluminum cup than for the water. The correct answer, therefore, is (B).

59. The ideal gas law states that the absolute pressure P of an ideal gas is directly proportional to the Kelvin temperature T and the number of moles n of the gas and is inversely proportional to the volume V of the gas [$P = k(nT/V)$]. Therefore $(PV)/T$ is equal to a constant if the number of moles of gas is kept the same [$P_1 V_1/T_1 = P_2 V_2/T_2$]. Solving for T_2, [$T_2 = (P_2 V_2 T_1)/(P_1 V_1) = 1{,}500$ K]. The correct answer, therefore, is (C).

60. During each half-life, the number of radioactive atoms is reduced by a factor of two. For the radioactivity of the sample to be reduced to 1/8 (1/2 → 1/4 → 1/8) of its original value, the time span has to be three half-lives [3 × 1,500 years]. The correct answer, therefore, is (D).

61. A significant feature of the photoelectric effect is that the maximum kinetic energy of the ejected electrons remains the same when the intensity of the light increases, provided the light frequency remains the same [$hf_o = KE_{max} + W_o$]. As the light intensity increases, more photons per second strike the metal, and consequently more electrons per second are ejected. Since the frequency is the same for each photon the energy of each photon stays the same. The ejected electrons always have the same maximum kinetic energy, but there are more electrons ejected. The correct answer, therefore, is (C).

62. In the Bohr model of hydrogen, the radii of the allowed orbits are given by $r_n = n^2 a_o$. For $n = 3$, $r_3 = 9a_o$. The correct answer, therefore, is (D).

63. When nuclear fission occurs, a massive nucleus divides into intermediate nuclei whose binding energy per nucleon is greater than that of the original nucleus. The correct answer, therefore, is (B).

64. The region of greatest nuclear stability is where the binding energy per nucleon is a maximum. The maximum occurs for mass numbers close to $A = 56$. The correct answer, therefore, is (C).

65. Alpha decay occurs when an unstable parent nucleus emits a $_2He^4$ particle. $_{92}U^{238} \rightarrow {}_2He^4 + X$. Mass number and charge are conserved. Thus, the daughter nucleus $X = {}_{90}Th^{234}$. The correct answer, therefore, is (A).

66. Gamma rays are highly energetic and highly penetrating. Because of its high atomic number ($Z = 82$) and high density (11.3 g/cm^3), lead is typically used to shield gamma ray sources. The correct answer, therefore, is (D).

67. Option (A) is the equation of a hyperbola. Option (B) is the equation of a straight line. Option (C) is the equation of a parabola with vertex at $y = b$. Option (D) is the equation of a circle of radius a. The correct answer, therefore, is (C).

68. When the curve in answer (D) is extended to a complete parabola, there are two values of y for every value of x. That is, y squared is directly proportional to x [$y^2 \propto x$] or y is directly proportional to the square root of x [$y \propto x^{1/2}$]. The correct answer, therefore, is (D).

69. One would most likely vary the length, which becomes the independent variable, and measure the period, which is dependent on the length. The correct answer, therefore, is (B).

70. When the ammeter-voltmeter method is used to measure resistance, the ammeter is connected in series with the resistor since the ammeter has a small resistance, and the voltmeter is connected in parallel with the resistor since it has a high resistance. The correct answer, therefore, is (C).

71. The size of one Kelvin is identical to that of one Celsius degree. There are 100 divisions between the ice and steam points on both scales. The correct answer, therefore, is (B).

72. Chlorine gas is instrumental in the destruction of the stratospheric ozone layer. Freon contains chlorine, and benzene is very toxic. The correct answer, therefore, is (B).

73. Ionizing radiation is radiation capable of removing an electron from an atom. X-rays are a form of ionizing radiation. Options (A), (C), and (D) all involve the use of x-rays. NMR uses magnetic fields and radio waves, which are not forms of ionizing radiation. The correct answer, therefore, is (B).

74. Volcanoes and earthquakes must be considered, because the stability of the site is of critical importance for ensuring that the radioactive waste will not be reintroduced into the environment. For the same reason, the site would be chosen to be free of groundwater. The underground site would be least affected by the climate. The correct answer, therefore, is (A).

75. Radon is a major contributor to natural background radiation. There is a growing concern about radon as a health hazard because it can be trapped in houses, entering primarily through cracks in the walls and floors in the foundation and in the drinking water. The entry of radon can be reduced significantly by sealing the foundation against the entry of the gas and providing good ventilation so that it does not accumulate. The correct answer, therefore, is (D).

Chapter 19

Are You Ready? Last-Minute Tips

▶   ▶   ▶   ▶   ▶   ▶   ▶   ▶   ▶   ▶   ▶   ▶

Checklist

Complete this checklist to determine if you're ready to take your test.

- ❏ Do you know the testing requirements for your teaching field in the state(s) where you plan to teach?

- ❏ Have you followed all of the test registration procedures?

- ❏ Do you know the topics that will be covered in each test you plan to take?

- ❏ Have you reviewed any textbooks, class notes, and course readings that relate to the topics covered?

- ❏ Do you know how long the test will take and the number of questions it contains? Have you considered how you will pace your work?

- ❏ Are you familiar with the test directions and the types of questions for your test?

- ❏ Are you familiar with the recommended test-taking strategies and tips?

- ❏ Have you practiced by working through the practice test questions at a pace similar to that of an actual test?

- ❏ If constructed-response questions are part of your test, do you understand the scoring criteria for these items?

- ❏ If you are repeating a Praxis Series™ Assessment, have you analyzed your previous score report to determine areas where additional study and test preparation could be useful?

The Day of the Test

You should have ended your review a day or two before the actual test date. And many clichés you may have heard about the day of the test are true. You should

- Be well rested

- Take photo identification with you

- Take a supply of well-sharpened #2 pencils (at least three)

- Eat before you take the test, and take some food or a snack to keep your energy level up

- Be prepared to stand in line to check in or to wait while other test takers are being checked in

You can't control the testing situation, but you can control yourself. Stay calm. The supervisors are well trained and make every effort to provide uniform testing conditions, but don't let it bother you if the test doesn't start exactly on time. You will have the necessary amount of time once it does start.

You can think of preparing for this test as training for an athletic event. Once you've trained, and prepared, and rested, give it everything you've got. Good luck.

Appendix A
Study Plan Sheet

Study Plan Sheet

See chapter 1 for suggestions on using this Study Plan Sheet.

STUDY PLAN						
Content covered on test	How well do I know the content?	What material do I have for studying this content?	What material do I need for studying this content?	Where could I find the materials I need?	Dates planned for study of content	Dates completed

Appendix B
For More Information

▶   ▶   ▶   ▶   ▶   ▶   ▶   ▶   ▶   ▶   ▶   ▶

For More Information

Educational Testing Service offers additional information to assist you in preparing for The Praxis Series™ Assessments. *Tests at a Glance* are available to download, at no cost, from The Praxis Series Web site, **www.ets.org/praxis**. The *Registration Bulletin* is also available without charge (see below to order). You can obtain more information from our Web site: **www.ets.org/praxis**.

General Inquiries

Phone: 609-771-7395 (Monday-Friday, 8:00 A.M. to 7:45 P.M., Eastern time)
Fax: 609-771-7906

Extended Time

If you have a learning disability or if English is not your primary language, you can apply to be given more time to take your test. The *Registration Bulletin* tells you how you can qualify for extended time.

Disability Services

Phone: 609-771-7780
Fax: 609-771-7906
TTY (for deaf or hard-of-hearing callers): 609-771-7714

Mailing Address

Teaching and Learning Division
Educational Testing Service
P.O. Box 6051
Princeton, NJ 08541-6051

Overnight Delivery Address

Teaching and Learning Division
Educational Testing Service
Distribution Center
225 Phillips Blvd.
P.O. Box 77435
Ewing, NJ 08628-7435

NOTES

NOTES